Fifth Edition

By Marion Hepburn Grant

IN AND ABOUT

Hartford

ITS PEOPLE & PLACES

Ellsworth S. Grant
Fifth Edition Editor

The Editor is most grateful to Carol Peterson and Frances Hoxie of The Connecticut Historical Society for their editorial services. Ms. Peterson laboriously updated most of the entries and Miss Hoxie proofread the text and compiled the Index. Additional thanks are due to Christopher Bickford, the Society's Director, for his valuable suggestions on format and to Kate Steinway and Paige A. Savery, for their diligence in finding and furnishing the illustrations. All photographs are courtesy of The Connecticut Historical Society except when otherwise noted.

Ellsworth S. Grant

The
Connecticut
Historical
Society

The dramatic cover photo by Larry Nagler of Hartford, reflecting the Travelers Tower in the Gold Building on Main Street, exemplifies Hartford past and present.

TABLE OF
CONTENTS

Marion's guidebook was truly a labor of love. More than anything else she wrote, it embodied her unique perspective of where Hartford was going as well as where it had been. Its birth was accidental. Many years ago, when Newton Brainard was the head of a moribund Chamber of Commerce, she suggested to him that Hartford needed a guidebook for visitors. "But Marion," he exclaimed, "we don't want visitors." Despite the rebuff she nurtured the idea. In 1964 she met with the director of a local foundation to seek funding for establishing the Urban League of Greater Hartford. As she was about to depart, having won his approval of a $5,000 grant, she happened to mention that Hartford also needed a guidebook. "All right," he said, "I'll give you $5,000 for that too!"

The project, under the auspices of the Coordinating Council for the Arts, a volunteer predecessor to the Greater Hartford Arts Council, almost foundered. The grant was insufficient to support a professional writer, so Marion took over the task of researching, writing and even marketing the book. Connecticut Printers of Bloomfield agreed to print it at cost. The first edition, which appeared in 1966, was sold out before it left the press. It consisted of two small volumes, one called "Tours and Tales," the other "Calendars and Keys." Two more editions soon appeared, the proceeds from each going to finance each printing. Finally, with 20,000 copies in circulation, Marion decided to revamp the format. "Calendars and Keys" was discontinued because it became outdated so quickly. The time had come, moreover, to find a new publisher because of the demise of the Coordinating Council. The Guidebook account was turned over to The Connecticut Historical Society as a self-perpetuating fund, and in 1978 the fourth and largest edition of 5,000 copies appeared. At the time of her death Marion was working on the fifth edition.

According to the *Hartford Advocate*, the Guidebook "remains a repository of tasty historical tidbits about the city. But *In and About Hartford* is more—it is the embodiment of Grant's optimistic vision of the city, which integrates Hartford's past and future with its present."

Photo courtesy of Laurie Johnson.

The modern city of Hartford is only three decades old. Clustered between the Connecticut River on the east and Asylum Hill on the west is an array of office towers that proclaim the prosperity of a state with the highest per capita income in the country. Approaching the city on I-91, the visitor has a spectacular view of the entire downtown area—a metropolis that suddenly seems to rise in various colors and shapes from the surrounding suburbs and meadows of the Connecticut River Valley. It is a compact city, bustling, changing, growing, clogged with traffic, short on adequate housing, ethnically diverse with a predominantly black and Hispanic population, and long on tradition and accomplishment.

Hartford, having celebrated its 350th anniversary, is poised to enter the 21st century from the vantage point of economic stability, innovative corporate management, concerned neighborhoods, and strong support of the city's cultural and recreational assets. To grasp the uniqueness of Hartford takes more time and energy than most visitors have. From your hotel you can take a one or two-hour walking tour that will encompass most of the landmarks that are closely identified with Hartford's past and present:

The Connecticut River

Old State House

Travelers Tower

First Congregational Church &
Ancient Burying Ground

Wadsworth Atheneum

City Hall & Public Library

Bushnell Park

Bushnell Memorial Hall

State Capitol, Library &
New Legislative Office Building

Civic Center

Such a tour, however, omits, because of distance, several other important landmarks that every visitor will want to see. First and foremost, the Mark Twain and Harriet Beecher Stowe houses; Armsmear, the home of Samuel Colt, and the Church of the Good Shepherd; Aetna Life Insurance Company, the largest colonial office building in the world, and the Cathedral of St. Joseph across the street; The Connecticut Historical Society; and in season Elizabeth Park.

Although the Guidebook tells you where to go and what to see, it has deliberately avoided suggestions of where to eat or shop. This information is readily available from the:

Greater Hartford Convention &
Visitors Bureau 522-6766

Downtown Council 728-3089

Hartford Courant Calendar,
published every Thursday

Connecticut or *Hartford* magazines

For outdoor entertainment for both children and adults you might consider the Bushnell Park Carousel; a visit to one of the area's wineries or orchards; a riverboat cruise from Charter Oak Landing; or the Valley Railroad steam train and boat ride in Essex. For indoor tours you might consider one of the many historic homes and museums; a backstage tour at the Bushnell; the Connecticut Regional Market; Mystic Marine Life Aquarium; the State Capitol; or the Travelers Tower observation deck.

The name Hartford was taken from Hertford (pronounced Hartford or Harford) on the river Lea in Hertfordshire, England, birthplace of the Rev. Samuel Stone, Thomas Hooker's assistant and the first to be named on the Indian deed to Hartford in 1636.

Since 1571 the arms of Hartford in England have been a "hart" or stag standing in a "ford" or stream. In the background of the English seal is an arch very reminiscent of our own Hartford's Civil War Arch.

The first seal of American Hartford was designed in 1785. It emphasized the importance of the Connecticut River to the inhabitants of those times. The river is represented by the figure of an old man crowned with rushes seated against a rock, holding an urn with a stream flowing from it; at his feet a net, and fish peculiar to the river lying by it, with a barrel and bales; over his head an oak growing out of a cleft in the rock; and around the whole thing the words "Sigillum Civitatis Hartfordiensis" ("Seal of the City of Hartford").

In 1852 a new city seal was designed and approved by the Common Council. It is somewhat like the seal of old Hertford in that it shows a "hart" standing in a "ford." At the base of the shield in which the hart is emblazoned is a fruitful grapevine, symbolizing the state, and at the top is an American eagle, symbolizing the nation. Oak leaves, symbolizing freedom, embellish the side of the shield, and below is a streamer with the words "Post Nubila Phoebus" ("After the Clouds, the Sun"). Around the whole seal are the words "Seal of the City of Hartford, Connecticut."

Mark Twain once observed that Hartford is the "city of the historic and revered Charter Oak, of which most of the town is built!"

This is quite true.

If there had been no Royal Charter, and thus no Charter Oak, there would have been no Hartford, Connecticut. It would probably have been Hartford, Massachusetts, or Hartford, New York, or perhaps Hartford, New England! For without the legal strength of the old Royal Charter and the self-rule it guaranteed, the little colony of Connecticut would no doubt have been absorbed by one of its bigger neighbors very early in its history. For this reason the Charter Oak, which supposedly hid the Royal Patent during the dark days of the Andros regime (1687-89), is a vital symbol of Connecticut's passion for independence; in fact, it is the symbol of Connecticut's very existence.

The Royal Charter of Connecticut was a wonderfully liberal document. It gave the Connecticut Colony a remarkable amount of political freedom from the mother country. Both the procuring of the Charter and the defending of the Charter demanded a tremendous amount of courage and legal acumen from many generations of Connecticut citizens. Practically speaking, the little colony did not have much of an excuse for separate existence. But it did exist, and it did endure, thanks to the legal base provided by the charter and the legal skill of the citizens who protected it.

It is no accident that the first American law school was founded in Connecticut! And it is not strange that Oliver Ellsworth of Windsor should have been appointed third Chief Justice of the U.S. Supreme Court.

From the beginning, the Puritan pioneers of Connecticut had a keen respect for the law. Before he moved from Massachusetts Bay to the new Connecticut frontier in 1636, Thomas Hooker, that most practical of preachers, made quite sure that his settlement would enjoy the same protection from English law. He did not wish his new Biblical Utopia to be snatched from him and his followers, once trees had been cleared and homes built! The best existing title to the lands of the Connecticut River was the Warwick Patent issued by the Council of New England to Robert, Earl of Warwick, a nobleman sympathetic to the Puritan cause. The Council was composed of a group of wealthy Englishmen interested in developing land and trade in this area. Since the territory the Patent purported to cover had never been surveyed, it was necessarily a rather imprecise document! John Winthrop, Jr., son of the Governor of Massachusetts, was the Earl's American agent. Therefore, Thomas Hooker took great pains to make his settlement proper in the estimation of Winthrop and the Patent he represented.

Hooker also requested the authority to make laws in the new colony, for, in the words of the day, "when there are people to sit down and inhabit, there will follow upon occasion some cause of difference." Since Hooker recognized all the legal claims of the Warwick Patent, Winthrop in turn allowed the first General Court of Connecticut to be located in Hartford and gave Hooker and his congregation wide authority to make laws, issue decrees and even to wage war.

It must be remembered that in those days Connecticut was a long, long way from Massachusetts. This factor of distance made local self-government both essential and possible.

The Pequot War of 1637 was the first test of the colony's capacity for survival. After victory over the hostile Pequot Indians had been achieved, the colonists were able to return to the problems of building their settlements in Hartford, Windsor and Wethersfield. On May 31, 1638, Thomas Hooker gave a memorable speech to the General Court in Hartford in which he declared, "... the choice of public magistrates belongs unto the people, by God's own allowance!"

Because of this speech, Hooker is hailed by historians as one of the founders of American democracy. He deserves this honor. He certainly planted here important new concepts of government, seeds of democracy, that would grow and blossom for future generations. But, as a 17th century Puritan, Thomas Hooker was no advocate of "pure" democracy or total religious freedom. He required that everyone in his colony attend the Congregational Church. There was no other, and if anyone tried to start one, he was expelled. By "the people" Hooker meant reliable, church-going, land-owning Englishmen. Women

and servants were never included, although of course they attended church. Blacks, Indians, Dutchmen, Jews and Quakers, too, were definitely not "the people."

In Puritan Massachusetts, also a single-church colony, the franchise was limited to church "members" only, and church membership was limited to the "saints," those Congregationalists who, because of a particular mystical religious experience, were able to prove to the other saints of the church that they were indeed one of God's "elect," destined for salvation after death. Salvation was the major desire of every devout Puritan. In Massachusetts, too, everyone had to be a church-goer even when not allowed to be a church member. The stocks or worse were the rightful punishment for anyone who did not attend the Congregational Church.

Thomas Hooker did not like certain aspects of the Massachusetts system. He thought too much unlimited power was vested in the chief saints, i.e., the clergy and civil magistrates. He also thought the method of selecting Puritan saints was dubious. It was too easy for artful hypocrites to gain church membership by feigning a saintly religious experience. He noted that many hard-working Congregationalists were being denied church membership because they were too honest to pretend to be spiritually "elected by God," however much they might long for salvation or the vote.

In the new Connecticut Colony, Hooker and his followers were progressive in that they did not legally limit the franchise to the proven saints. They included Congregationalists whom they called "admitted inhabitants" and "freemen." The first were allowed to vote in town elections, and the second were allowed as well to vote for colony officers and to run for office. It was comparatively easier, too, in Connecticut to become a saintly church member.

It is hard for us today to realize that Hooker was, for his time and religion, remarkably open-minded and humanistic. His basic values and concepts started a chain reaction of great significance to this country. However, the voters of Hooker's day were more like stockholders in a single corporation than free citizens in a democracy. "Saints," "admitted inhabitants" and "freemen," all land-owning English Congregationalists, were required to have made a definite investment in the common enterprise of building a Biblical Utopia in the wilderness.

Thus, Connecticut, although more liberal than Massachusetts, was not as radical as Rhode Island where Roger Williams preached and practiced pluralistic religious liberty and genuine personal freedom that would ultimately prove to be impractical for his time in history. Hooker's genius was to strike a conservative, yet workable and dynamic balance between the two extremes. To this day, the genius of Connecticut reflects the personality of this remarkable man who could realistically encompass both continuity and change.

Extremes of wealth and poverty were rare in the Connecticut Colony. Everyone worked. There were a few household slaves, but slavery was not economical and thus not widespread. Since vast opportunities existed on the new Connecticut frontier, industrious young Englishmen were able to rise rapidly to comparative affluence and influence. As most of them derived from a modest social rank in the mother country, they would never have had such opportunities in class-ridden England. So, although this was not an "ideal" democracy, born perfect but fragile from a philosopher's brain, it certainly was a tough, practical self-government, incomplete but ever-growing, from the roots up, nurtured by the talents of the individual inhabitants and their constantly expanding Utopian dream.

In 1639, the Fundamental Orders, drafted presumably by Roger Ludlow, the best lawyer in the colony, were adopted by the General Court in Hartford and became Connecticut's first constitution, the legal basis of government until the Royal Charter was procured.

In 1658, Oliver Cromwell, Puritan Protector of England, died. Worse still, Charles II was restored to the throne. These events were a severe shock to the Puritans of Hartford, for they placed in doubt the authority of the Warwick Patent, legal basis of their Fundamental Orders. Desperate for fear a Royal Governor would now be sent to rule Connecticut, as was the case in most of the American colonies, the practical Yankees took stock of their plight. Now that there was once more a king in England, they must have a Royal Charter that would protect their unique self-government.

In 1657, John Winthrop, Jr., had been elected 5th governor of Connecticut. So, on July 23 of 1662 this gentleman was commissioned by his constituents to go to England on the delicate mission of procuring a liberal Charter. Winthrop was a man of rare charm and sharpest intellect. Despite the disfavor in which Puritans were held in the mother country, he adroitly maneuvered his way into royal circles. No one really knows how he managed the brilliant coup of obtaining the Charter. But an existing document from Connecticut colonists to King Charles gives a hint. The "game" was to make the English think that Connecticut was utterly unimportant and impoverished. The colonists described their settlement as "a place remote from the Christian world ... a desert difficultly subdued, no way improvable for subsistence but by great cost and hard labor, with much patience and cares ..."

The new Royal Charter, a document written largely by Winthrop himself, contained practically all the freedoms of the old Fundamental Orders. It also vastly increased the colony's geographical area. Connecticut in those days was bounded on the east by Narragansett Bay, on the south by Long Island Sound and the Atlantic Ocean, on the north by Massachusetts, and on the west by the Pacific Ocean! So, once more, Connecticut's legal basis for self-government was assured.

As long as Charles II was king, everything went smoothly. But when he died in 1685 and was succeeded by his autocratic brother, James II, the Yankees in Hartford knew they were in for trouble again. James had a distressing new plan for the colonies of New York and New England. He wished to consolidate them into one great Dominion of New England under one Royal Governor, Sir Edmund Andros. New Hampshire and Massachusetts had already lost their charters. In 1686 Rhode Island's patent was suspended, and this once-independent little colony fell under Andros's control. Only Connecticut remained to be absorbed.

In Hartford a number of writs were received by Connecticut's governor, Robert Treat, from Andros demanding submission of the colony and surrender of the Charter. But somehow the Yankees managed to dodge and delay.

Finally news was received that Andros was coming personally to take over the government. On October 26, 1687, the Royal Governor set out from Boston with a retinue of 75 men. The Yankees met him when he crossed the river at Wethersfield and politely escorted him to Hartford where he was given an official welcome.

Next morning royal and colonial officials gathered in the second-floor assembly room of Sanford's Tavern on King Street, now Main. They sat at a large table, Andros surrounded by his advisors and ensconced in the official Governor's chair, Treat flanked by his assistants. The Charter in its wooden box reposed on the table in front of Governor Treat.

All day they argued the matter. Treat gave a long and impassioned speech describing the struggles and sufferings of the little colony. Many other people spoke. Since October days are short, candle-light was soon required to carry on the bitter business. But when the actual moment came for the Charter to be handed over to Andros, a very peculiar "accident" took place. One report states that Andrew Leete of New Haven fainted after giving a last, desperate speech for the preservation of Connecticut, and fell upon the candles, dashing them to the floor.

At any rate, in the words of an early historian, "The lights were instantly extinguished and one Captain (Joseph) Wadsworth of Hartford, in the most secret and silent manner, carried off the Charter and secreted it in an old oak tree ... The candles were officially relighted, but the patent was gone, and no discovery could be made of it, or of the person who carried it away."

The chagrin of Andros may well be imagined. But he was not thwarted from taking possession of the colony itself. Andros allowed Governor Treat to be on his advisory council, but he ruled the new Dominion of New England with an iron hand and suspended most of the liberal laws.

One of his most distressing acts was to declare invalid all land titles secured under the old Charter. As for Indian deeds, he stated they were worth no more than "the scratch of a bear's paw."

The Yankees were forced to endure this despotism for two unhappy years.

Then, in 1688, James II, as unbending as his Royal Governor, finally incurred the wrath of the English Parliament. In a political upheaval named the Glorious Revolution, this Catholic monarch was removed from power and replaced by his Protestant daughter, Mary, and her husband, William of Orange. The Dominion of New England was dissolved and Andros was arrested and returned to England.

On May 9, 1689, the freemen of Connecticut voted to "restablish the government as it was before ... according to the old Charter." And so it remained until revised in the Constitutional Convention of 1818.

Connecticut was unique among the 13 original colonies in maintaining self-rule up to the outbreak of the American Revolution; with the brief exception of the two harsh years under Andros. When war was declared, Connecticut's Governor Jonathan Trumbull, being the only governor still elected by his constituents, was also the only governor to side with the colonists. All the others became Tories, including Benjamin Franklin's own son, royal governor of New Jersey.

The English were so angered--and impressed--by Trumbull's stand that for many years they derisively called all patriotic Americans "Brother Jonathan." The English were also surprised when this "unimportant" little colony, under the expert management of the army's Chief General of Supply, Hartford's Jeremiah Wadsworth, was among the first in providing the revolutionary forces with soldiers and first in supplying beef, oxen and salt, second in pork , and third in flour, grain, horses and rum! Connecticut was also a prime source of firearms, cannon and gunpowder. From

Valley Forge, Washington wrote to Trumbull, "The care of your legislature in providing clothing and necessaries of all kinds for their men is highly laudable and reflects great honor upon their patriotism and humanity."

In 1788 Jeremiah Wadsworth started this country's first woolen mill in Hartford. At the time of Washington's inauguration, the President and the entire Connecticut delegation wore suits made from cloth manufactured in this mill.

During the Constitutional Convention in Philadelphia, Connecticut's old Royal Charter served as a model and Connecticut lawyers provided much skillful legal talent, particularly in framing the famous Connecticut Compromise that was so essential to the successful outcome of the Convention.

Equally important were Connecticut's grass root citizens who had been trained in their many town meetings to the duties as well as the privileges of democracy. Most of them were Federalists, great admirers of George Washington, but suspicious of Thomas Jefferson and his radical ideas. These village citizens, as well as their leaders provided a stability and solidity to both the American Revolution and the new American nation that were vital to the success of both. The Connecticut Colony's emphasis was on community responsibility, personal commitment, common sense and "steady habits." As the franchise in this state has been gradually broadened to include people of other religions and races, and even members of the female sex, the freedom to vote has always ultimately been based upon that deemed best for the community as a whole. Even in modern times, "radical change" in Connecticut is approached with a paradoxically practical as well as idealistic emphasis.

Mark Twain was right. Hartford is the "city of the historic and revered Charter Oak, of which most of the town is built!"

And because of the unique, historic and successful struggle for constitutional self-government that took place in this city and state, symbolized by the Charter Oak, Connecticut is proudly called "The Constitution State."

1600

The Indians who lived in Hartford before the coming of the white Europeans were the Saukiogs whose name meant Black Earth because the land in this area was exceptionally fertile. (In Wethersfield, Farmington, Windsor and East Hartford lived the Pyquags, Tunxis, Poquonocks and Podunks.) All of these small, relatively peaceable tribes belonged to the Algonquin Federation. Around the turn of the 17th century (1600) the territory of the Connecticut Algonquins was invaded by a fierce tribe of Pequots from the north. The Pequots, whose name meant Killers of Men, were a branch of the warlike Mohawks who lived along the Hudson River. The Pequots soon subjugated the Algonquins and established a headquarters near the modern town of Mystic on Long Island Sound.

1614

Adrien Block, a Dutch navigator employed by the Dutch West India Company, became the first white man to explore the Connecticut River. He sailed up as far as the falls at modern Enfield and named it the Fresh River because its waters were so pure for drinking. The Indians, however, called it the Quonitockut ... the Long Tidal River ... a name which the English settlers later developed into Connecticut.

1616

An epidemic, probably measles or smallpox, decimated one-third of the Indian population of New England. This fact greatly facilitated the conquest of the area by the Europeans.

1631

Wanginnacut, Chief of the Podunks (East Hartford), traveled with some braves overland to visit the English settlers at Boston and Plymouth. The Indians urged the Puritans to settle in Connecticut so that they could become their military allies against the invading Pequots.

1632

Edward Winslow of Plymouth explored the Connecticut for possible trade and settlement.

1633

June. Dutch traders bought land from the Pequots at the future site of Hartford. They erected a fort and trading post named House of Good Hope at Dutch Point.

September. William Holmes of Plymouth, guided by friendly Podunk-Algonquins, defied Dutch guns at Dutch Point and sailed up the river and founded Windsor where he built a trading post and palisade.

John Oldham of Massachusetts Bay explored the Connecticut, traded and made friends with the Pyquag-Algonquin Indians of Wethersfield.

1634

Oldham and a few companions built temporary housing and passed the winter at Wethersfield. In the spring more settlers came from Massachusetts Bay by boat.

1635

Lured by glowing reports of the fertility of the Connecticut River Valley, 60 families, including women and children, set out from the Massachusetts Bay Colony to Windsor. They started their journey in late autumn and were soon troubled by cold weather and lack of food. The river froze, and a provision ship sent to sustain them was blocked by the ice. Part of the group made the bitter journey overland back to the Bay Colony, and a few went down river to seek for the ship. They fortunately found a fishing boat that transported them back home. The remaining settlers endured what is known to history as "the starving time." They survived only with the help of friendly Indians.

Determined not to repeat the mistakes of some of the Windsor settlers, the Rev. Thomas Hooker of Newtown (Cambridge) Massachusetts, sent 24 young "Adventurers" to the Hartford area to prepare the way for his new colony. They purchased their land from the Saukiogs and thus disputed both Pequot and Dutch ownership of the land.

A fort was erected at Saybrook Point at the mouth of the Connecticut, and a Puritan colony established by English proprietors under the military leadership of Lion Gardiner.

A group of Puritans from Dorchester, Massachusetts, joined the Windsor colony and expropriated the land of the Plymouth settlers.

A virulent epidemic of smallpox decimated the Poquonocks in Windsor. Almost one entire tribe was wiped out.

1636

In June the Rev. Thomas Hooker and his Puritan followers journeyed overland to Connecticut, settled Saukiog and named it Newtown.

1637

Newtown was renamed Hartford.

The Pequots, under the leadership of Chief Sassacus, harassed all the English in the Connecticut Valley. In April at least six men and three women in Wethersfield were slain by a large raiding party, and two young girls were kidnapped. The Saybrook Fort was in a virtual state of siege, and one Saybrook youth was roasted alive by the Indians. Many others were captured, tortured and killed. Thoroughly frightened and equally determined, the settlers gathered at Hartford on May 1st and declared war on the Pequots. By June the war was won by the English with the aid of Mohegan (renegade Pequot) allies. Sassacus fled north to the Hudson where he was murdered by his kins-men, the Mohawks, and his head was returned to Hartford for the price of a reward.

1638

The New Haven Colony was established by devout Puritans.

1639

The Fundamental Orders were drawn up and adopted by Hartford, Windsor and Wethersfield. First Constitution of the Colony.

1640

Farmington was founded

1642

Simsbury was founded

1644

The Saybrook Colony joined the three up-river towns of the Connecticut.

1649

Charles I was beheaded. Oliver Cromwell became Lord Protector of England.

1650

A Code of Law for the Connecticut Colony was drawn up and adopted by the Legislature at Hartford.

1654

The Dutch Fort was "sequestered" and the Dutch left Hartford.

1658

Oliver Cromwell, Puritan Protector of England, died and Charles II was made king of England.

1662

John Winthrop, Jr., fifth governor of Connecticut, went to England to obtain a Royal Charter. His success was vital to the future independence of the colony. .

1675-1676

King Philip's War. The Indians, under King Philip, chief of the Wampanoags of Massachusetts and Canonchet, chief of the Narragansetts of Rhode Island, tried to unite to fight the English. But they failed because they were still too divided. Philip was betrayed by an Indian, and Canonchet was captured. Before Canonchet was dismembered, piece by piece, by his Indian captor, he uttered the historic words, "I like it well. It is better to die before my heart is soft and before I have spoken anything unworthy of a chief."

1685

James II succeeded his brother Charles II to the English throne. He decided for military reasons to amalgamate all the colonies of New England into one Dominion of New England.

1687

Sir Edmond Andros was appointed Royal Governor of New
England by King James. He recalled all former Royal
Charters from the colonies, but the Connecticut Charter
was hidden in the Charter Oak.

1688

King James was deposed in England in the Glorious
Revolution and replaced by his daughter, Mary and her
husband, William of Orange. Andros was arrested and
returned to England, and the Dominion of New England
was dissolved.

1689

It was voted in Hartford to carry on the Connecticut
government as it had been before under the Royal Charter.

1693

Glastonbury separated from Wethersfield and became an
independent township.

The City of Hartford should be viewed both as an
archeological "dig" and a frontier.

An old industrial city that is evolving into a post-
industrial metropolis, Hartford today is alive with new
construction, new activities and new people. (Ethnically the
city includes as diversified a racial and cultural mix as can
be found anywhere in the world.)

Architecturally it is an astonishing conglomerate of
Colonial, Georgian, Federal, Greek Revival, Gothic,
Victorian, Italianate, and Modern.

Best known as the Insurance City of the nation,
Hartford is the Capital Region's dynamic hub of finance,
marketing, aircraft and precision manufacturing, industrial
research laboratories, computer and communications technologies and government. Because it is a state capital
and because it has an extensive urban park system and a
wealth of medical, educational, recreational and cultural
facilities, almost half of the city's land is tax exempt. Even
so Hartford's economic base is exceptionally sound.
Efforts are being made to create the types of urban
housing that will attract as residents the people who
work in the city but presently live in the suburbs.

Stimulated by the creation of a glamorous Civic
Center, Hartford is now almost as busy after dark as
during the daylight hours. Unique historic buildings are
being restored and millions have been spent on new construction by both the private and public sectors of the
community.

Founded by English Puritans in 1636 and first
named Newtown, Hartford has always been a purposeful
beehive of idealistic dreamers and hard-working doers.
The Puritan pioneers were inspired by a Utopian vision
of building a truly Christian community in the virgin
wilderness of the Connecticut River Valley. A few Dutch
fur traders had preceded the Puritans to this area in 1633.
They had built a trading post, House of Hope, at the
junction of the Park and Connecticut rivers, a section still
called Dutch Point. Since the Dutch were concerned
mostly with exploiting the rich fur resources of the valley,
not with building a permanent settlement, they were not

23

accompanied by their families. Naturally they viewed with alarm the arrival of the prolific and determined English men and women who claimed this land for themselves. For almost 20 years the Dutch and English struggled for possession of the Connecticut frontier. Finally out-numbered, out-worked and out-fought, the Dutch traders sailed down-river to seek out new fur country. They expressed their chagrin by calling the English victors Jankes (pronounced Yankees), a Dutch diminutive of the word Jan (John) that still has the double meaning of "robber" or "pirate."

Piratical as the Yankees may have seemed to the ousted Dutch, those vigorous Biblical folk started here a new civilization of world-wide consequence. Alexis de Tocqueville, the great 19th century French sociologist, called Connecticut in 1831 "one very great miracle," a tiny spot on the map of the world, yet a mighty influence upon the character of the new United States because of the creativity and strength of the state's inhabitants. Tocqueville noted with amazement that one-third of the men then in the U.S. Senate and one-fourth of those in the House of Representatives had been born in Connecticut—a state which, he said, had produced the clock peddler, the schoolmaster and the senator: "the first to give you the time, the second to tell you what to do with it, and the third to make your laws and civilization."

Modern Yankees, stemming from many nations and races, have added to the scope and reality of the Puritan's Utopian dream by bringing to Hartford a rich variety of cultures. All Yankees share a common historical experience. They also share a common spiritual purpose. No matter when their ancestors arrived from foreign ports, all have been inspired by an optimistic faith that, with the help of God and a personal willingness to work hard, life in this world could be improved.

The Yankee talent for practical idealism is well expressed in the insurance business which must be both innovative and conservative at the same time.

The practice of insurance started in Hartford back in the 18th century when the town was a busy river port. Captains and merchants used to gather down by the wharves on the Connecticut River especially at Morgan's

Coffee House, an establishment run by J. Pierpont Morgan's grandfather. There the men would make agreements to share risks and profits on cargoes of ships going forth to trade overseas. The insurance business began informally in Hartford in 1794 under the leadership of its most influential merchant and financier, Colonel Jeremiah Wadsworth. He and three other men of financial substance and moral integrity started a fire insurance company. It began as a partnership of gentlemen, with the insuring partners changing as one partner left and others joined. In each case the personal fortunes of the insurers were pledged to pay the claims in the event of loss.

Hartford's merchants and bankers certainly were not unique in their early involvement with marine and fire insurance. This was being done in many sections of the new nation. Hartford's uniqueness lay in building a solid reputation for keeping solvent, keeping promises to pay losses, keeping together in times of disaster, and in keeping up with the new types of insurance. Since "keeping up" has been so vital to the growth of insurance in this city, it is not surprising that local companies have pioneered a great number of insurance "firsts" by anticipating changing social conditions without abandoning their basic insistence on absolute fiscal integrity. These "firsts" include the first travelers, steam boiler, automobile, and airplane insurance, and the first insurance policy for astronauts. They have also pioneered "safety first" since in Hartford all disasters are necessarily "doubly mourned"!

The city's oldest active insurance concern is the Hartford Fire Insurance Company. Founded in 1810, it is now part of the Hartford Insurance Group. In December of 1836 a terrible fire broke out in New York City. Nearly 700 buildings were destroyed. When Eliphalet Terry, president of Hartford Fire, received news of this calamity, he rushed to the Hartford Bank to make sure that all drafts made on his company would be honored. He pledged his personal fortune to cover possible debts and was certain that all members of his board of directors would do likewise. Then, despite the freezing weather, he took off for New York in a horse-drawn sleigh. When he arrived, he found that most other insurance companies had collapsed under the burden of gigantic claims. The burnt-out populace was in despair believing all insurance policies to be worthless. To the unhappy homeowners and merchants Terry made the dramatic announcement that the "Hartford" stood ready to pay all claims in full. Confidence was restored, Hartford's reputation for reliability burgeoned, and Mr. Terry did not return to his home town until he had sold a large amount of new insurance!

The same scene was repeated in New York eleven years later. Again Hartford companies kept their promises. When Chicago was gutted by fire in 1871, Marshall Jewell, board member of the Phoenix Fire Insurance Company, governor of Connecticut, and president of the Jewell Belting Company, lost no time in going personally to that bereaved city to guarantee the soundness of Hartford's concerns. Standing on an old crate amid the smoking ruins, he calmed the fears of policyholders. To one prominent merchant he wrote out his personal check for $20,000 to cover losses guaranteed by the Phoenix.

After the San Francisco earthquake and fire, insurance claims were truly staggering. In the U.S. Senate one senator sadly commented that no American fire insurance company now could possibly be sure of solvency. Challenged, Morgan G. Bulkeley, senator from Connecticut and president of the Aetna Life Insurance Company, rose quickly to his feet. He pointed proudly to Hartford's history of reliability, and then added fiercely, "I do unhesitatingly affirm that Hartford companies will pay in full every claim made against them."

And they did--thanks to the loyal support of Hartford banks and other local insurance companies.

As government and business today endeavor to cope with brand new problems posed by the crisis of cities, the development of atomic energy, the exploration of space, and a massive social revolution, Hartford's sturdy old insurance companies are daily challenged to tailor new techniques and new concepts of insurance protection and company investments. Corporate citizenship is now a high priority in the business community.

Often overlooked is the fact that Hartford was the manufacturing center of New England from the Civil War until about 1960, a period of 100 years. Several hundred plants, some large like Colt's and Pratt & Whitney Machine

Plan of The City of Hartford.
Engraving, 1824.

Tool, employed in total more than the banks and insurance companies. They made a variety of metal products like guns, typewriters, fasteners, steam turbines, and machinery. Their names and products were house-hold words: Colt revolvers, Royal and Underwood typewriters, Fuller brushes, and Silex coffee makers. One by one, starting in 1958, the factories moved to the suburbs, merged with other companies or simply went out of business. Nonetheless, in Connecticut manufacturing still accounts for a sizable chunk of the work force, between 25 and 30 percent. Post-industrial Hartford has become a service-dominated economy, with three out of four employed in government, insurance, banking, wholesale and retail trade, and other service-type enterprises.

More important, however, than all the billions and statistics are the civic affection and creative concern bestowed upon Hartford by many generations of able, loyal citizens. Churches, schools, hospitals, museums, public parks, gardens, statues, monuments, and homes, large and small, all combine to make Hartford a very attractive city.

In 1868 when Mark Twain first came to Hartford he wrote, "Of all the beautiful towns it has been my fortune to see this is the chief ... You do not know what beauty is if you have not been here."

More than a century later, this is still true.

Oil painting, "Hartford in 1824"

In the 17th century, when the first Puritan pioneers migrated to New England, it was their custom to start each settlement by designating as the nucleus of their new community a common area for the general use of the townsfolk. Around the edge of this Common they placed their house lots, beyond which lay the open land for farming and pasture. No doubt this arrangement had many advantages, not only for augmenting the spiritual and political cohesiveness of the town, but for mutual protection against Indian attack. In 1635 when Hartford (originally Newtown) was laid out by the stalwart young Puritan "adventurers"or scouts who preceded the settlers who arrived the following year, Newtown's Common was bounded east and west by present Main Street and Columbus Boulevard and North and South by Kinsley Street and Burr Mall. Within the Common the Puritans constructed their first Meeting House. Thus, for many years, the area now known as Thomas Hooker Square was known as Meeting House Square. Because the Puritans' house of worship was also used as the new settlement's Town Hall, the Meeting House was the vital core of their theocratic community in which church and state were always joined as one. Although the original Meeting House was soon outgrown and presented to Hartford's spiritual leader, Thomas Hooker, to be used as a barn, new meeting houses were always built in approximately this same area to accommodate the town's religious and political life. Nearby taverns also served from time to time as gathering places for the colony's political and business leaders.

The northeast corner of the Hartford Common was the site of the town's jail, or "house of correction," first constructed in 1640 and flanked by a whipping post and the customary stocks. The southeast section of the Common was used for many years as an out-door market, and in the northwest section there was a town well and pump that supplied the tiny settlement with water. Some portion of the Common was also used as Hartford's first burying ground.

The Connecticut Colony originally consisted of only three towns... Hartford, Windsor and Wethersfield. From the beginning Hartford was looked upon as the center of the colony, so the Hartford Meeting House served as the

OLD STATE HOUSE

800 Main Street
Thomas Hooker Sq
522-6766

The Old State House also serves as the city's Visitor Information Center.

Hours:
Open 7 days a week
Monday through Saturday
10:00 a.m.-5:00 p.m.
Sunday 12:00-5:00 p.m.
Closed major holidays.

Museum Shop:
An exciting gift shop, concentrating on Connecticut things with the flavor of a country store. Items for students range in price from $1.00 to $3.00.

Admission:
Free, with suggested donation.

Tours:
Guided tours or self guided tours are available. Special emphasis is placed on the history and architecture of the building.
For information about special events, educational programs, and guided tours please call 522-6766.
The Old State House pulses day and night with lively events: jubilees, festivals and celebrations, including the Fourth of July and seasonal celebrations of Hartford's ethnic communities; free concerts each week all summer; holiday programs and family entertainment for young and old; Chamber Music plus — the Old State House's ensemble-in-residence performing year 'round in the Court Room; changing exhibitions of art, antiques, crafts, history and technology, political debates, forums and appearances by aspiring candidates.

colony's first supreme political body, then known as the General Court. The two other major political jurisdictions within the present State of Connecticut were the Saybrook Colony and the New Haven Colony. Saybrook joined Connecticut in 1644 and New Haven in 1665. Unfortunately New Haven submitted to being annexed to Connecticut with great reluctance, having failed to obtain from the English king a Royal Charter that was vital to her own political sovereignty. The fact that Connecticut in 1662 had succeeded in winning from King Charles II a very liberal and powerful Royal Charter forced this alliance with New Haven.

In 1698 Connecticut's unicameral General Court was remodeled into a bicameral General Assembly consisting of an Upper House that included the governor and his assistants and a Lower House composed of delegates from all the towns in the colony. In order to placate New Haven, the General Assembly met alternately in Hartford and New Haven, so both towns shared the honor of being the colony's political capital. In 1717 New Haven built a handsome State House for the use of the General Assembly, and three years later Hartford did the same. By 1720 the Connecticut General Assembly consisted of 89 men... 12 in the Upper House and 77 in the Lower House. So for many years Hartford's plain, wooden capitol building, measuring 70 feet long and 30 feet wide, was quite adequate. Sixty years later, however, a vastly expanded 200-man General Assembly began to complain bitterly about the cramped and unsanitary facilities of their meeting place in Hartford.

In April of 1783, when the war-weary citizens of this city received the happy news of a provisional treaty with Great Britain, they celebrated the successful termination of the American Revolution with a great parade and many fireworks. During the festivities the wooden State House was accidentally set afire and much of the roof was destroyed. Only the heroic exertions of volunteer firemen prevented the building from being totally demolished. Although the roof was repaired, the fire and the obvious inadequacy of the meeting place spurred the town fathers into deciding, in 1792, that a larger and much more elegant capitol must be constructed. A letter from Connecticut

Governor Jonathan Trumbull Sr.'s artist son, John, to Oliver Wolcott, Jr., dated September 30, 1792, reads: "A new State House is to be built here next year upon a design of Mr. Bulfinch, which I think is worth executing in the best materials..."

Charles Bulfinch of Boston was one of the most illustrious architects of his day. He later designed and built the capitols in Boston, Massachusetts, and Augusta, Maine. The Capitol in Washington, burned by the British in 1814, was subsequently rebuilt after Bulfinch's designs.

One of the chief promoters of the Hartford State House of 1792 was Jeremiah Wadsworth who had served as Commissary General for George Washington during the American Revolution. As Hartford's wealthiest merchant, Colonel Wadsworth contributed the first and largest subscription to the building fund for the new structure... all of $500. Other leading citizens followed suit until a total of 51 donors had contributed $3,600. The State then added more funds that brought the total up to $13,600, but even this amount was insufficient to meet the building costs. In 1793, therefore, a public lottery was authorized to raise funds since the descendants of the Puritans did not regard lotteries as gambling but rather as a kind of voluntary tax quite suitable for financing worthy causes. Unfortunately, the lottery was almost a complete failure. Finally two men, Jeremiah Halsey and Andrew Ward, proposed to the General Assembly that they would furnish and finish the Hartford State House if they were given the funds already raised and a strip of western land between New York and Pennsylvania that was known as the Connecticut Gore. This Gore was claimed by Connecticut through the Royal Charter of 1662. The General Assembly was sold, and the Hartford State House was finally completed and furnished at an estimated cost of $52,480. In true Yankee fashion, the former wooden State House was not demolished to make room for the new, but moved over to Church Street and converted into a rooming house.

Bushnell Park

*Tour telephone: 240-0222.
Tours: Monday through
Friday, 9:30 am to 3:00 pm,
departing every 30 minutes
with the exception of 12 noon.*

Until 1871 Hartford shared with New Haven the honor of being a capital of the State of Connecticut. That year the citizens voted to have this city be the sole capital. A special Board of Capitol Commissioners then was created by the General Assembly and charged with the responsibility of bringing about the removal of Washington College, now Trinity, to its present site to make way for the new Capitol building; finding an architect; choosing a design; and having a new State Capitol constructed within a budget of $1,000,000. The only plans submitted upon which all the commissioners seemed able to agree were those of architect Richard M. Upjohn of New York City. His "Gothic Castle" came strictly within the budget. However, it was topped with a Tuscan clock tower which was disagreeably unfamiliar to Yankee commissioners accustomed to Bulfinch domes.

On March 12, 1872, the *Hartford Times* editorialized in distress, "Nobody would ever imagine such a building to be intended for a State House. All would require a sign board, painted in big letters, over main entrance, as follows:

THIS IS A STATE HOUSE
These plans are architectural delirium tremens ...
Our own preference — doubtless an uneducated
one — had inclined towards a dome rather than
a clock tower as more expressive of the sentiments
and character of a Capitol."

Even so, on October 10th a contract was signed to construct the building with James Goodwin Batterson, president of a local granite works and architectural firm as well as president of Travelers Insurance Company. Batterson immediately went to work and began laying the foundations of the new building according to Upjohn's design. Then, in May of 1873, responding to public clamor in the press, the General Assembly ordered all work on the construction of the building halted until its design could be reconsidered. In July a newly elected governor dismissed the first Board of Capitol Commissioners and appointed a new five-member board chaired by Alfred E. Burr, the fiercely pro-dome editor of the *Hartford Times*. Within the next year another $1.5 million was appropriated by the

Legislature to the new Capitol's budget to make the structure larger and fireproof ... and also to replace the original clock tower with a "more imposing tower or dome." Upjohn agreed to the dome and was officially put in charge of the Capitol building project.

With Upjohn's alterations approved and the additional monies appropriated, work on the building commenced again in 1875. By March of 1878, although the building was not entirely complete, the Legislature met for its first session in its new home. The public reaction was frankly ecstatic. Somehow the new Capitol which had cost more than $2.5 million expressed the optimism and opulence of its time in history. The agonies of the Civil War were over ... the industrial North had defeated the agricultural South on the field of battle ... a brave new world lay ahead.

A short while later, however, the citizens were shocked to learn that some serious cracks had opened up in the supporting piers of the Capitol's golden dome, and questions even arose as to whether the dome itself might collapse. After bitter controversy, the situation was ultimately corrected by pouring ten tons of lead into the crevices behind the piers. Another crisis arose when it was found that the $14,000 winged state, the Genius of Connecticut that graced the peak of the dome, was insecurely mounted.

Even so she remained there until she was finally removed in 1942. Despite the loss of the Genius the Connecticut State Capitol was registered as a national historic landmark 29 years later.

On June 12, 1973 the Connecticut State Capitol Preservation and Restoration Commission was created. A year later funds were appropriated to restore and renovate the Capitol.

If the state flag is flying over the west wing of the Capitol the governor is in his or her office.

The State Capitol is decorated with extensive exterior sculpture. On July 30, 1908, after remarking that one generation will crucify its reformers while the next generation will build them monuments, Hartford artist Charles Noel Flagg stated, "When all the work here mentioned is completed, the north front of the Connecticut State Capitol will present a collection of public sculptural decorations perhaps unequaled in the United States."

The twelve statues that encircle the dome of the Capitol represent Agriculture, Commerce, Education, Music, Science, and Force. The sculptor was John Quincy Adams Ward.

As mentioned, a statue that used to top the dome was called the Genius of Connecticut. The Genius, a winged female figure, was created in 1877-78 by New York sculptor Randolph Rogers in his studio in Rome, and cast in bronze in the Royal Foundry in Munich. Soon after the lovely Genius was mounted on the peak of the golden dome, someone noticed that she had not been securely attached to her lofty perch. When the wind blew, she teetered dangerously from side to side! Since she stood 17' 8" tall, exclusive of wings, and weighed 3.5 tons, the legislators who convened in the halls and chamber below were profoundly bothered by her wobbly ways.

Year after year the lawmakers debated the fate of the Genius, but they could not make up their minds what to do about her. Finally Charles Hopkins Clark, a former editor of the *Hartford Courant*, made fun of their indecision by challenging them to choose between "a loose woman over their heads or a fallen woman in their midst!" Even so, no decision was made until October 6, 1938 when, following the Great Hurricane, Governor Robert A. Hurley ordered the Genius removed by the W.P.A. Four years later, during World War II, she was melted down for scrap metal to be used for armaments.

In 1878 when Randolph Rogers delivered the bronze Genius to James Batterson, the builder of the State Capitol, he included as a gift the original plaster model. Batterson, in turn, gave the model to the State. For many years the model was displayed in a niche in the north lobby where, as time went by, she gradually deteriorated. Anticipating the coming American Bicentennial, Governor Thomas Meskill decided to have the model restored. Under the direction of Edward J. Kozlowski a Glastonbury sculptor, Casimir Michalczyk, was commissioned to undertake the project. On April 26, 1973 the restored Genius was unveiled and placed in the Rotunda of the Capitol. In 1965 he

Genius of Connecticut.

created the first engineering mock-up for the Apollo A-1 power cell and has done countless designs for other aerospace programs. His sculptures, water colors and paintings have been shown in numerous museums.

In the east lobby of the Capitol there is a statue of Revolutionary War hero, Nathan Hale by Karl Gerhardt. Like sculptor Michalczyk, Gerhardt also worked in a local industry. He designed machines for Pratt & Whitney Machine Tool Company.

Besides statues, numerous fascinating artifacts and plaques may be seen that commemorate important historical events in Connecticut's history. The League of Women Voters is on hand to conduct tours.

LEGISLATIVE OFFICE BUILDING

Capitol Avenue

Between the State Armory and the Capitol has risen an impressive and expensive new monument for the processing of state legislation in the most efficient and up-to-date manner. Oriented toward the 100-year-old Capitol, the five story Legislative Office Building features blocks of Texas granite and a copper mansard roof. A planted terrace spans the I-84 ramps, connecting it with the grounds of the Capitol, and a moving walkway beneath the highway provides handicapped access. The heart of the building is the large atrium with brass-railed galleries. The state shield, a hand-carved 2,700 pound piece of granite, is mounted at the second level. The warm cherry wainscoting is reminiscent of colonial Connecticut. Above it, subdued pinks, grays and ivory complement the dominant rose shade of both marble and steel.

Ten hearing rooms open directly off the atrium, which are scaled for committees and crowds of different sizes. At the east end a dramatic gold-leafed eagle rests on a polished granite column. Each of the double-leaved cherry doors facing the atrium is embellished with representations in wood of the Charter Oak, mountain laurel, the Old State House, and other symbols. For the first time in the state's history all senators and representatives have their own offices, located on the third and fourth levels. On the fifth floor is a roomy legislative library. The entire building has been designed with television and radio in mind; video screens at each entrance display the time and location of hearings and other events. There is also a public dining facility.

*The State's new Legislative Office
Building. Photo courtesy of
Barbara D. Zuna.*

THE CONNECTICUT STATE LIBRARY

Capitol Avenue

HOURS: Monday through Friday 8:30 a.m.-5:00 p.m.; Saturday 9:00 a.m. 1:00 p.m. (except holiday weekends). Closed Sundays and Holidays.

The Connecticut State Library is the principal library of the state government and the focal point for state-wide library activities. It provides service to the General Assembly, the various State executive departments, the judicial department, and to the entire State. It promotes library development in the State, works to improve library standards, recommends legislation concerning libraries, and tries to foster a climate of acceptance and under-standing of libraries and the value of library service.

The reference and research collections are free to the public but are not available for loan. Borrowing services are provided to other libraries through interlibrary loan and from three service centers.

The major part of the book collection is located in the Connecticut State Library and Supreme Court Building, opposite the State Capitol, 231 Capitol Avenue, Hartford. A granite structure consisting of three wings, it is an adaptation of Italian Renaissance style of architecture. The State Library occupies the east wing of the building. It contains the main reading room and the historical records section from which various services are provided to the public. The Connecticut Supreme Court, the highest State court, occupies the west wing of the building.

In the courtroom is a mural, painted by Albert Herter, depicting the adoption in 1639 of the Fundamental Orders of Connecticut. These were the first rules by which the Colony of Connecticut was governed. On permanent display in Memorial Hall are the original Charter, framed in wood from the Charter Oak, granted to Connecticut in 1662 by Charles II; the "original" copy of the Constitution adopted in 1965; and portraits of Connecticut governors. A part of the valuable Joseph C. Mitchelson Coin Collection, the Colt Collection of Firearms and the table upon which President Abraham Lincoln signed the Emancipation Proclamation are also on display. (The Colt Collection is recognized to be one of the most famous collections of firearms and related material anywhere in the world. It contains numerous valuable letters, documents, books and other memorabilia as well as approximately 1,000 firearms that tell the long history of the company that Sam Colt founded.)

The general and special collections of the Library
contain 435,000 bound volumes, two million manuscripts,
a million pamphlets, microfilms, maps, pictures, and other
memorabilia. The basic collections are in the broad subject
fields of law, the social sciences, history and genealogy, and
the official state archives, including the original records of
the Colony and the State beginning with the first record
of the General Court on April 26, 1636.

The law collection is extensive. It includes statutes,
reports and digests of the United States and of all the states,
and Connecticut Public Acts and General Statutes from
earliest days. Connecticut legislative committee hearings
on proposed legislation since 1900, Attorney General's
opinions, Departmental regulations, and a large number
of law journals are also on file.

The history and genealogy material is exceptional. A person wanting to trace his Connecticut ancestors can come to the Library and find numerous records and indexes. The famous Barbour Collection records births, marriages, and deaths in all Connecticut towns prior to 1850. The Library has a large number of probate records—wills, inventories of estates for many Connecticut towns. Both collections are completely indexed. Also indexed are Connecticut church records from the 1600's to the 1900's, early U.S. Census records, cemetery headstone inscriptions, and family Bible records.

The Library maintains war records of Connecticut residents, an extensive collection of Connecticut newspapers, pictures of Connecticut, and early automobile catalogs.

The Library is responsible for the distribution and exchange of official state documents and reports, and the sale of U.S. topographic maps of Connecticut. It is an official regional depository for U.S. publications, and a depository for documents of other states. Photoduplication and rapid copy facilities, microfilm and microprint equipment implement the services of the State Library. The Library acquires and displays in a museum the important artifacts which reflect the long, outstanding history of Connecticut, such as military relics, Indian handicrafts, and other objects of historical interest.

The Library was "established" in May, 1854, when the Connecticut General Assembly authorized the appointment of the first State Librarian. It was his responsibility to assemble in the Old State House the materials housed in the various State offices and to establish and administer the State Library. The State Library was moved in 1878 to the newly completed State Capitol where it remained until its transfer to the State Library and Supreme Court Building on November 28, 1910. Construction of an extensive addition to the building was completed in February, 1968.

Other functions of the library include the examination of town records for preservation and safe-keeping. A Records Center for the storage of infrequently used records of state agencies is located in Rocky Hill.

Connecticut State Library

STATE ARSENAL AND ARMORY

360 Broad Street

On June 28, 1904 the Municipal Art Society of Hartford was formed "to conserve and enhance in every practicable way the streets, public buildings and public places in Hartford; and to stimulate interest in the scenic, artistic and architectural development of the city..." Charles Noel Flagg, Hartford's well-known painter, was one of the chief promoters of this new society.

The Municipal Art Society's first project was to urge the State of Connecticut to purchase Hartford's deteriorating old railroad round-house situated on the western edge of Bushnell Park, remove it, and build in its place a handsome new State Arsenal and Armory which "would form a part of the splendid group of buildings which will one day surround Bushnell Park." After much effort the Society succeeded in persuading the State to agree to its proposal. Then, in 1905, talented New York architect Benjamin Wistar Morris, was retained to draw up plans for the new building. (Morris later designed the home office of the Connecticut Mutual Life Insurance Company.) The young architect was a Trinity graduate, son of the Episcopal Bishop of Oregon and son-in-law of Hartford's unofficial "city planner," the Rev. Francis Goodwin. Thus both his professional and social credentials were exemplary!

The new State Arsenal and Armory was completed in 1909 and proved an invaluable facility as well a great addition to the city's architectural appearance. In 1916 the U.S. Navy's first blimp, DN-1 was assembled here. The blimp had been built in New Haven the year before, but this armory was the only state building large enough to contain the inflated airship while it was being rigged!

Until the Hartford Civic Center was constructed in 1975 the Armory's vast auditorium area, capable of seating 10,000, was used for all major State and City functions and exhibits. The prestigious Governor's Ball is still held here as are many large shows. This is also the headquarters for the Air National Guard, the Army National Guard, Civil Preparedness, the Army Advisors Office, the Horse Guard and Foot Guard, and a private Officers' Club for American Veterans.

This is the residence of the Governor of Connecticut. Located on six acres of ground, the house contains nineteen rooms. It was acquired by the state for the chief executive in 1943 and first occupied in 1945.

The house was built in 1909 by Dr. George C.F. Williams whose family was closely connected with the Capewell Manufacturing Company, a venerable Hartford enterprise. It cost $43,000, an enormous sum in those days. The architects Andres, Jaques, and Rantoul of Boston, and the builder, Robert Porteous of Hartford, had recently designed and built the handsome Hartford Club on Prospect Street in the city.

Because Prospect Avenue dividing Hartford and West Hartford was still a dirt thoroughfare, Dr. Williams tried to persuade the city fathers to curve the road west so that he could have a larger front yard. Unfortunately a neighbor, Robert Schutz, president of the Smyth Manufacturing Company, objected strenuously and insisted that the new road must be straight. Obviously, Mr. Schutz won the argument.

In 1916 two wings were constructed on the north and south sides of the house and, in 1927, an additional maid's room was added. On both occasions Smith and Bassett of Hartford were the architects.

METROPOLITAN DISTRICT COMMISSION

555 Main Street
278-7850

Tours: The West Hartford Water Purification Plant off Farmington Avenue in West Hartford and the Reservoir #6 Water Purification Plant in Bloomfield off Route 44 are open for group tours during weekday working hours. The M.D.C.'s Hartford Water Pollution Control Plant in the South Meadows area and three smaller sewage treatment plants in Rocky Hill, East Hartford and Poquonock, are also open for tours, if scheduled in advance. Call the above number for appointments and further information on facility tours.

Recreation Opportunities: The roads and grounds around the West Hartford and Reservoir #6 Water Purification Plants are lovely places to walk, hike, bicycle, jog and cross-country ski. They are open 8:00 a.m.— 8:00 p.m. in the summer and from 8:00 a.m. to dark in the winter months. No boating, swimming, fishing or skiing are allowed in the five small reservoirs that comprise the West Hartford/Bloomfield system, nor are such activities allowed in the M.D.C.'s two major sources of drinking water: The Nepaug Reservoir in Collinsville and the Barkhamsted Reservoir. Swimming, boating and fishing are allowed on a seasonal basis at the M.D.C.'s Lake McDonough

The Hartford headquarters building for the Metropolitan District Commission, completed in 1977, was developed by the Bushnell Plaza Development Corporation. The architects were Russell, Gibson von Dohlen of West Hartford, and the contractors were W.J. Barney Corporation of Groton, Connecticut.

The M.D.C. is the oldest regional body in Connecticut engaged in activities of a public works nature. It was the "brain child" of Charles A. Goodwin, son of the Rev. Francis Goodwin who personally brought about the creation of Hartford's extensive park system. The son was as visionary, civic minded and practical as the father. His mission was to provide Metropolitan Hartford with an ample, high quality water supply. This radical concept is best described in Mr. Goodwin's own words written in 1930: "The establishment of a Metropolitan District within the County of Hartford makes a change of policy in Connecticut respecting the operation of certain essential public functions.

In the past we have had local governments and state government. Matters of local importance have been left in the hands of towns. The state functions have been steadily widening. There are, however, certain public needs which are in no sense statewide and yet which involve two or more communities and are not strictly local.

The increasing complications of modern life, the crowding together of individuals in great cities involve an interdependence between the central city and the suburban communities requiring a common government as to certain functions which, while responsive to local demands, is free from obstructions of governmental units."

After almost 10 years of struggling to pass the essential legislation, Mr. Goodwin, a lawyer in the firm of Shipman and Goodwin, was finally successful. (No doubt he learned the important lesson of patience and persistence from his wife's grandfather, Horace Bushnell, as well as from his own father!) In 1929 the Metropolitan District Commission was created by an Act of the General Assembly, and on July 1, 1930 Mr. Goodwin became the District's first chairman. He served until January 1, 1949 when he retired at his own request. It was during this period when the political genius of Charles Goodwin and the engineering genius of Caleb Mills Saville created the major portion of the present plant of the M.D.C. Saville Dam in Barkhamsted memorializes the great engineer.

In 1948 the American Office of the old Russia Insurance Company on Broad Street, designed by Edward Hapgood of Hartford and built in 1915, became the first headquarters of the M.D.C. This unusually handsome building was supposedly a small scale duplicate of the Russian company's home office in Petrograd. Old Hartfordites recall the two Russian bears that used to flank the front entrance. The bears are now the property of the Science Museum of Connecticut in West Hartford. In 1968 the building was destroyed to make way for the new Y.W.C.A., and the M.D.C. moved into temporary quarters on Hartford Plaza. Ten years later, in February 1978, the M.D.C. moved into its current Main Street headquarters building.

Today the M.D.C., with an annual budget of over $50 million, supplies water to some 400,000 people in eight member towns (Hartford, East Hartford, Windsor, Bloomfield, Newington, Wethersfield, Rocky Hill and West Hartford), plus Glastonbury and portions of Farmington and South Windsor. Average daily consumption is 60 million gallons of water, which was first fluoridated in 1960. Industry too is a major consumer of clean water, so Hartford's Space Age industrial plants could not exist without the services of the M.D.C.

The M.D.C. opened it first sewage treatment plant in Hartford in 1938. Today the District maintains a sewage treatment system, including secondary treatment, in Hartford, Rocky Hill, East Hartford, and Poquonock. These water pollution control plants process a daily average of 65 million gallons of waste water from a population of some 360,000 people.

(formerly Compensating Reservoir) facility off Route 219 in Barkhamsted. The lake is open from Memorial Day through Labor Day. Fishing and boating opportunities are also available at the West Branch Reservoir approximately six miles north of Winsted on Route 8.

For further information on the operations and services of the Metropolitan District, contact the M.D.C.'s Public Information office between 8:00 a.m — 4:00 p.m. at 278-7850.

HARTFORD MUNICIPAL BUILDING

550 Main Street

In 1910 when the great J. Pierpont Morgan built and dedicated the Morgan Memorial wing of the Wadsworth Atheneum in honor of his father, he was not pleased by the fact that the neighborhood just across the street from the lovely new museum was an ugly slum. So he bought up most of the property on this block, removed the slums, then presented the land to his native city with the proviso that the area be made a place of beauty. Because the present Old State House, which had been used as Hartford's City Hall since 1873, was becoming cramped for space, the city fathers decided that they would construct on this cleared land a handsome new Municipal Building. Davis and Brooks, architects, created plans that were late Georgian in style to complement the Morgan Memorial and the Old State House. The new building was dedicated in 1914 and completely occupied by the following year. Two large murals on the south wall of the first floor depict historic scenes from Hartford's early years.

If you enter from Burr Mall and find your way up the magnificent staircase, you can actually stand on the frosted glass ceiling of the bottom level. A feeling of spaciousness is provided by the glass gallery which makes up the roof of the building.

Fountains, Municipal Building, 550 Main Street

These two fountains were designed by Davis and Brooks, architects of the Municipal Building, in 1914.

THE FEDERAL BUILDING

450 Main Street

Designed by architects Prentice and Frid and constructed in 1963, the Federal Building stands on the former homesite of Connecticut's illustrious political "boss", Democrat John Moran Bailey, and the former site of the Parma Restaurant where Democrats met for political caucuses. The Parma is now located at 271 Sheldon Street.

The Federal Building contains the offices of numerous Federal agencies including the Federal Bureau of Investigation and the Internal Revenue Service. Here, too, are the U.S. Courts and the offices of Federal Judges and Congressmen.

Photo courtesy of Laurie Johnson.

Hartford's preeminence as a financial center second in importance only to Boston and New York rests on the solid foundation of two basic commercial ideas that derived from the Puritan heritage of its capitalists during the late 18th and early 19th centuries. These were: sound credit and calculated risk.

Even the first settlers shared a double-barreled vision of the good life. On the one hand they were concerned with spiritual salvation; on the other, they appreciated the need to survive and prosper. In fact, worldly success was often viewed as a sign of being "elected" to sainthood. The basis of the famous Puritan work ethic was the conviction that godliness must be demonstrated by usefulness. The famous 17th century Puritan divine, Cotton Mather, said every Christian had two callings, first to serve the Lord and then "a personal calling, or a particular employment, by which his usefulness, in his neighborhood, is distinguished ... this that he may glorify God, by the doing of good for others, and the getting of good for himself."

This credo amounted to practical idealism. A Congregationalist was a person with his head in the clouds but his feet on the ground. He did not countenance aggrandizement or exploitation. To the contrary, ostentatious display of wealth was deplored, and the obligation to care for the "deserving poor" was mandatory. For the most part, Hartford citizens were neither very rich nor very poor. Instead, they aspired to become a sober and sound middle class.

Nowhere was this credo better demonstrated than in banking and insurance. They both evolved out of the city's functioning as a busy river port and its dependence to a large extent on maritime trade with the West Indies and coastal cities. Captains and merchants used to gather down by the wharves on the Connecticut River, especially at Morgan's coffee house, an establishment run by J. P. Morgan's grandfather. It served as both a club and chamber of commerce, where important business matters were discussed and decided, the proprietor's advice and assistance always sought, and agreements were made to share risks and profits on cargoes of ships going forth to trade overseas.

Today, 46 insurance companies are located in the Greater Hartford area with assets approaching $120 billion. Annual premiums amount to more than $7 billion. Altogether, they employ 46,000, including 6,000 Aetna Life employees who work in its magnificent new Middletown facility.

In 1791 an Act was passed by the U.S. Congress authorizing the establishment of a U.S. Bank with branches to be opened in eligible cities. Hartford's merchants, led by Colonel Jeremiah Wadsworth, a personal friend of Alexander Hamilton, justly considered that a commercial bank in Hartford would particularly benefit the development of the area. The city's businesses had been limited by the fact that specie was scarce in those days, so they were often forced to resort to barter ... a very awkward method of trade for Hartford's many sea captains who were heavily involved in commerce with the West Indies. The fact that a local bank would be allowed to print money was a most attractive prospect.

In 1792 Hartford's first bank was chartered. Noah Webster, the great lexicographer, was one of the Hartford Bank's original petitioners, and John Caldwell, a leading merchant and grandfather of the future Samuel Colt, became the bank's first president.

The 26-story skyscraper that is now the headquarters was designed by Welton Becket of California, constructed by the George A. Fuller Co. of New York, and completed in June, 1966.

Connecticut National is one of the two largest commercial banks in Connecticut. Now merged with the Shawmut Bank of Boston, the combined banks have assets of nearly $28 billion.

CONNECTICUT NATIONAL BANK

777 Main Street
Tel: 728-4336
Public Information

The bank's Corporate Services Center was designed by architect Charles DuBose Associates, built by Industrial Construction Company of Newington, and opened in December of 1971.

Created as a technical building to house all departments that are computer related, the Center houses employees who process banking transactions on the most advanced computer systems.

The building, which has an exterior of large precast concrete panels, consists of five floors of working area and two floors used for parking. Each floor is approximately 36,000 square feet in size. At first glance the lack of windows is evident (there is one row of windows on the top floor). The closed environment helps to control the building's temperature and humidity.

CONNECTICUT NATIONAL SERVICE CENTER

150 Windsor Street

CONSTITUTION PLAZA COMPLEX

Management Office
100 Constitution
Plaza
527-2636

Opened in 1962-64, this $40 million complex was Hartford's first major urban renewal project in modern times. It replaces over 12 acres of run-down ethnic neighborhoods. Columbus Boulevard recalls the numerous Italians who used to populate this thoroughfare then known as Front Street.

Financed by Travelers Insurance Company, Constitution Plaza includes banking, broadcasting, commercial and hotel facilities. The architect for the project was Charles DuBose and the landscape architects were Sasaki, Walker & Associates Inc. The Plaza's name celebrates the world's first written constitution that was drawn up in Hartford in 1639.

The Plaza is the focal point of many community-wide festivals. Events such as The Taste of Hartford, a variety of outdoor concerts and a lovely Festival of Lights are held here. Of great historical significance was this nation's first Ecumenical Easter Sunrise Service that was celebrated here for the first time on April 10, 1966. More than 10,000 Roman Catholic, Orthodox and Protestant Christians participated.

Broadcast House 3 Constitution Plaza

The home of WFSB-TV3, it is the largest and most complete facility of its kind in Connecticut. The architects were Fulmer & Bowers of Princeton, New Jersey.

Fountain on Plaza Constitution Plaza, Hartford

Created by Masao Kimoshita in 1962-64 under the direction of the plaza's architect Charles DuBose and landscape architects Sasaki, Walker and Associates, Inc., this fountain is unusual in that its waters are not tossed up into the air. Aware of the fact that the brisk breezes that frequently sweep over the plaza would blow the flying water in such a way that it would soak passing pedestrians, Mr. Kimoshita designed this fountain to resemble a mountain stream with waters flowing downward in a carefully controlled cascade!

Clocktower on Plaza Constitution Plaza, Hartford

This clocktower was designed by Masao Kimoshita in 1961-64.

Society for Savings, organized in Hartford in 1819, was the first institution of its kind in Connecticut and the sixth in the U.S.A. The bank was originally a philanthropic enterprise sponsored by Hartford's "Standing Order" to assist the new poor who were then migrating into the city. By receiving, investing and paying compound interest on small savings of working men and women, the early trustees of this mutual savings institution endeavored to teach their depositors habits of thrift that would be beneficial both to their own futures and to the future of the community as a whole. Daniel Wadsworth, Hartford's chief benefactor at that time in Hartford history, was the new savings bank's first president. Society's present headquarters were built in 1893, but the name of the architect is unknown.

Society has been in the forefront of bank data processing since 1961 when it became the first bank in New England and the third in the world to process teller transactions on-line. Today, it is the second largest savings bank in New England with assets of over $3.6 billion. In 1984 it converted to the stock form of ownership. It operates 38 branches throughout the state.

SOCIETY FOR SAVINGS

31 Pratt Street
727-5000

MECHANICS SAVINGS BANK

60 Pearl Street
525-8661

Chartered in 1861 and led by president James P. Foster, the Mechanics Savings Bank was designed especially to receive the savings of working people. In those days anyone with a "trade" was known as a "mechanic." Most of them worked in local factories like Colt's Armory.

In the early 1920s the bank constructed a headquarters at 60 Pearl Street, then purchased the building just to the east in the 1940s. In 1973-74 these two adjacent buildings were renovated under the guidance of Bernard Vinick Associates.

Mechanics is the seventh largest savings bank in Connecticut. In 1988 it occupied its new office that is part of the city's latest skyscraper, known as the "Blue Building." This 17-story structure represents the first example of creative zoning in Hartford: a non-profit art gallery called Art At 100 Pearl occupies the lobby space between two banks. The idea for a place where the public could be exposed to museum quality art works came from Helen Krieble Fusscas, owner of the Connecticut Gallery.

UNITED BANK

101 Pearl Street
520-3400

In 1964 the United Bank was created by combining the old Riverside Trust Co., Bristol Bank & Trust Co., and the Portland Trust Co. The latter was the oldest, having been founded in 1865. At the same time the First Connecticut Bancorp also was created combining the new United Bank & Trust Co., the Simsbury Bank & Trust Co., the New Britain National Bank, and the Pioneer Credit Corporation of Great Barrington, Massachusetts. James J. Preble became the first president of both new corporations.

The United Bank is now number nine of the 71 commercial banks in Connecticut. The bank's headquarters at 101 Pearl Street were completed in 1971. The architects were Jeter, Cook & Jepson and the contractor was Edward Packtor Company.

Opened for business July 24, 1858 as the State Savings Bank, this financial institution was originally located at 295 Main Street. Its first president was Chester Adams. It erected its own building at 39 Pearl Street in 1923.

In 1968 the bank merged with the Dime Savings Bank and a few years ago the combined institutions were acquired by the People's Bank of Bridgeport, the largest savings bank in Connecticut.

PEOPLE'S BANK

1 Financial Plaza
280-2636

Founded in Hartford in 1863, the Travelers Insurance Companies today are one of the largest multiple-line insurance companies in the world, and the largest in the nation. It is listed among the top 25 corporations in America. A pioneer in many different forms of insurance, the company wrote the first accident policy in the U.S.A. and was the first with automobile and aircraft liability coverage.

This is the company's fourth home office within the City of Hartford. The original portion of the building was constructed in 1907 on the former site of Sanford Tavern, a popular Hartford gathering place established by one Jeremy Adams in 1651 in which the famous Charter Oak incident occurred in 1687. Many additions to The Travelers corporate headquarters have been made since, the most interesting of which is the tower completed in 1919 under the direction of architect Donn Barber. It rises to a height of 34 stories, its pinnacle being 527 feet above the street. All around the cupola is a series of powerful projectors giving off a flashing red light, visible for many miles and serving as a beacon for aircraft. In the daytime the view from the top of the tower is spectacular.

Batterson Memorial Hall, located on the first floor right inside the Main Street entrance, is well worth a visit. A large seated statue of the company's founder, James Goodwin Batterson, created by sculptor Albin Polaska in 1919, exudes the man's dynamic personality. With his long white beard and little round belly Batterson looks like an aggressive version of Santa Claus! One of 12 children of a poor Bloomfield stonecutter, Batterson was an astonishingly versatile human being. He customarily slept only five hours a night and always made the most of his waking hours. In 1838, at age

THE TRAVELERS INSURANCE COMPANIES

277-0111
for information and services.

Tower tours are run every half hour, week-days only, 8 A.M.- 3:30 P.M., May-October, Batterson Memorial Hall is open all year round during office hours.

15, he was apprenticed by his father to a printer in Ithaca, New York. (His indenture is on display in the company museum.) Not surprisingly, he walked the 200 miles to his new job and took up his task as errand boy with zest. During the evenings, he devoted himself to the equivalent of a college course augmented by a heavy correspondence with Hartford friends who were attending college. One of his passions was Greek. (Many years later he became president of the Greek Club of New York and wrote his own translations of the *Iliad*, *Odyssey*, the *Lyrics of Anacreon*, and a number of Latin hymns.) His apprenticeship to the printer was terminated after only three years, however, because his father needed the young man's assistance in the family stone business. With characteristic energy and imagination Batterson vastly expanded the business into an organization of national renown. As both designer and builder of stone monuments, he erected the National Soldiers Monument at Gettysburg and others at Antietam, Galveston, San Francisco, and elsewhere. As a builder he provided the stone and much architectural know-how for both the National Capitol and the Library of Congress in Washington, the state capitals of Connecticut and New York (while erecting the latter he invented a turning lathe for polishing stone columns), and a number of impressive structures in Philadelphia and New York City including the Waldorf Astoria in Manhattan, and the Vanderbilt mansions in New York and Newport. At the same time he was extremely active in politics, became chairman of the State Republican Committee, and won Connecticut for Abraham Lincoln. These activities did not deter him from also becoming a much respected financier, a patron of the arts, a poet, one of the foremost Egyptologists of his day, and a fellow of the American Society of Civil Engineers!

In 1859, when a 36-year-old Batterson was on a business trip in England, he became intrigued by the subject of accident insurance as written by a number of English companies. On his return home he discussed this concept with friends who, four years later under his leadership, petitioned the Connecticut legislature for permission to form a corporation "for the purpose of insuring travelers against loss of life or personal injury while journeying by railway or steamboat." The following year the charter of this little Hartford company, the first casualty insurance company in North

America, was amended to include accidents of all kinds. When James Goodwin Batterson died in 1901 his pioneer project had grown to might proportions ... but it had been only one of the many interests in his surprisingly creative and productive life. The New York *Herald* noted in his obituary, "Certainly few more remarkable men ever lived in Connecticut. The country at large may well honor his memory as one of her greatest sons."

In 1962 plans were begun to develop the south side of the Travelers Insurance Companies tower building so that the area could be coordinated with the rebuilt Wadsworth Atheneum and redesigned city streets. The main entrance to the Travelers was relocated and the Tower Square complex created. The architects were Voorhees, Walker, Smith, and Haines of New York City, the builder George A. Fuller Company, and the site planners and landscape designers Sasaki, Walker & Associates of Watertown, Mass. The Tower Square complex was completed in 1964, the 100th anniversary of the founding of the company.

In 1970 a new 13-story office building and five-level parking garage were built on an 11-acre tract of land bordered by Prospect, Grove and Arch Streets and Columbus Blvd. This expansion was coordinated with the renovation of the Hartford Club. The architects and planners for the Travelers' addition were Rogers, Taliferro, Kostritsky and Lamb of Baltimore, the associate architect Charles DuBose of Hartford, and the contractor the Turner Construction Company.

TRAVELERS DATA CENTER

300 Windsor Street

No tours except by special arrangements. Call administrative offices: 277-3713

The Travelers Data Center is one of the most extensive data processing facilities in the world. It cost almost $20 million and covers 8 1/2 acres of land. A one-story building, it contains 200,000 square feet of space and was constructed to satisfy special air conditioning and electrical requirements of computer installation. The Center was created to consolidate all the company's growing electronic data processing under one roof, and is linked to major field offices across the country. Information requested by an office 3,000 miles away will reach the requester in approximately 90 seconds ... with extreme accuracy from a constantly updated file.

The building was designed by the New York architectural firm of Voorhees, Walker, Smith and Haines and the general contractor was George A. Fuller of New York City.

CONNECTICUT BANK & TRUST COMPANY

1 Constitution Plaza
244-5000

The Connecticut Bank, founded in 1814, is the second oldest commercial bank in Hartford. According to tradition, a prominent founder of this bank was an irate Episcopalian who had difficulty doing business with the Hartford Bank because it was dominated by Congregationalists!

This may well have been true. Burgeoning local business enterprises and the westward expansion were, in fact, creating pressing needs for additional financing. So Hartford's first bank was flourishing. The petitioners for a new bank quite reasonably contended that "it was more congenial to the true republican principles ... that a new bank be granted (a charter) ... thereby promoting competition which creates an increasing endeavour to accommodate the public ..."

The architects of its headquarters on Constitution Plaza were Kahn and Jacobs of New York City for the total building, and Carson and Ludkins of New York City for the section occupied by the bank. Of particular interest is the Calder mobile that hangs above the main banking floor.

Connecticut Bank's Operations Center is located at Founders' Plaza in East Hartford. The building was completed and occupied in 1971. The third floor of the Operations Center houses, with one exception, the bank's entire data processing department. This computer complex was designed by Charles DuBose Associates to provide sufficient space for both current and future computer needs.

Connecticut Bank is one of the two largest commercial banks in Connecticut. In 1985 it merged with the Bank of New England, headquartered in Boston. Assets total $32 billion.

Founded in 1866 when steam was becoming a major power source in the growing city of Hartford as well as the nation, Hartford Steam Boiler Inspection and Insurance Company with its Canadian affiliate, The Boiler Inspection and Insurance Company of Canada, provide insurance coverage and inspection services designed to detect accident-producing conditions in boilers, pressure vessels, and a wide variety of machines that use, generate or transmit energy.

With Radian Corporation, its subsidiary in Austin, Texas, Hartford Steam Boiler provides advanced technical, engineering, and scientific services, and related products for industry and government, primarily in the fields of environment, health, safety, chemical process technology, data acquisition and communications, and energy.

In 1982 the company moved to 1 State Street, its new world headquarters building. Designed by Skidmore, Owings & Merrill of Houston, Texas, to complement the city's architecture, the 24-story office tower is said to combine the "pride of craftsmanship" apparent in the stone exteriors of some of Hartford's older landmarks, such as the Old State House and the Richardson, with the sculptural form exhibited in the modern and glass buildings of the '60s and '70s.

HARTFORD STEAM BOILER INSPECTION AND INSURANCE COMPANY

1 State Street
722-1866

PHOENIX MUTUAL LIFE INSURANCE COMPANY

1 American Row
275-5000

Photo courtesy of Laurie Johnson.

Tours of the company may be arranged for high school students involved in work-study programs, but there are no tours for the general public. Lobby exhibits, however, are always open to the general public.

Organized in 1851, Phoenix Mutual insured only the lives of strict teetotalers during the first decade of its business existence. Today it is one of the five biggest in Hartford and one of the top 25 in the U.S.A. In 1978 the company reached $70 billion in life insurance in force.

The extraordinary elliptical glass skyscraper that is Phoenix Mutual's home office is technically known as a "lenticular hyperboloid." It was designed by architect Max Abranovitz of New York City, and is one of the world's few two-sided office building. With its curved glass walls creating an impression of weightlessness, the Phoenix building has excited wide acclaim and has won numerous international architectural awards.

Aetna Life Insurance Company (renamed Aetna Life and Casualty in 1967) was founded in 1853. The first president was Eliphalet Bulkeley who had also been the first president of Connecticut Mutual Life Insurance Company. An argument between Bulkeley and Major James Goodwin (father of Rev. Francis Goodwin) and J. Pierpont Morgan ended in victory for the latter. Undaunted, Bulkeley founded his own company. Durings its first year of operation, the Aetna paid 36 claims. Today the company is the largest diversified financial company based on assets in the U.S.A. It is also first among insurance companies in number of new individually-written corporate pension plans sold and premium income from fidelity and surety bonds; first among insurance companies in number of group dental policies written; the largest writer of individual tax sheltered variable annuities in the country; and fourth among casualty and property companies in amount of premium income; and has almost $100 billion of life insurance in force.

Eliphalet Bulkeley's youngest son, Morgan Gardner Bulkeley, became the third president of the Aetna in 1879, a position he retained until his death in 1922. A man of tremendous energy and wide interests, he excelled both as a businessman and as a politician. He entered Republican politics in 1875, first as a Hartford alderman, then as mayor, then as governor of Connecticut, then as a U.S. Senator. Perhaps the most dramatic event of his political career was the occasion when he was nicknamed "Connecticut's Crowbar Governor."

During the gubernatorial election of 1890 Bulkeley, who had decided not to run for a second term, was faced with a most unique dilemma. When the votes were counted neither the Republican nor the Democratic candidate for the office of chief-of-state had clearly been elected according to Connecticut's antiquated election law, because neither one had a majority of the votes cast. Because a fantastic number of "specked" or defaced ballots had been thrown out, both sides cried "Foul!" and claimed victory. In those days an election not decided within the state's election laws was thrown into the State Legislature for a decision. At that time the Democrats had a slight edge in the Senate, and the House was solidly Republican. Inevitably, therefore, the legislative decision was tied!

AETNA LIFE AND CASUALTY

151 Farmington Avenue
273-0123

Open for tours 9 A.M. to Noon, 1-3 P.M. Call for appointment.

Determined to obey the law, Governor Bulkeley then ruled that no new governor had been elected so that he, as incumbent governor, was forced to remain in office. The only man who did manage to win a majority in the legislative run-off was the Democratic candidate for state treasurer, Nicholas Staub. A fierce political battle then ensued between Bulkeley and Staub. Late in March, when a Democratic committee was given the use of the anteroom adjoining the governor's office, Staub persuaded the State Capitol's building superintendent to secure the door between that room and the governor's office with a large padlock. When Bulkeley found the door locked, he was so outraged that he sent for a crowbar and personally wrenched it open ... hence his nickname, the Crowbar Governor.

Equally incensed, Comptroller Staub then cut off Governor Bulkeley's funds, and the state soon ran out of money. The governor countered by pledging his entire personal fortune, backed by the assets of the Aetna Life Insurance Company, to finance the state. Finally, on January 5, 1891, the Connecticut Supreme Court handed down a unanimous decision that Governor Bulkeley, in the absence of a constitutionally chosen successor, remained the *de jure* as well as the *de facto* political leader of Connecticut. All indebtedness was repaid both to Bulkeley personally and to the Aetna. On October 7, 1891, however, the laws of Connecticut were changed so that the candidate receiving the highest popular vote for a state election could be elected legally.

Bulkeley Bridge was built by Morgan G. Bulkeley and named in his honor, and he saved the Old State House from destruction. His civic "good works" were legion. Not only the most powerful man in town, he was also the city's most passionate protagonist. He loved this "turf" in which his Yankee roots ran deep. The community was second only to his family in his personal concern. He loved Hartford's past, present and future because he wanted his children, and his children's children to enjoy a Hartford that was beautiful and prosperous.

Morgan Bulkeley Brainard, who followed in his uncle's footsteps, was equally devoted to the welfare of his city, as were other members of the family. It was under Mr. Brainard's leadership that this huge new office building for Aetna was built on Farmington Avenue in 1931. This was the first time in Hartford that a place of work was, in fact, a complete community containing dining, shopping, recreational and educational facilities. One of Mr. Brainard's chief reasons for including all these amenities was to provide his employees with a wholesome, company-subsidized luncheon. He had noticed many came to work without eating a proper breakfast, so he felt a good lunch would raise their efficiency and thus be both to the employees' and the company's best interests! Understandably, the Aetna is the largest building of Colonial design in the world. The architect was James Gamble Rogers of New York who commented, "My inspiration, or perhaps I should say my courage, was drawn from the former Connecticut State Capitol [now known as the Old State House]."

Of particular aesthetic interests are the executive offices and meeting rooms on the eighth floor. These rooms contain exquisite examples of old Colonial panelling and flooring and the antique furniture is of museum quality. The roof garden just off the executive offices is especially charming and affords a fine view of the city and the hills to the west.

In 1968 the company embarked upon a major addition to its home office. Chairman of the Board Olcott D. Smith explained, "The need for additional space is brought about by our rapid growth. Combined premium income has doubled in the last 10 years. The new facilities will help us provide better service to our field organization and to our policy holders." The architects were Kevin Roche, John Dinkeloo and Associates, designers of such well-known structures as the TWA Terminal at Kennedy Airport in New York City and the St. Louis Memorial Arch. The builder was McClosky & Co., Inc. of Philadelphia. The contemporary design of the new addition was described by Mr. Smith as a "mark of our commitment to the future. The design was chosen to accentuate the Colonial architecture of the present building and preserve the main entrance as the focal point. Great care was taken to achieve architectural harmony."

Aetna Casualty's Corporate Data Processing and Administrative Services are located in this new addition and in other portions of the home office. In 1955 the company pioneered in Connecticut an I.B.M. electronic "brain" called a "650 drum calculator." Because accumulating and managing information is a major activity of the insurance business, the company's data processing component is now vastly enlarged to cope with its millions of policies in force. Aetna Casualty's computers maintain financial data about every aspect of its operations, ranging from the number of paper clips a department orders to the performance of the company's investment portfolio!

Aetna's continued commitment to the welfare of Hartford was shown in 1975 when the company joined with the city and the Greater Hartford Chamber of Commerce to revitalize the urban core of the Capitol Region by creating the Civic Center. Aetna developed the $35 million shopping sector of the Civic Center complex and co-financed with I.T. & T. the new Sheraton Hotel adjoining the Center.

Aetna also has played a prominent role in the revitalization of several other districts in Hartford, while at the same time it has been sensitive to neighborhood preservation. In 1983, Aetna completed renovations of several historic buildings on Capitol Avenue in conjunction with the Frog Hollow Living History Project. (In earlier times, this area was called Frog Hollow as a result of the legendary frog population that resided in a marsh near the corner of Ward and Broad streets.) The renovated facilities now house the company's Corporate Administration and Corporate Personnel departments. Exhibits in the lobbies of these new offices chronicle the evolution of the machines and products manufactured more than a century ago in the industrial district along Capitol Avenue.

The 1984 completion of the Aetna Institute for Corporate Education on Farmington Avenue, across from the company's home office, further exemplifies Aetna's ability to serve the community while advancing its own interests. The Institute is located only a short distance from the homes of Mark Twain and Harriet Beecher Stowe, on a plot once owned by Thomas Hooker, the founder of Hartford. The area, called Nook Farm, was a prosperous and socially influential literary community in the nineteenth century. The Institute is an educational center that uses state-of-the-art technology to ensure that the company's 55,000 employees have access to materials and information to enhance their professional abilities and understanding of the financial services industry.

The Aetna Institute also provides hotel services for employees from distant field offices while in Hartford and includes 387 beds, 26 classrooms, two dining rooms, a fitness center and a library. The company retained a physical connection to the historic value of the neighborhood by renovating Hasting's Farm, an 1892 residence, and integrating it into the design of the complex. The interior serves as the facility's central offices.

Along with its investment in Hartford's past, Aetna is clearly concerned with the future of the city's neighborhoods and residents. No discrimination as to race, creed or sex is tolerated by the management. Aetna's support of Asylum Hill Inc. and its investment in the renewal of Congress Street are further examples of the company's commendable corporate citizenship.

Built in 1931, the home office of Aetna Life & Casualty Insurance Company is the largest building of colonial design in the world.

HARTFORD INSURANCE GROUP

Hartford Plaza
547-5000

*Museum Hours: 9:00 A.M. - 4:00 P.M. M-F
Group tours by appointment. Call (203) 547-4979*

Founded in 1810 as the Hartford Fire Insurance Company, The Hartford is Connecticut's oldest existing insurance firm. Its home office complex on Hartford Plaza occupies 10 acres of land that used to be the site of the city's first public reservoir as well as the original campus of the American School for the Deaf, now in West Hartford. The original home office, at 690 Asylum Avenue, was designed by the Boston firm of Edwin Sherrill Dodge and constructed in 1921. A 22-story office tower, designed by Skidmore, Owings and Merrill, was completed in 1967. There is also a nine-story North Plaza building which houses data processing and related functions.

The Hartford Exhibit, a multi-media display area that traces The Hartford's 175-year business history is located in the atrium of the Tower Building. The company's symbol, the stag, stems from a 16th century seal used by the English town of Hertford, for which Hartford, Connecticut was named. The particular pose of the insurance company's stag was taken from the popular English painting, Monarch of the Glen, by Sir Edwin Landseer in 1851. The museum is named in honor of Herbert P. Schoen, former chief executive officer.

The Hartford was purchased by ITT Corporation in 1970. Five years later, ITT joined forces with Aetna Life and Casualty to build the new Sheraton Hotel adjoining the Hartford Civic Center, a major addition to the economic viability of downtown Hartford. The Hartford is active in the Greater Hartford community through numerous corporate contributions and community service programs.

In 1984, The Hartford Insurance Group had worldwide revenues of more than $5.7 billion. One of the nation's largest international insurance companies, The Hartford ranks ninth among insurers in the nation.

For many years, the Pulitzer Prize-winning poet Wallace Stevens was an executive with The Hartford Insurance Group. Those who knew and respected him as a businessman were often quite unaware of his accomplishments as a poet, and vice versa!

Founded in 1846, Connecticut Mutual is the oldest life insurance company in the state and the sixth oldest in the nation. A pioneer in many fields, the founders played a variety of key roles in expanding the insurance industry. Its first president also became the first president of Aetna Life and Casualty. One of its founders became the first president of Phoenix Mutual and another an early president of Connecticut General.

When young J. Pierpont Morgan left his home town for New York City to establish his great financial empire, Connecticut Mutual of Hartford became his first account. This was not remarkable because his uncle, James Goodwin, was president!

After the death of James Goodwin in 1878, Colonel Jacob Greene succeeded him. A native of Waterford, Maine, Colonel Greene was a veteran of the Civil War and a former Indian fighter. A gentleman of absolute honesty and strong convictions, Colonel Greene played a vital role in the company's history during a very difficult period. During his term of office a shady method of selling insurance became popular in this country. It was the Tontine system developed by an Italian, Lorenzo Tonti, a system of betting on an individual's chances of survival. Colonel Greene despised it as nothing better than "pure gambling, a deplorable life and death numbers game." He stated firmly that his company would have nothing to do with Tontine. Connecticut Mutual paid a heavy price for Greene's fiscal integrity and personal determination. In 1878 when he became president it ranked second in the list of leading life insurance firms in the United States. By 1905, after the so-called "30-years war" between the pro-Tontine and anti-Tontine life insurance companies, it ranked fourteenth. That year, however, Colonel Greene was finally vindicated. On July 20th W. W. Armstrong of New York State commenced his famous investigation of the insurance industry. Week after week sensational revelations of insurance corruption made newspaper headlines. In the end the Tontine companies were thoroughly discredited, and Colonel Greene and his company were revealed as shining examples of fiscal virtue.

Connecticut Mutual has a long tradition as an exemplary corporate citizen. Through the Connecticut Mutual Life Foundation, major contributions are made annually to

CONNECTICUT MUTUAL LIFE INSURANCE COMPANY

140 Garden Street
727-6500

Tours by appointment. Call Personnel Department.

organizations dealing directly with the social problems of Hartford. A special investment program channels funds into socially-desirable projects that do not meet normal market criteria as to interest return and/or risk.

Since Connecticut Mutual's home office building, designed by Benjamin Wistar Morris, was constructed in 1926, several new wings have been added. The most recent additions were completed in 1972 and house a complete training center and fully equipped television studio. The Lord's Hill Lounge contains an interesting display of company historical memorabilia. The azalea bushes and wide lawns that surround the building are particularly lovely.

At the beginning of the 1980s, Connecticut Mutual diversified and now offers a broad range of financial products and services nationally.

Photo courtesy of The Travelers Companies.

Greater Hartford is known world-wide as the Insurance Capital. Following is a list of Connecticut-chartered and licensed insurance companies, arranged by groups, that are headquartered in the Capitol Region. Note that many are over a century old.

1853
AETNA LIFE & CASUALTY GROUP
Aetna Life & Casualty (parent company)
Aetna Casualty & Surety Company
Aetna Casualty & Surety Company of America
Aetna Financial Services, Inc.
Aetna Life Insurance Company
Aetna Variable Annuity Life Insurance Company
Automobile Insurance Company of Hartford, Connecticut
Standard Fire Insurance Company

1865
CIGNA GROUP
Connecticut General Life Insurance Company
CIGNA Life Insurance Company
Connecticut General Fire & Casualty Insurance Company
Aetna Insurance Company
Century Indemnity Company

1846
CONNECTICUT MUTUAL LIFE INSURANCE COMPANY

1831
COVENANT GROUP
Covenant Mutual Insurance Company (parent company)
Covenant Corporation
Covenant Insurance Company

1831
COVENANT NATIONAL LIFE INSURANCE COMPANY
(subsidiary of New England Mutual Life Insurance Company)

1810

HARTFORD GROUP

Hartford Fire Insurance Company (parent company)
Hartford Accident and Indemnity
Hartford Life and Accident Insurance Company
Hartford Variable Annuity Life Insurance Company

1866

HARTFORD STEAM BOILER INSPECTION AND INSURANCE COMPANY

1871

NATIONAL FIRE INSURANCE COMPANY
(subsidiary of Continental Casualty)

1841

ORION GROUP

Security Insurance Company of Hartford
Fire & Casualty Insurance Company of Connecticut
Connecticut Indemnity Company
EBI Indemnity Company
Security Reinsurance Company
Orion Excess Insurance Company

1887

PATRONS MUTUAL INSURANCE COMPANY

1851

PHOENIX GROUP

Phoenix Mutual Life Insurance Company (parent company)
Phoenix General Insurance Company

1867

SAFEGUARD INSURANCE COMPANY

1863

TRAVELERS INSURANCE GROUP

Travelers Corporation (parent company)
Charter Oak Fire Insurance Company
Phoenix Insurance Company
Travelers Indemnity Company
Travelers Insurance Company
The Travelers Life and Annuity Company
Travelers Life Insurance Company

Pratt & Whitney Company,
Flower Street, c. 1911.

Until the 1830s, there was only minimal growth in manufacturing in the Hartford area, especially as compared to New Haven (arms), Waterbury (brass), New Britain (hardware) and Plymouth (clocks). The city's economy was still river-oriented, but new enterprises were adding to its prosperity. In 1820, when the population totaled around 7,000, there were, besides several blacksmiths and cabinet-makers, three cotton and woolen mills, six tanneries, five potteries, two tin shops, 15 shoemakers, six book binderies, eight distilleries, two hat shops, two looking-glass makers and four coppersmiths.

The introduction of steam power after 1815 revolutionized not only transportation on land and water but also accelerated the growth of manufacturing and completely changed the living style of workers. Mills and factories, using stationary steam engines, could be located anywhere, and the city was the logical place because of the proximity of the labor supply. In turn, the factories attracted hordes of newcomers. Hartford rapidly became urbanized, nearly doubling in size from 1820 to 1840 and more than doubling from 1840 to 1860, with clusters of multistoried factories, smoking chimneys and dingy slums nearby.

Among the earliest users of steam were the brothers Alpheus and Truman Hanks, who started the Hartford Iron Foundry in 1820. Noted for making the first cast iron plow, this foundry later became Woodruff & Beach, famous for its steam engines. Among their achievements were a gigantic 250 horsepower engine for Sam Colt's Armory and a double-piston pump for the Hartford Water Works. Considered an engineering marvel in 1855, this pump lifted water from the Connecticut River all the way up to the public reservoir on Lord's Hill, now the site of the Hartford Insurance Group. Hartford residents drank river water until 1876 when the Connecticut became too polluted and new reservoirs had to be built in West Hartford.

The lifeline between steam engine and machinery was the leather belt. The old Jewell Belting Company, founded by Pliny Jewell in 1845, made leather belts of all sizes for Hartford's plants. Jewell was the third such enterprise in the nation and, for many years, the largest belting company in the world.

Detail of Lithograph of Hartford showing the Park River and Rifle Avenue (New Capitol Avenue), 1864.

Our industrial strength can be attributed to the mastery of precision metal working and, in particular, to the rapid growth of the machine tool industry beginning in the middle of the last century. A significant part of that growth took place in New England--mainly in Windsor, Vermont; Providence, Rhode Island; and Hartford, Connecticut. The machine tool, which creates all other tools and even replicates itself, enabled the system of interchangeable parts invented by Eli Whitney of Hamden and Simeon North of Berlin to be brought to a state of perfection, which in turn made possible the spread of mass production for every conceivable human need.

The start-up of the Sharps Rifle Company in 1852 opened up what became the Capitol Avenue industrial center that would subsequently accommodate such great enterprises as Weed Sewing Machine, Pope Manufacturing, Pratt & Whitney Machine Tools, Arrow Hart & Hegeman, Underwood Typewriter, and Hartford Machine Screw. For a long while Capitol Avenue was called Rifle Avenue.

After the Civil War the Weed Sewing Machine Company settled down on Capitol Avenue and soon became, next to Colt's, the largest manufacturer in the city. From 1876 to 1881 George Fairfield served as Weed's president, during which period occurred two events that had a significant impact on the future of metal working as well as on Hartford's industrial prosperity. One was the fortuitous meeting with Colonel Albert A. Pope of Boston which quickly led to Weed's entry into making Pope's "Columbia" high-wheel bicycle, the first commercial self-propelled vehicle in America. By 1890, the sewing machine market having collapsed, Weed made nothing but safety bicycles; Colonel Pope assumed complete control and changed the firm's name to the Pope Manufacturing Company.

The other event was the coming together of the inventor Christopher Spencer and Fairfield in 1873 over the former's latest and, as it turned out, most epochal invention. Inside the Weed factory the genius from Manchester built the first single-spindle automatic screw machine. It proved to be the birth of not only the screw machine industry in America but, three years later, resulted in the founding of Hartford Machine Screw, now a division of Stanadyne in Windsor.

The progress in interchangeability of machine parts made by Elisha Root at the Colt Armory was extended further by Francis Pratt and Amos Whitney in their machine tool enterprise, begun in 1860. Prior to 1900 the partners designed an astonishing variety of machines--lathes, boring mills, shapers, planers, vertical drills, grinders, die sinkers, profilers, presses, power hammers and various cutting machines. No other machine tool builder, before or since, could match this record. Before World War I, Pratt & Whitney Machine Tool was the largest company of its kind. Like Root, Amos Whitney also excelled in teaching hundreds of apprentices to become journeymen and to start other businesses.

In 1897 Colonel Pope and the inventor Hiram P. Maxim made history when they offered to the public the first electric carriage in America. Under the headline "Horseless Era Comes," the *Courant* welcomed the Mark III car which had an operating radius of 30 miles and a top speed of 12 miles an hour. The following year Maxim had on the road a four-wheel vehicle with a two-cylinder air-cooled engine that traveled from Hartford to Boston, with repeated stops due to frightened horses and dreadful roads.

Had Henry Ford remained a farmer, the capital of Connecticut might also have become the automobile capital of the United States instead of Detroit. Hartford made up for it by becoming the number one manufacturer of aircraft engines. In 1925 Frederick Rentschler and George Mead designed and built the first successful air-cooled airplane engine, the renowned Wasp, in the old Pratt & Whitney complex on Capitol Avenue. Today Pratt & Whitney Aircraft is a division of United Technologies.

Between 1860 and 1960 Hartford inventors and entrepreneurs established the city as the foremost manufacturing center in New England. Through brainpower they overcame the state's lack of natural resources. From the opening of the U.S. Patent Office in 1790 until 1930 Connecticut received more patents per capita than any other state, about one per thousand citizens. Apparently, there was only one thing a Yankee could not invent even if he put his hand to it; over the grave of Jonathan Kilbourne in Colchester is this epitaph:

"He was a man of invention great
Above all that liv'd nigh;
But he could not invent to live
When God called him to die."

New forms of energy undergirded Yankee ingenuity. After steam power came gas for illumination in 1848, then electricity in the 1880s, generated by the burning of coal and oil.

By 1960, the factories which for 100 years had provided plenty of entry-level work were disappearing. Employing more people than the insurance companies, they had been turning out such varied products as horseshoe nails, counters, organs, pay telephones, machine tools, screw machine products, electric switches, Colt guns and Maxim silencers, and glass-blowing machinery. As their multistoried buildings became obsolete, many found it necessary to move where there was ample space for more efficient one-story operation and for employee parking. Others went out of business or left the state entirely--like Fuller brushes and Royal and Underwood typewriters--eliminating over 10,000 jobs. As a result, the majority of jobs are now to be found in the insurance, finance, distribution and government sectors.

COLT ARMORY

150 Huyshope Ave

No tours.

The star-spangled, blue onion dome that has topped Colt's Armory for over 100 years is a Hartford landmark. In the 1920s the stars were removed, probably for reasons of economy. However, in 1976 a mysterious benefactor contributed over $5,000 to restore the dome to its former glory. Originally painted on the dome, the new stars are made from aluminum and fastened on with bolts. Why did Colonel Samuel Colt, descended from a long line of Connecticut Puritans, embellish his new factory with this odd piece of Byzantine brilliance? For many years it was rumored to be the gift of a grateful Turkish sultan who particularly appreciated the efficiency of Colt revolvers. Actually it was just one more example of Colt's talent for flamboyant showmanship. Because he admired the onion domes he had seen on his trips to Russia and Turkey he simply had one made to attract attention to his new business enterprise. He also used onion domes to decorate his personal residence, Armsmear.

When Colonel Colt constructed his gun factory here in 1854, it was the largest privately owned armory in the world. The original portion was entirely destroyed by fire in 1864, two years after his death, and completely rebuilt. The gilded colt that stands atop the dome no doubt symbolizes the colonel. The colt carries a broken spear, partly in its mouth, partly on the ground, an ancient symbol of the war horse carrying on the battle after its master has fallen.

Samuel Colt, whose gun peddling made him a world traveller, brought many new ideas back to Hartford. While in Holland he admired the dikes the Dutch built to create additional land. Because the South Meadows in Hartford were regularly inundated each year by spring floods, the area had not been used for building. For a relatively small sum of money, Colt purchased the low-lying South Meadows, constructed a dike to keep out the flooding river, and created what was probably the first industrial park in the nation. This included not only well-paid jobs in his armory, but nearby housing for his factory workers and managers as well as his own fine home. Colt also provided his employees with a clubhouse, educational programs, and a stimulating assortment of recreational activities, both cultural and sporting. In fact, the creation of Colt's new industrial enterprise stimulated the changeover of Hartford's economy from the West Indies trade to manufacturing.

Under the dynamic leadership of Sam Colt and his able
superintendent, Elisha K. Root, Colt's Armory became much
more than just a gun factory. It was this country's first
"school" of applied mechanics, a fountainhead of mass production that has revolutionized the material fate of the world.
Attracted by the vitality and the genius of these two great
inventors, brilliant young men flocked to this city to learn
from them. Colt and Root used the new steam power that
was replacing the old-fashioned water power. They were
also very liberal in buying only the best machinery, provided
it operated with efficiency and economy. Specialized
machines, like well-trained, healthy workers, soon paid for
themselves. As a young man traveling in the South, Colt
noted with disgust the use of slave labor. His disapproval
was not humanitarian but economic. To his Yankee mind,
the slaves were woefully inefficient. He predicted, quite
correctly, that the southern part of the United States would
not grow in industrial importance until the southern
work force was healthier, better educated and more
realistically motivated.

New inventions at Colt's Armory were a frequent occurrence, and the intellectual atmosphere of the place was scintillating. Since the opening of the U.S. Patent Office in 1790, Connecticut has received more patents per capita than any other state in the nation. The Colt Armory was a major stimulant to these "firsts." Graduates of the armory then went forth as engineering and manufacturing missionaries to set up new factories in Hartford and all over the world.

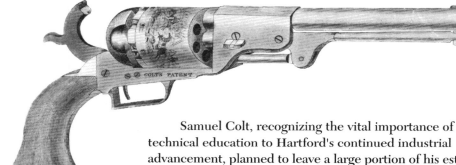

courtesy of The Colt Collection, The Hartford Public Library.

Samuel Colt, recognizing the vital importance of technical education to Hartford's continued industrial advancement, planned to leave a large portion of his estate to found a Hartford Institute of Technology. However, the short-sighted city fathers were so antagonistic toward him and his enterprise that he changed his will in disgust. Even so the city gradually became a major center of manufacturing. A fantastic number of useful things besides guns were eventually made here: machine tools, chucks, gauges, counters, sewing machines, bicycles, automobiles, pneumatic tires, typewriters, screws, horse nails, electrical devices, castings, silencers, and numerous components of the great aircraft industry, to mention just a few. In fact, most of the major machine tool businesses throughout the U.S.A. have their roots in the old Colt Armory.

Excellent exhibits of Colt firearms may be seen at the Connecticut State Library and the Wadsworth Atheneum.

United Technologies Corporation is a diversified, high-technology industrial giant with corporate headquarters in this building. Its subsidiaries design, develop, manufacture and market a broad variety of technological products for individual, commercial and governmental customers all over the world.

UTC is composed of four operating groups: Pratt & Whitney Aircraft (headquartered in East Hartford), Otis (North American Operations headquartered in Farmington), Essex, and Systems and Equipment (headquartered partially in Hartford and partially in the southern part of Connecticut) which world-wide employ more than 133,000 people and operate over 180 plants. More than 30 of the plants and 44,000 of the employees are located outside of the United States. UTC is the largest employer in New England and, in the Hartford area alone, has a work force of over 30,000 men and women. Some are employed at Pratt & Whitney Aircraft and at UTC's Research Center in East Hartford, some at Hamilton Standard in Windsor Locks, and some at the two plants of the Power Systems Division in Farmington and South Windsor.

UTC is the world's leading designer and builder of jet engines, elevators and escalators. It also is the largest U.S. manufacturer of wire and cable products, the largest independent producer of wiring assemblies and circuitry for the automotive industry, and a world leader in helicopter design and manufacture. Because the keystone of UTC's corporate strength is its ability to advance new technologies, numerous other exotic products are constantly being created by its four operating units.

Few residents of Greater Hartford realize that Pratt & Whitney Aircraft's Willgoos Turbine Laboratory in East Hartford is the world's largest privately-owned installation for testing air-breathing powerplants and high-powered rotating machinery. There, in 1961, Pratt & Whitney Aircraft revolutionized the aircraft industry by using this unique facility to develop the world's first commercial turbofan jet.

UNITED TECHNOLOGIES CORPORATION

1 Financial Plaza
728-7000

Hamilton Standard, a subsidiary of UTC's Systems and Equipment Group, played a vital role in the world's first successful moon shot, the Apollo program, by developing space suits and backpacks for the pioneer astronauts. The Power Systems Division built fuel cells for their spaceships. Today, Hamilton Standard is equally involved with the space shuttle which will be in operation during the 1980s and 1990s. New types of space suit/life support systems are being developed for future astronauts to wear when they work outside their spaceship in earth orbiting flights. Environmental control equipment is being built for the shuttle's orbiter, a combination spaceship and aircraft, and the European Spacelab, a manned laboratory which will be one of the orbiter's payloads.

United Technologies Research Center in East Hartford employs scientists, engineers, technicians, and supporting personnel. The corporation spends record millions on research and development. This type of commitment springs from the corporation's basic belief that technology, properly and conscientiously managed, is our best hope for overcoming the economic and social problems faced by human beings in this world today.

Turn to Bradley Air Museum for a history of the development of the aircraft industry in the Hartford area.

Completed in 1974, One Financial Plaza is one of the largest rental office buildings in Connecticut with a total area of 630,000 square feet. Other businesses and banks besides United Technologies Corporation are also located here. Architects for the structure were Neuhaus and Taylor of Houston, Texas, and the consulting architect was Connie Nannpier. The builders were Gilbane Building Company of Providence, Rhode Island; the developers are Connecticut Financial Associates; and the managers are Cushman and Wakefield of New England.

The building includes a garage for 1,200 automobiles and a landing pad for helicopters on the roof.

SOUTHERN NEW ENGLAND TELEPHONE

111 Trumbull Street
527-6373
information.

Tours by appointment are available at the Central Office, on Trumbull Street, Hartford. There is an historical exhibit at 227 Church Street, New Haven. The company will provide educational programs for schools as well as a great variety of films including one on the life of Alexander Graham Bell. Call the business office in your area for educational programs and materials.

"It is my heart-warm and world-embracing Christmas hope and aspiration that all of us, the high, the low, the rich, the poor, the admired, the despised, the loved, the hated, the civilized, the savage, may eventually be gathered together in a Heaven of overlasting rest and peace and bliss, except the inventor of the telephone."

Mark Twain

When Mark Twain was a resident of Hartford he turned down an opportunity to become an investor in a new-fangled invention called a telephone. (Instead he spent large sums of money on an ill-fated typesetter which led to his eventual bankruptcy.) In 1878, however, the famous author did become one of the first in Hartford to have a telephone installed in his home. It was a party-line phone on the same circuit as the *Hartford Courant*, the *Courant's* editor Charles Dudley Warner, Senator Joseph Hawley, and a Mr. Hubbard. Each of the four privileged customers paid $5 a month for the service.

Today Greater Hartford ranks first in the nation with the percentage of telephones per household.

Without doubt the fantastic revolution in communications is basic to the creation of our Space Age society. The Southern New England Telephone Company continues to play a major role in this communications revolution. SNETCO's 10-story Communications Center on Trumbull Street, designed by Hartford architect Louis Drakos, was opened February 2, 1973. It was built to house an Electronic Switching System as well as a new Long Distance Switching Center. Together with the Long Lines department of AT&T, SNETCO invested $9.2 million over a three-year period in this equipment which combines electronic control with electro-mechanical hardware. The entire installation and building cost nearly $20 million.

The creation of this Communications Center with its super-sophisticated equipment has almost doubled the number of long distance calls that can be handled in Hartford. It now directs some 40,000 calls per hour out across the state and nation and can be expected to handle twice that volume in the near future.

SNETCO's pioneering communications services are absolutely vital to Space Age Hartford's prosperity and continued growth. The new communications Center was a significant factor in American Airlines' decision to move its reservations center into this area.

In 1886 William Gray of Hartford invented the first coin operated telephone in the world, the Gray-Pay Telephone.

Back in the 1870s the offices of several important textile concerns which operated mills in outlying towns and villages were located in the City of Hartford. One of those was the Willimantic Linen Co. headed by Austin Dunham and his son Austin C. Dunham. In 1878 young Dunham made history by installing a six-lamp arc system in one of his mill buildings, the first instance in which electrical lighting was used in an industrial establishment.

This use of electricity for lighting stimulated wide interest and attention. A Hartford friend of A. C. Dunham was a youthful alderman named Morgan Gardner Bulkeley whose father was president of the Aetna Life Insurance Company. Bulkeley shared Dunham's enthusiasm for electricity as the essential new power source for Connecticut's burgeoning manufacturing economy, so he decided to seek public support. September 17, 1879 happened to be the anniversary of the Civil War Battle of Antietam. It was also the day when the battle flags of the Civil War were going to be carried from the old Hartford arsenal to the State Capitol where they were placed in permanent display cases. Following a grand parade and a glorious picnic on the grounds of Bushnell Park, Bulkeley planned to entertain the gathered throngs with a spectacular display of "outdoor illumination." With the aid of A. C. Dunham he had arc lights placed strategically about the Capitol and on top of a number of buildings that edged the park. A huge electrified lantern was also placed atop the Capitol dome, and two more within the dome itself.

From 7 o'clock until 10 the delighted spectators in Bushnell Park watched the fantastic arc lights as they illumined the surroundings and the night sky. "Now and then,"

NORTHEAST UTILITIES

HELCO became part of Northeast Utilities in 1966 and was subsequently merged into one of NU's other subsidiaries, The Connecticut Light and Power Company. Headquarters are located on Selden Street, Berlin. Call 665-5000 and ask for the Community Relations Department for information on educational materials. The company has an excellent library of films on energy, careers, conservation, the environment, safety and general interest topics that are available free of charge. Films are available in 16 mm and in 1/2" VHS. The company also makes available career education, safety programs, teacher workshops and resource kits and speakers. A free booklet listing the films and educational programs is available.

Groups wishing to tour the Connecticut Yankee Nuclear Power Station at Haddam Neck should make arrangements in advance. Call 267-9279. The Connecticut Yankee Energy Information center is open all year, Monday-Friday 9 a.m. to 4 p.m. From July 1-August 31, the center also is open Saturdays from 10 a.m. to 5 p.m. and Sundays from noon to 5 p.m. The center is closed on all major holidays. Write Northeast Utilities, P. O. Box 270, Hartford, CT 06141-0270 or call (203) 665-5189.

the *Hartford Courant* reported the following day, "the light would strike some unexpected spot and there would be a slight scream and a lively scramble as some affectionate couple ... beat a hasty retreat."

The "illumination" not only increased public interest in electricity but in young Morgan Gardner Bulkeley who in the next city election was elected mayor of Hartford.

In 1881 A. C. Dunham and M. G. Bulkeley became the prime movers in procuring the charter that created The Hartford Electric Light Company. The interests of both men in the development of the company never flagged. Their combined managerial, inventive, financial and political talents were essential to the new company's great success.

HELCO, over the past 100 years, has pioneered many "firsts," both technical and managerial. The company has always been "on the move" into an ever-expanding future. In 1965 HELCO, The Connecticut Light and Power Company and Western Massachusetts Electric Company through ownership by Northeast Utilities initiated formal proceedings toward affiliation. On July 1, 1966 the consolidation went into effect. The union was of considerable historic interest because it was the first holding company to be created under the Public Utility Holding Company Act of 1935.

In 1977 another "first" was achieved by NU. On August 18 Connecticut Yankee nuclear power plant in Haddam Neck set a record for the longest continuous operation by any nuclear power in the world. In August 1984, the plant completed a new world record with 417 days of continuous operation, surpassing a mark set by the Maine Yankee nuclear power plant in 1978. NU owns 44 percent of Connecticut Yankee and oversees its operation.

This type of praise means a lot to Space Age Connecticut whose economic survival depends upon adequate sources of power. But perhaps the laconic statement of a neighboring East Haddam dairy farmer is even more heartening to the managers of Connecticut Yankee. "It makes juice. It puts nothing harmful in the milk. It has a proven operating crew and a fine safety record. It doesn't worry me one bit."

By 1987, nuclear power accounted for approximately two-thirds of the power used by customers of Northeast Utilities.

Founded in 1848 as the Hartford City Gas Light Company, CNG is this community's oldest public utility. Many years, expansions, mergers and acquisitions later the company has become a major pioneer coping with the energy and pollution problems of modern times.

In 1962 CNG led the nation by constructing in downtown Hartford a steam and chilled water plant, the world's first investor-owned facility of this type, and began providing year-round climate control service to Constitution Plaza. This single facility, located on Columbus Boulevard, prevents the pollution otherwise inevitable from many individual boiler plants.

Ten years later CNG in cooperation with United Technologies introduced the world's first experimental natural gas fuel cell home, thus demonstrating the feasibility of an energy service using a power source that produces electricity direct from natural gas.

More than one-third of this country's total energy is supplied by natural gas piped to this part of the nation from gas-rich fields in Louisiana and Texas. When energy supplies became tight in the 1970s CNG spearheaded a major "energy banking" operation by constructing in Rocky Hill an $8 million liquified natural gas plant that stores 1.2 billion cubic feet. Altogether, CNG serves 134,000 customers in 21 communities. A non-regulated subsidiary, Affiliated Resources Corporation, supplies 13,000 customers with heating and cooling services, including all of the major downtown buildings; it also markets propane.

CNG's $12 million operating and administrative complex on Columbus Boulevard consists of a wedge-shaped office building, a covered parking lot and drive-in teller window for customers and a new operating plant. The two buildings were designed by the Hartford architectural firm of Frid, Ferguson, Mahaffey & Perry "to emphasize energy conservation."

CONNECTICUT NATURAL GAS CORPORATION

100 Columbus Boulevard
727-3000

CAPEWELL HORSENAILS, INC.

1395 Blue Hills Ave.,
Bloomfield
242-3650

This old company, still the largest supplier of horse nails in the world, is one of the few remaining artifacts of the ingenuity and genius that created this city's once burgeoning industrial past. There was a time, roughly between 1854 and 1959, when Hartford was a major center of manufacturing. These factories, in turn, provided jobs for hardworking immigrants who lived in the ethnic neighborhoods that made the city itself a colorful and prosperous "port of entry" for the poor but ambitious.

Back in 1865 a young inventor from Cheshire, Connecticut named George J. Capewell went calling on the wealthy Williams family of Hartford to see if they would be interested in backing his latest invention, a machine that could automatically form horseshoe nails. Up to this time all horseshoe nails were laboriously made by hand by local blacksmiths. Capitalist A. W. C. Williams decided to back the inventor, and the company was established on Sheldon Street. In 1881 the first machine-made horse nails in the world were actually produced and soon found a ready market. Nine years later the company moved to the corner of Governor Street and Charter Oak Avenue. Unfortunately in 1903 a disastrous and extremely costly fire destroyed the old factory.

Undaunted, the management announced that a new factory would immediately be constructed. "The new plant will be 50 feet high from the ground floor and will measure about 350 x 100 feet and will present an entirely different appearance from the old structure, being of a much more ornamental design. It will be as nearly fireproof as the most skillful engineering can provide. The whole structure will be made of steel and brick with concrete floors and roof throughout. It will be equipped with water towers on top of the building, to be used in case of fire inside. The thickness of the walls will not be less than 12 inches. The building will be large enough to accommodate the 1,000 employees engaged by the company in all capacities, being three stories high and so constructed as to provide for large window space which will make the workshop of the most perfectly lighted kind." At this time the company was operated by Dr. George C. F. Williams, a nephew of A. W. C. Williams. After Dr. Williams's death in 1933 he was succeeded by his son, Staunton Williams, whose former home on Prospect Avenue is now the mansion of the Governor of Connecticut.

During World War I a severe shortage of male factory workers prompted a major social innovation on the part of some factory owners in Hartford. Up to this time females were not often employed on machines in local industries. Yankee factory owners, however, evolved a practical solution to their labor problems. An article in the Hartford *Courant*, March 3, 1918 describes Capewell's pioneering day nursery "for the small children of the women who work at the plant and have no other suitable place to leave them ... At first thought it might seem that a nursery in a factory is a peculiar institution, but there is little question that the care of their children is a big asset in the mother's eyes ..." After this breakthrough, hiring women on machines became commonplace.

The horse nail business peaked in 1912 at which time the company had factories in London and Toronto as well as Hartford. However the automobile, also pioneered in this city, relegated the horse to a minor role as a common carrier which resulted in a great decline in production until 1955. Then an increased interest in pleasure riding and horse racing started a modest but steady annual increase in the sale of horse nails.

During World War II Capewell began producing forgings for parachute harness fittings and also metal cutting saws, as well as remaining the sole supplier of horseshoe nails for the free world. One of its earliest horse nail machines went to the Smithsonian in 1964 as an example of the first machine capable of transforming steel by cold rolling instead of heating.

In 1974 Capewell became a division of Stanadyne, a Windsor-based conglomerate. In 1985 Mustad, a Swedish manufacturer, bought the horsenail division and moved it to Bloomfield as a separate entity.

> "For want of a nail the shoe was lost.
> For want of a shoe the horse was lost.
> For want of a horse the rider was lost.
> For want of a rider the battle was lost.
> All for the want of a horse shoe nail."
>
> Benjamin Franklin, 1758

For three and a half centuries Hartford's churches and synagogues have played a key role in enabling newcomers to become stable, productive citizens. New immigrants were often poor, lonely, frightened and disorganized. They naturally tended to join forces with those of similar background to create places of worship in which their own language was spoken and native traditions observed. This was essential to their becoming rooted in the city. The religious institutions became the immigrants' extended families, their support groups. Within them fraternal clubs and societies were formed, all related to the particular ethnic heritage. Ministers, priests, and rabbis taught the newcomers how to behave in their new environment, assisted them in finding employment, and even advised them on the responsibilities of citizenship. Thus the poor were empowered spiritually, economically, and politically. With the recent arrival of Vietnamese and other Asians the process of assimilation and upward mobility still continues, making Hartford one of the most inclusive societies in the Northeast.

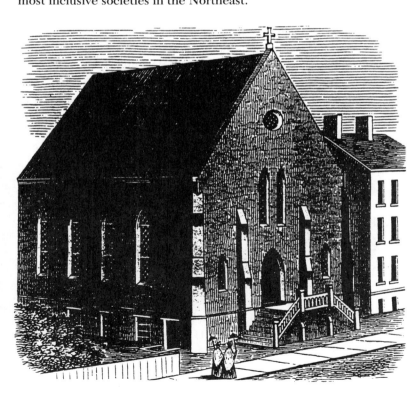

*Church open noon to 3:00 pm
daily, Burying Ground always
open. No admission charge.*
249-5631

Center Church, Hartford's First Church of Christ, Congregational, was "gathered" at Newtown (now Cambridge), Massachusetts in 1632. The following year the congregation's leader and first pastor, Rev. Thomas Hooker, arrived in Massachusetts from England. Two years later the church moved as a body to the west bank of the Connecticut River. There the Puritan settlers founded another Newtown, renamed Hartford in 1637 in honor of Hertford, England, birthplace of Hooker's assistant, Rev. Samuel Stone.

The church's first two meeting houses (1636 and 1638) were located in what is now Thomas Hooker Square. The third meeting house, completed in 1739, was located on the present site on the corner of Main and Gold streets. A simple wooden edifice, 66 feet long and 46 feet wide, it was topped by a wooden tower that protected a town bell that the first settlers had carried with them through the wilderness from Newtown, Massachusetts. From the beginning this bell played a central role in the life of the town, summoning Hartford's inhabitants both to worship and to town meetings and announcing other important community events. The third meeting house was typical of all New England meeting houses in the early 18th century. The plan for the structure is said to have been prepared by a Mr. Cotton Palmer of Rhode Island, not an architect but a builder, who was paid the munificent sum of one pound for his services!

It was in this building that the new United States Constitution was ratified in 1788 ... church and state still being one at that time in Connecticut history.

In 1807 the fourth and present meeting house of the church was built on the site of the third at a cost of $32,014. Daniel Wadsworth is reputed to have been the amateur architect. This probably is true, as the previous pastor of the church had been his grandfather, Rev. Daniel Wadsworth, and because his father, Colonel Jeremiah Wadsworth, Hartford's wealthiest merchant, had taken his son on many trips to England. The young Daniel could have admired the Christopher Wren church, St. Martin's-in-the-Fields, which the fourth meeting house of Hartford's First Church closely resembles. Some of the timbers of the first three meeting houses are said to have been incorporated into this structure. The steeple is 185 feet high and encloses a belfry in which was placed the venerable old bell. This bell had been recast in England in 1727 and was recast again in 1841. However, it still includes materials of the original bell carried to Hartford by the Puritans of 1636. It weighs approximately 3,450 pounds and bears the inscription "Holiness unto the Lord."

In 1850 the pulpit of the church was extended to the west over an additional portion of the land granted by the town from the Ancient Burying Ground. The interior of the sanctuary is very lovely and quite traditional, except for the Tiffany stained-glass windows.

Center Church House was constructed on Gold Street in 1905 as a headquarters for the educational and social work of the church. It was around this time that a great many Armenians started migrating to Hartford, driven from their own country by successive waves of persecution by both Turks and Russians. They settled in a small area behind the present State Library. Although they started out in a variety of humble occupations, their strong neighborhood and family cohesiveness and their love of hard work and book-learning enabled them to create a remarkably dynamic community that soon improved itself economically. The Armenians belong to the Gregorian Church which is not Roman Catholic, Orthodox, or Protestant. Too few in number and originally too poor to build their own church, they began attending Center Church where they were most welcome. Many Armenians are still Congregationalists for this reason.

Center City Church is an active member of the Center City Churches Inc. ministry. While Center Church remains almost totally white and middle class, it has begun to attract suburban residents who want to take part in the church's urban ministry. Center Church has also made efforts to attract those who work in the city, but leave for home by nightfall. Mid-week services, concerts, and lectures are offered.

The Ancient Burying Ground

Hartford's Ancient Burying Ground is the very Gethsemane and Golgotha of the city's historic past. To this burying ground for 167 years were borne the last remains of some of the community's most exalted religious and civic leaders. It has been reliably estimated that when, as promised, the Angel Gabriel shall sound his trumpet on the final Judgment Day above the graves of this ancient cemetery, more than 6000 individuals will answer the call. How is this possible?

First, because this burying ground used to be much larger. On January 11, 1640, Hartford's town fathers, exercising the right of eminent domain, voted to lay out a town burying lot that extended approximately from Main Street on the east to Lewis Street on the west, and from Pearl Street on the north to Gold Street on the south. Second, because Hartford's early settlers followed the traditional English custom of placing graves in any available portion of the churchyard regardless of family relationship. Gravediggers would simply probe the hallowed soil with an iron rod to find a space below ground where, by reason of non-occupancy or occupancy long past, they could safely undertake to make room for a newcomer. Thus, over the years, bodies were often laid one upon the other, and individual graves and grave markers became displaced or lost. Today the markers over the graves in this cemetery do not necessarily guarantee that the deceased actually lies in the earth below. The ancient gravestones are more accurately memorials to the dead, not gravestones as we understand their significance today. For example, when people inquire about the grave of Hartford's famed founder, the Rev. Thomas Hooker, they are shocked to learn that the true site of the great man's resting place is uncertain. We know only that Hooker, like most of the founders and early inhabitants of Hartford, was buried in what used to be a much larger cemetery.

Because Hartford's Ancient Burying Ground occupies a prime site in the Center City, its former boundaries have been constantly encroached upon during the last three centuries. From the beginning the cemetery was used for more that just a place to inter the dead. As in England, it doubled as a pasture. As early at 1652 a "pale fence" was erected around the area to keep grazing sheep, horses, and cattle from straying. However, in 1664 a law was passed sternly stating that residents must "at no time suffer hogs" to enter and root about in this hallowed portion of town.

The cemetery's first major boundary encroachment was made by the First Church Society (Congregational) when, on December 18, 1712, the society petitioned the town "for the liberty to set a meeting house either in part of or in whole on the burying lott." The present brick church, constructed in 1807, is even larger than its predecessor. Because the bones of the Rev. Thomas Hooker and Connecticut's first governor, John Haynes, presumably lie underneath the building, the two men are memorialized by two large brownstone plaques on the outside of the church's west wall. This is not a sacrilege but an honor, much as the most renowned English dead are buried within churches. A handsome table tablet in the cemetery also memorializes Hooker. In 1836 a committee chaired by Daniel Wadsworth erected a tall brownstone obelisk that listed the names of the 163 first settlers of Hartford. If they were not killed in the wars with the Indians or drowned at sea, their bones probably lie here.

The second major encroachment on the cemetery's boundaries was made when a school was constructed on Main Street just north of the church. The general attitude of the town fathers may best be judged by a vote that was taken in 1756 stipulating that the burial lot should be cared for at "as little expense as may be to the town." Then in 1785, these frugal Yankees voted that the entire eastern portion of the cemetery along Main Street "may be disposed of for erecting stores." When James Mooklar, a Pearl Street barber, was given permission to extend his shop six feet onto the graveyard, he actually "took considerable more of the town's land than he had liberty under vote of the town," for which infraction of the law he was simply charged back rent!

By 1807 new cemeteries had been laid out in the southern and northern sections of Hartford, and the Ancient Burying Ground ceased to be used except for occasional interments. By then Main Street stores extended well into the graveyard, and only a few citizens, like Daniel Wadsworth and his friends, took much notice of the place. In 1887, when the Waverly Building was constructed on the present site of the United Technologies Building, the workmen unearthed numerous coffins and countless old bones.

In the 1890's Gold Street, which bordered the southern boundary of the Ancient Burying Ground, had degenerated into a grubby 16-foot alley filled with slums "where the moral

as well as material filth desecrated the very atmosphere."
Nobody seemed to be able to do anything about this unfortunate condition until Emily F.S. Holcombe, wife of John
Marshall Holcombe, president of the Phoenix Mutual Life
Insurance Company, decided to clean up both Gold Street
and the decrepit old cemetery. Mrs. Holcombe herself was
regent of the local chapter of the Daughters of the American
Revolution. On October 31, 1898, she managed to persuade
the D.A.R. ladies to join her cause. She also enlisted the
support of her pastor, Rev. George L. Walker of the First
Church, Congregational, as well as the backing of her husband and the city's most prominent businessmen and
political leaders. In fact, she pursued her goals with such
zeal and skill that she was soon affectionately dubbed "The
Gold Street Woman."

At first she met with considerable resistance from the City Council, so she clearly pointed out that Gold Street was "a disgrace to the vicinity and a source of offense to the locality, (a place) upon which, from the windows of the tenements, old shoes, tin cans, and excremental filth are often thrown ..." Then she demanded, "Is there not public spirit enough in Hartford to accomplish this result (of cleaning up Gold Street) in honor of the fathers whose graves lie so dishonored close to our very doors? If it is impossible to secure appropriations from the city, does not the voice of duty call upon individuals to accomplish such a work?"

She eventually did receive the necessary support, so Gold Street's slums were removed, the street itself widened, and the cemetery greatly improved. In the process, however, even more remains of former generations were unearthed. Although most of these relics were treated with proper respect and replaced within the graveyard, some were carelessly carted away to the dump. At long last, on April 21, 1899, a triumphal gathering was held on Gold Street to celebrate the accomplishments of Mrs. Holcombe and her cohorts. The Colt Band played suitable music, speeches were made by local ministers and politicians, and the assembled crowd sang in unison, "Praise God From Whom All Blessings Flow."

The D.A.R. ladies further improved the cemetery by enclosing it with an impressive iron fence which cost $100,000 and was designed by architects McKim, Mead & White of New York. A handsome gate on Gold Street memorializing Connecticut's first governor, John Haynes, was presented by his descendants, the Misses Stokes of New York City. Emily Seymour Goodwin Holcombe, after her death, was appropriately interred in the historic burying ground that she had worked so hard to save and restore.

In 1952 Edward M. Day and a few other members of the First Church erected the Main Street gate to the cemetery. This gate honors Hooker and all the other founding fathers. A few years later the City of Hartford, the Connecticut Historical Commission, and the Society of the Descendants of the Founders erected a standing plaque on the Main Street side of the cemetery on which a few words give a brief account of the city's history. Finally, in July 1976,

United Technologies Corporation, on behalf of its employees, placed a plaque on the Gold Street entrance telling how they "undertook the rehabilitation and continued maintenance of the Ancient Burying Ground, where lie some of Connecticut's earliest settlers, as a contribution to the City of Hartford in this our Nation's Bicentennial Year."

In greater Hartford there are many old Congregational churches like Center Church with adjoining ancient burying places like this one. A number of articles and books that have been written on the subject of gravestones as an early New England art form may be found at The Connecticut Historical Society.

Typical of the epitaphs found on these old gravestones are the following:

> Death is a Debt
> To nature due
> Which I have Paid
> And so must You

> My Friends most Dear
> As You Pass by
> As You are now
> So once was I
> As I am now
> So you will be
> Prepare for Death
> And Follow Me

To which an irreverent wag is reputed to have replied:

> To follow You
> I'm not content
> Until I know
> Which way You went.

In December 1983 the Society of the Descendants of the Founders of Hartford established the Ancient Burying Ground Association to raise money for the restoration of the cemetery. A new founders' monument was erected to replace the old obelisk. Four years later the AGBA became a separate corporation and is engaged actively in the restoration of 124 brownstone and marble markers.

The living history of St. Patrick - St. Anthony parish is a remarkable series of stories within the larger one. Originating in 1829 as the first Roman Catholic parish in Connecticut, it was then named "Most Holy and Undivided Trinity." The church building itself had just been purchased from Hartford Episcopalians, and the Catholics had moved it to Talcott Street. Unbeknown to Trinity's handful of parishioners -- some Irish laborers and a few Protestant converts -- the parish's halting start represented the beginnings of what was to become the Archdiocese of Hartford. These pioneer Catholics had the first resident pastor ever appointed for the state, Rev. Bernard O'Cavanagh. Back then, Connecticut was under the jurisdiction of the Bishop of Boston, Benedict Fenwick. It was after 1837, however, when Rev. John Brady took over Trinity parish, that the pace of Catholic development quickened. Over the next 15 years, its growth paralleled Hartford's transportation boom, which attracted a large Irish immigration. The net result was the construction of a new church at the present site, which was renamed in honor of St. Patrick to reflect a strong Irish presence of over 3,000 parishioners. When the new church was dedicated on December 14, 1851, Trinity Church on Talcott Street was closed. In 1853, during a local episode of anti-Catholicism, the abandoned church was burned in a fire that claimed all the first baptismal records. The marriage register, however, was saved and is today in the possession of St. Patrick - St. Anthony parish. It is the oldest Catholic document in the state, and dates to December 1829.

The elegant Gothic edifice that was the St. Patrick Church of 1851 was constructed of brownstone from Portland, Connecticut. This building was the culmination of Father Brady's work at the parish of St. Patrick. In 1854 this busy priest, who by now had won the respect of the whole Hartford community for his interest in education and temperance, and to whom city Protestants had even lent money for his new church, died of cholera.

Brady's parishioners defied the bishop with whom Brady was feuding at the time of his death and buried their beloved priest as he had requested - adjacent to the main entrance of the church. A brownstone monument with Celtic cross was soon erected by the parish to mark his grave. It remains today. Ten feet beneath the memorial is a

ST. PATRICK - ST. ANTHONY CHURCH

285 Church Street
246-6874

97

four-foot high flagstone vault built by Father Brady's parishioners to house his coffin. The epitaph on the monument above closes with the words, "through his apostolic labors this cathedral was erected." Brady and his flock had thought that their new church would eventually become the Cathedral for the new Hartford diocese, which had been established in 1844. However, Hartford's geographic center was seen by church authorities as moving westward, thus leaving St. Patrick's behind. Sadly, the church that Father Brady built burned to the ground on a January night in 1875.

The church that presently stands on the site (the corner of Church and Ann streets) was dedicated on November 26, 1876, during the pastorate of Father James Hughes. He had taken over for Brady in 1854 and was a fittingly energetic successor. Like the church of 1851, the current structure is of Portland brownstone and almost identical in size. Most of the present windows are original to the building. The newspapers of 1876 had termed them "of the finest Cathedral stained glass" from New York.

Father Hughes' parish in the 1870's experienced its greatest growth spurt...his congregation often numbered between 4,000 and 6,000. Once again, the size of the parish reflected yet another era of economic prosperity in Hartford with plentiful job opportunities for its largely Irish constituency.

Like Brady, Father Hughes was a builder. Besides the church, he oversaw the construction of a new school, convent, social hall, and orphanage. The last three institutions were housed in one large building which occupied the site of the present St. Patrick - St. Anthony rectory built in 1959. The parish still preserves the touching records of Father Hughes' orphanage discontinued in 1916. The Sisters of Mercy taught in the parish schools from 1852 to 1958. In fact, it was this religious order's original mission in Connecticut. The Christian Brothers had taught the boys of the parish from 1866 to 1885, after which the sisters resumed that responsibility as well.

By the late 1950's and early 1960's, the parish began to suffer the effects of vast population shifts in Hartford, resulting from local redevelopment. In 1956, for the third time in its long history, fire ravaged the church, but did not destroy the building. The steeple, however, was lost. Not long after the tragedy and because of changes in the city, the then

Archbishop Henry J. O'Brien decided to merge the parish
with another historic Catholic community, that of St.
Anthony on Talcott Street. The former Church of
St. Patrick was rededicated under the patronage of both
saints. The old church received a new name and new energy
in 1958. Thus, as can been seen on the present church's cornerstone (to the right of the main entrance), the year "1958"
is listed along with "1851" and "1876" as a founding date of
this church. Appropriately resting on this new cornerstone
and almost totally effaced is the original cornerstone. It is
not known whether this stone dates from 1876 or 1851.
Once the two faith communities were joined, the Italian-
Americans of St. Anthony, a parish which dates back to 1893,
lent their spirit to the revitalizing of old St. Patrick's. They
enhanced the parish with another of the great ethnic traditions of Hartford. The spirit of this ongoing renewal still
pervades the life of St. Patrick - St. Anthony parish. In the
midst of an ever-changing downtown Hartford, Connecticut's oldest Catholic congregation continues to adapt to
the needs of those around it. The church remains as a symbol of the community's   faith. It is an integral
part of Hartford's   history.

**CATHOLIC
INFORMATION
CENTER**

(Old St. Paul's Church)
125 Market Street
522-0602

In 1854 the City Missionary Society of Christ Church Cathedral (Episcopal) constructed this curious little brownstone building which three years later became St. Paul's Church. Father Charles Fisher served as pastor from 1857 to 1876, ministering to the needs of the immigrants who were beginning to settle in the area. The newcomers were chiefly German Lutherans who worked in the local factories. In 1880 the German Lutherans organized their own Church of the Reformation and purchased this building from the Episcopalians. Rev. Edmund F. A. Houtel was the Lutherans' pastor. For the next 17 years German-language Sunday services and a Saturday German school were held here.

Many Italian immigrants began coming to Hartford in the 1880's. They, too, settled along Front and Market streets and, being Roman Catholics, attended St. Patrick's Church on Church Street. Like all newcomers to the city, they longed to have their own church in which their native tongue was spoken. Finally, in 1894, the first Mass for Italians families was said in a vacant store on Morgan Street. Four years later St. Anthony's parish was organized, and the Italians first rented, then purchased, this brownstone building from the Lutherans who had moved into a new church on Charter Oak Avenue.

Under the leadership of Father Andrew Kelly, the burgeoning Italian community eventually built a basement church on Talcott Street, which was dedicated on October 31, 1921. This brownstone building became a recreation center and was renamed Casa Maria. In time the Italians also built a rectory, a convent, and a library on Market Street. Although a number of Jewish and black families lived in this neighborhood, most of the residents were

Italian, so this part of town became known as "Little Italy."
In the words of Armando Perretta, who grew up here, the
East Side was "a city within a city in whose boundaries one
could obtain anything to sustain life." Most of the men
worked in the factories or in construction, some became
push-cart peddlers and cobblers, others opened grocery
stores, pastry and ice cream shops, restaurants, and even
banks. Some, like Tony Zazzaro and Rocco Pallotti, achieved
fame as politicians, and a few like Bat Battalino and Willie
Pep rose to the top in the boxing world.

On March 19, 1936, the East Side was dealt a mortal
blow by the Great Flood which inundated Hartford. Once
again the Casa Maria became St. Anthony's Church while the
church on Talcott Street was repaired. Then, in the 1940's,
the Filippini Sisters came to Hartford to take charge of the
Italians' parochial school, and the Casa Maria provided five
classrooms.

In the 1950's, when plans were being made to build
Constitution Plaza, all the residents of the old ethnic neighborhoods on the East Side were relocated into other parts of
the city. Under the leadership of Father Alexis Riccio, St.
Anthony's parish was merged in 1958 with St. Patrick's on
Church Street. Almost all the old tenements and other
buildings, with the exception of Casa Maria, were torn down.
This durable little brownstone structure was purchased by
the Archdiocese of Hartford and, once again, was put to good
use. The archdiocese operates a book store, library, information center, and diocesan school offices on the site. Its
history as a house of worship for three successive denominations reflects in part the changing nature of the area's
ethnic population.

**ANCIENT
GRAVESTONE**

125 Market Street

Urban renewal and the passage of more than two centuries have not disturbed the graves of Norman Morison, a Hartford physician, and his son, Allan. The tiny graveyard is protected by a small enclosure at the northwest corner of the brownstone building at 125 Market Street that has been used as a church by three religious denominations at various times and is now owned by the Catholic Archdiocese of Hartford.

Dr. Morison was born in Scotland in 1706, graduated from the University of Edinburgh, and migrated to Connecticut around 1733. He settled in Wethersfield, then moved to Hartford where he purchased a home on the east side of Main Street. His two-acre house lot stretched from Main to Market Street. In 1745 Dr. Morison served as a physician to the British forces when they attacked Cape Breton in Nova Scotia. The next year he was chief surgeon for Captain William Whiting's company of foot soldiers during an expedition against the French in Canada.

In 1759 an epidemic of smallpox broke out in Hartford. Dr. Morison's son, Allan, contracted the disease and, much against his father's wishes, was sent to a "pest house" on the outskirts of the town, where he subsequently died. When the doctor was informed that the boy, as a carrier of the disease, could not be interred in the town's graveyard, he buried his son at the end of his own garden in a little iron-fenced plot and arranged with his attorneys that the grave would be protected forever. Two years later the father contracted "epidemic pneumonia" at age 55, after treating an afflicted friend, and died. He then was buried next to his son. In 1795 Dr. Morison's grandson directed in his will that all future owners of the site must preserve the two graves.

The property changed hands through the years. A brownstone building (now the Catholic Information Center) was erected, keeping the graves intact on the side of the building. Allan's gravestone still stands as part of a wall and the physician's grave is marked by a horizontal slab. In 1879 another restriction was placed on the property: "Deed to be void if buildings are used for other than religious purposes." Despite the ravages of time and radical changes in land use, the deeds are still honored.

This plaque was placed on the wall outside of G. Fox & Company's warehouse on September 9, 1973, by the Prince Hall Grand Lodge of Connecticut, Free and Accepted Masons. It marks the "Site of the Talcott Street Congregational Church. Established 1826. First Negro Church in Hartford." It also honors the church's first pastor, a "Recognized Leader in the Underground Movement and Early Fight for Negro Civil Liberties, Outstanding Minister Dr. James W.C. Pennington, 1840-1855."

Born a slave, James W.C. Pennington as a youth escaped from a plantation in Maryland. He fled to Connecticut where influential friends assisted him to acquire an excellent education. He eventually became a very popular Congregational pastor. While on a trip to Europe Pennington was given a doctorate by the University of Heidelberg.

When the Fugitive Slave Law was passed by the U.S. Congress in 1850, all runaway slaves in the northern states were required to be returned to their southern owners. This included Dr. Pennington, whom John Hooker of Hartford subsequently purchased from his Maryland master for $150. Hooker was a brother-in-law of Harriet Beecher Stowe. Before freeing his distinguished slave, John Hooker kept the deed of sale for two days before legally freeing Pennington, simply to experience the unique sensation of "owning" a Doctor of Divinity!

PENNINGTON PLAQUE

N.W. corner of Talcott & Market streets

HOLY TRINITY ROMAN CATHOLIC CHURCH

53 Capitol Avenue
246-4162

Attracted by job opportunities in local factories, Lithuanian Roman Catholics began settling in Hartford in 1890. Responding to the fact that these newcomers were scattered and without a parish, Rev. Joseph Zbrys of New Britain began coming to Hartford every Sunday to say Mass in the Lithuanian tongue. For $12 a month he rented a large room for religious services. By 1900 the Lithuanians had become sufficiently unified to obtain their own property at 41 Capitol Avenue for $10,000. A beautiful small chapel was erected, a building that was later to become the convent of the Sisters. This chapel was completed and consecrated as Holy Trinity Church on August 18, 1903.

The present church building was designed by architects Whiton and McMahon, and the cornerstone was laid in 1915. For over a decade, however, worship was conducted in the basement until the superstructure was completed. Builder William O'Neill began the upper church in 1925. It was dedicated March 18, 1927. Byzantine, Romanesque, and Lithuanian traditions shaped this parish church. The wood carvings made by hand and arranged along the interior walls of the sanctuary are particularly attractive.

In 1924 Holy Trinity pioneered the establishment of a Roman Catholic high school in Hartford. Thirty-eight years later the Bishop decided to build three new Catholic high schools, so Holy Trinity finally closed its doors in 1964. Today the majority of the families that comprise the loyal congregation of this church live in the suburbs.

105

During the American Revolution two outstanding Polish patriots, General Casimir Pulaski and General Tadeusz Kosciuszko, came to the aid of General George Washington and the American army. Pulaski was mortally wounded in a battle at Savannah, Georgia. Kosciuszko ultimately returned home, but before he departed the Americans rewarded him with American citizenship, the thanks of Congress, a pension, and a considerable amount of land. He in turn made a unique bequest to the new United States: "I, Tadeusz Kosciuszko, being just in my departure from America, do hereby declare and direct that, should I make no other testamentary disposition of my property in the United States, I hereby authorize my friend, Thomas Jefferson, to employ the whole thereof in purchasing negroes from among his own or any others and giving them liberty in my name, in giving them an education in trades or otherwise, and in having them instructed for their new conditions." Before his death in 1817 Kosciuszko emancipated his own Polish serfs, but there is no reliable record of what happened to his philanthropic bequest to American negro slaves.

During the last quarter of the 19th century, Polish immigrants, fleeing war and persecution in their mother country, began arriving in the U.S.A. Most of them were poor peasants almost totally lacking in education and skills. They were, nevertheless, more than willing to work in even the lowliest jobs. Like most European newcomers, their great dream was to own their own land. Since this was not possible until they acquired sufficient money, they found employment in Hartford's labor-hungry factories. Settling down chiefly along Sheldon, Woodbridge, Union and Governor streets, and later along Huyshope Avenue, they were able to walk to most of the places in which they worked. These included Colt Patent Firearms, Allen Manufacturing, Capewell Manufacturing, Emhart, Atlantic Tool, and other "shops." The three-story brick tenements in which they first lived were stark structures with small rooms and no inside toilet facilities. The only available water was a cold water tap located in the hallway on each floor of the building and used by all the roomers. Although their rents were lower than in other parts of the city, payments were high in proportion to their factory wages. Some

collected as little as $2.75 a week for 54 hours of work.

At first the Poles, being Roman Catholic, attended nearby St. Peter's Church on Main Street. Because the congregation of this church was solidly English-speaking Irish, the Polish newcomers longed for a priest of their own. For a while the bishop provided them with a Polish priest from New Britain who arrived every Sunday to say Mass in their native tongue. Because the Irish by then dominated the Hartford police force, friction sometimes developed between the two ethnic groups.

In 1899 a new priest, Father Stanislaus Musiel, came to Hartford to minister to the Polish residents who attended St. Peter's. Under his leadership they formed the Society of St. Stanislaus. Three years later a separate Polish parish was organized, and the first official Polish pastor, Father Lozowski, was installed. The Poles then purchased a lot on the corner of Charter Oak Avenue and Governor Street and erected a small wooden church which they named Sts. Cyril and Methodius. The new church was consecrated on April 5, 1903. They also built a Polish Catholic school where their children could use the Polish language and keep alive the history and customs of their ancestors.

During World War I many more Polish immigrants came to Hartford. They settled down in the Polish "ghetto," attracted by their fellow countrymen and the Polish church and school. The great majority became factory workers. In 1913 a new organization, the Polish National Alliance, was formed to assist both newcomers and older residents. Two years later a new Romanesque church building for Sts. Cyril and Methodius was constructed on Governor Street to accommodate the expanding congregation. The interior is very beautifully decorated with traditional Polish iconography, including a chapel of the "Black Madonna" which recalls a medieval miracle.

Because the Polish immigrants to Hartford were industrious and saving, their children and grandchildren made great progress economically, moving out of the "ghetto" usually in groups, to contiguous suburbs like Newington, Wethersfield, East Hartford, and Glastonbury. Some went even further into the country and purchased the little farms about which their immigrant ancestors had dreamed. There they became invaluable truck farmers supplying the city folk with excellent fruits, vegetables in season, and poultry, pork, and lamb through out the year.

The Poles, however, did not make as rapid advancement politically. The fact that their parents had come from three different sectors of a constantly invaded and divided mother country ... Austrian, German and Russian ... kept them politically divided here for quite a while. Eventually they did manage to develop a common "Polish" front which was essential to their political effectiveness. Walter Sidor was the first Polish American to be a judge of the Hartford City Court (1950) and was the first to be appointed a Superior Court Judge (1966) from the Hartford area. Attorney Joseph Ryter was the first Connecticut Congressman of Polish descent serving from 1945 to 1947. Mary Mazurek Heslin, who had been on the City Council for a number of years, served as Deputy Mayor from 1973-1974 and then went on to become the Commissioner of Consumer Protection for the State of Connecticut. In 1977 William Bieluch became a Connecticut Superior Court Judge and Zbigniew Brzezinski the first National Security Advisor of Polish origin.

Today the congregation of Sts. Cyril and Methodius still includes some urban residents. Most, however, are now suburbanites, children and grandchildren of the residents of the old ethnic neighborhood.

On July 13, 1790, the Rev. Freeborn Garretson, preaching to a Methodist gathering in Hartford, found his listeners ill-behaved and "fast asleep in the arms of the wicked one." The following day Methodist Bishop Asbury wrote in his diary about the deplorable state of his denomination in this city. "I rode 14 miles to the city of Hartford and preached once more in Rev. Strong's church (Congregational) and I roared out wonderfully on Matt. 11: 20-30: `Come unto me all ye that labor and are heavy laden and I will give your rest.'" This suggestion was apparently taken so literally that four years later the Bishop added to his diary, "I can scarcely find a breathing of living, holy spiritual religion here except amongst a few women in East Hartford."

All was not lost, however, because in 1820 the First Methodist Episcopal Church was organized in Hartford, and on May 24th of the following year a church was dedicated at the corner of Trumbull and Asylum streets. Rev. Benoni English was the first pastor. Methodism prospered in the city, and on April 4, 1860 a new and much larger church was dedicated on Asylum Street opposite the site of the old Bond Hotel.

Believing that a second ecclesiastical society was needed in the south end of town, the Methodists in 1851 purchased the Old South Public School building which stood on the present site of St. Peter's Roman Catholic Church. South Park Methodist, however, failed to progress until a new church was established on Hayden Place with Brother N.G. Cheney as the first pastor. In 1874 the foundation of this brownstone edifice was laid, and the congregation greatly expanded. For many years it was a very busy church supported by a sturdy residential neighborhood.

In 1981, due to a decreasing membership, South Park Methodist Church was put on the market for $275,000. Funds from the sale went to the new church to be housed at First-St. Paul's on Farmington Avenue. It was the second merger of two Methodist churches since 1975 when St. Paul's Church on Park Street merged with the First Methodist Church to form First-St. Paul's Church. St. Paul's Church and property were sold at that time to a Portuguese congregation. The new congregation has evolved into The United Methodist Church of Hartford.

SOUTH PARK INN

(The Old South Park Methodist Church)
75 Main Street

CENTRAL BAPTIST CHURCH

457 Main Street
522-9275

On March 23, 1790, 16 city residents organized the First Baptist Church of Hartford (now Central Baptist). The first sanctuary of this new denomination literally arrived floating down the Connecticut during a spring flood! The buoyant building belonged to some up-river Methodists. Because returning the church to its original congregation proved to be very expensive, the thrifty Baptists purchased it from the Methodists and set it up on Market Street, where it served their congregation for many years.

In 1807 the Baptist pastor and his flock became involved in a very heated controversy about singing in the sanctuary. The pastor held that all types of church music were sinful. Nevertheless his congregation overruled him by voting for "an ordinance of singing" which required all musically talented members to attend church so they could participate in the choir.

Soon after the War of 1812 the Baptists enlarged their little church, installed a basement, and erected a tower with a bell. In 1824 the basement of this church became the first classroom of the Episcopalians' new Washington College, now Trinity College.

A few years later the Baptists built a new church on Main Street where the Cheney Building (Brown Thomson's) now stands. In 1834, 55 members broke away and formed Hartford's South Baptist Church. The congregation of the First Church continued to grow, however, and in 1865 the members built another church on the corner of Main and Talcott streets. In 1909 Italian and Russian missions were formed within the church to welcome Baptists from those countries and to assist them in adjusting to America. Meanwhile the South Baptists constructed a second sanctuary on the corner of Main Street and Linden Place. Finally in 1922, both First and South Baptist decided to join together once again, so on December 18 they voted to unite under a new name: Central Church of Hartford, Connecticut. In 1925 the cornerstone of the present church building was laid.

Today Central Baptist continues to play a vigorous role in the center city. The church runs a day-care center for working mothers, a job training program, an adult church-academy, and every Sunday the Hispanic Baptist Church meets in the Center Church Chapel. Central Baptist is one of the ten members of Center City Churches Inc.

SOUTH CONGREGATIONAL CHURCH OF HARTFORD

277 Main Street
249-8627

The Old South Church, Second Church of Christ Congregational, was formally organized by 31 members of the First Church (Center) in 1670 after a protracted doctrinal dispute involving the so-called Half-Way Covenant and church government. Rev. Samuel Stone, second pastor of the First Church, favored a practice that allowed the baptism of children whose baptized parents had never fully united themselves with the Church but desired baptism for their children. Stone also favored a slightly more aristocratic, or Presbyterian, form of church government. An opposition faction within the First Church led by Elder Goodwin disagreed. This faction held that relaxing the traditional baptismal requirements would lead to an inferior class of church membership. They also championed the older, more democratic form of purely Congregational church government. In 1658 some members of the First Church had disagreed so strongly with Pastor Stone that they left Hartford, pioneered northward into the wilderness, and founded Hadley, Massachusetts. In 1663 after Stone's death, Rev. John Whiting became the new pastor, with Rev. John Haynes as his associate. These two strong-minded men continued the dispute, Whiting being "declaredly Congregational" and opposed to the Half Way Covenant, and Haynes leading the opposition.

From the very beginning of the settlement of Hartford by the Puritans there had been a slight but definite division in town between the inhabitants on the north side of the Little River and those on the south side in close (and unfriendly) proximity to the Dutch at "the Hollanders'" fur trading post. Fortunately the Dutch left Hartford in 1654, and the whole area fell into the hands of the English. Thus in 1669 Rev. Whiting and his followers decided to settle the dispute within the mother church by requesting a "friendly parting" and by forming a second society on the south side of the Little River. Whiting's proposal was greeted with sorrow but understanding by the congregation of the mother church, because the church fathers realized that the church building would either have to be enlarged or the congregation divided anyway to fit the needs of the town's rapidly expanding population. Therefore, since the Second Ecclesiastical Society Congregational within Hartford was formed in the spirit of friendship, the life of the town was actually enhanced by the event.

The first two buildings of the new South Congregational Church were simple wooden structures that closely resembled the early meeting houses of the First Church. The first sanctuary stood on the approximate site of the present Federal Building and, strange to say, the second was placed almost in the middle of Main Street. The third and present meeting house stands on the former house lot of Rev. Thomas Buckingham, South Church's second pastor.

This handsome brick sanctuary was dedicated in 1827. There was no formal architect. Two local builders, Colonel William Hayden and his brother-in-law Captain Nathaniel Woodhouse, designed and constructed the church. Years later Henry Valentine, a member of the congregation and a direct descendant of Captain Woodhouse, discovered in his attic an old builders' guide that was no doubt used in lieu of an architect, as the Corinthian columns, capitals, frieze, and many other architectural details of the South Church are identical to those described in the book. The use of a builders' guide by New England contractors was very common at that time in Hartford's history.

In 1847 the facilities of South Church were augmented when a separate lecture room was built just north of the sanctuary. Six years later the roof of the lecture room was turned about 90 degrees and lifted, a second floor was added, and the whole structure connected to the main sanctuary under the direction of architect Minard Lafever. In 1960 the church fathers employed architect Henry Kelly, brother of J. Frederick Kelly, Connecticut's most revered authority on colonial architecture, to undertake a major expansion of the church's facilities, including a chapel, Sunday School, kitchen and offices. The exquisite wood carvings and the terra-cotta plaques in this new addition are the work of Hartford's sculptress Frances Wadsworth. In 1967 the ceiling of the old sanctuary was restored, and an interesting discovery was made. Apparently the original ceiling of the church had been higher and flatter than the present one. In one high corner of the building, now hidden, was found a terra-cotta Tree of Life ... the tree was an oak tree, like the Charter Oak.

South Church today is a lively center for civic, cultural and service organization meetings of many kinds. There are concert performances each season. The church choir is outstanding. South Church is one of the few Congregational churches that did not merge with the United Church of Christ, preferring to retain its historic free Congregational status. For the same reason, South Church cooperates with, but is not a part of, Center City Churches Inc.

In March of 1977 South Church and portions of the adjacent neighborhood were listed in the National Register of Historic Places.

ST. PETER'S CHURCH

160 Main Street
525-2683

St. Peter's Church was established in 1859 when the entire population of Hartford numbered all of 28,000 people. At this time the only Roman Catholic church in town was St. Patrick's because their first church, Holy Trinity on Talcott Street, had been destroyed by fire. St. Peter's parish included all the territory south of the Park River in Hartford as well as the Town of Wethersfield. The new church's first pastor was Rev. Peter Kelly, a native of Ireland, who had been serving as a curate at St. Patrick's. His congregation also was Irish, impoverished immigrants who had been forced to leave their native land because of the potato famines. In Connecticut they became the poorest of laborers, chiefly occupied with digging canals, building railroads, and other rough employments. The Irish women, when not raising large families, served as domestic workers in the homes of the wealthy. Nevertheless, the Irish, thanks to their unique cohesiveness, their diligence, and their talent for politics, prospered.

The first building in which St. Peter's parish gathered was a brick structure that had been built in 1830 as a public school. Twenty-one years later it had been sold to the Methodist-Episcopalians and used by them as a church. Five years later it was rented as a Free Masons Chapel, then sold to the Roman Catholics. After a few renovations it was formally dedicated by the Rt. Rev. Francis P. McFarland on Sunday, December 1, 1859. As soon as their new church was refurbished, the Catholics began to construct a parochial school which was opened in 1860 with 200 students. The principal was John Gaffney who, with three lay women, taught all the classes. Their salaries were paid by the public school District Committee, but the students bought their own textbooks.

114

St. Peter's second pastor was Rev. John Lynch, who undertook the construction of a new church to accommodate his rapidly expanding congregation. The building of the new church was unsurpassed for ingenuity because it was placed on the exact site of the old one. This feat was accomplished by constructing the walls of the new building outside the walls of the original one. The cornerstone for the new edifice was laid in June 1865, but Father Lynch never failed to celebrate Mass every Sunday at St. Peter's. During the final week of construction the parishioners prayed one Sunday within the walls of the old church. Then, during the next few days, the walls were removed so that the following Sunday the parishioners prayed within their new church.

The architect for the new St. Peter's was John Murphy of New York City, who had been an associate of Patrick C. Keely. Keely had just designed a new Portland brownstone sanctuary for Asylum Hill Congregational Church and later became the architect of the original Portland brownstone Cathedral of St. Joseph on Farmington Avenue. John Murphy appropriately faced the French Gothic sanctuary of St. Peter's with Portland brownstone, and inside, the walls were painted lavender, the chestnut moldings installed, the gas jet lighting system modernized--the church had everything but its steeple, a condition fueling Mark Twain's remark that Hartford with its over-zealous church building and under-size construction budgets, had transformed itself "to the city of sawed-off spires." A south tower and spire were not added until 1926. The brownstone facade and dual spires lend a Gothic air to the neighborhood. The Star of Bethlehem is featured in the rose window as a symbol of the friendship between Father Peter Kelly and Rabbi Isaac Meyer, leader of the state's first synagogue, Charter Oak. When St. Peter's was dedicated on July 26, 1868, the huge building measuring 80 by 180 feet was one of the largest churches in Connecticut, with its sanctuary being one of the largest in the country. It cost $200,000, an enormous investment for a poor Irish congregation when a laborer's daily pay was $2.20 and domestic workers received $3 a week. However, the spiritual strength, and eventual political and economic strength the Irish derived from this glorious nucleus of their modest neighborhood manifested their importance in the years ahead.

In 1886-87 the interior of St. Peter's was renovated by John LaFarge of New York City, one of the foremost American decorators of that time. La Farge commissioned Renaissance-inspired wall paintings by Adolph Khuen and Louis Lamprecht. Today this interior, preserved intact, is considered to be one of the finest examples of 19th-century decoration in the state.

An encounter between St. Peter's Parochial School, the town's District School Committee, and Father John Lynch was of historic significance. When the parochial school was first opened, the public school District Committee provided only Roman Catholic teachers. After a few years, however, more and more Protestant teachers were added to St. Peter's staff until at least half of them were Protestants. This fact disturbed Father Lynch, because the Protestant teachers insisted upon using the King James translation of the Holy Bible rather than the Douay translation preferred by Roman Catholics. When the Catholics intimated that the King James version was a "secular" book, the Protestants were astonished and outraged! This reaction, however, had nothing to do with the separation of church and state. Both Catholics and Protestants assumed that religious instruction was absolutely essential to the proper education of a child in any type of school ... public, private, or parochial. Their dispute simply concerned biblical texts.

Because Father Lynch was unable to persuade the District Committee to insist that the teachers at St. Peter's use the Douay Bible, the Irish took care of the problem at the next District Committee election by voting into office a committee that was more sympathetic to their view. The old committee was furious so, before they retired, they appointed a Miss Parsons to St. Peter's teaching staff. A determined Protestant, Miss Parsons began her teaching duties every morning with lengthy prayers and reading from the King James Bible. This, of course, outraged Father Lynch. The new district School Committee tried, but failed, to transfer Miss Parsons to another school. Finally, in desperation, the Roman Catholics withdrew their children from her class and sent them to another school. So until her term was completed, Miss Parsons continued to read her Protestant version of the Holy Bible to an empty classroom. The following spring of 1866 the Catholics withdrew completely from the public school system, and Catholic nuns took over all teaching responsibilities. It is interesting to note that Hartford's great educator, Henry Barnard, sided with the Roman Catholics in this controversy. He agreed with an item that appeared in the *Hartford Times* on July 27, 1868 that deplored "the insane bigotry of a few hot heads in the South School District."

St. Peter's Greek Revival rectory just north of the church was built around 1840 for Ellery Hills of Hills, Rising and Childs, shoe manufacturers. (Hills's brother was the architect.) In 1850 the mansion was sold to Ira Peck, a local merchant. The Peck family continued to live here until 1902, when the building was purchased by St. Peter's parish. The Henry Barnard home just south of the church was purchased as a convent for the Daughters of the Holy Ghost in 1900 after Barnard's death.

No doubt the most famous of St. Peter's sons was John Moran Bailey, who graduated from St. Peter's School in 1918 and went on to become the head of the Democratic Party in Connecticut from 1947 until his death in 1975. Mr. Bailey also served as chairman of the Democratic National Committee from 1961 to 1968. As a boy young John lived at 450 Main Street (the present site of the Federal Building) with his parents Dr. Michael and Louise Moran Bailey. The Bailey home was the same architectural style as the nearby McCook homestead. Next door to the Baileys was the original Parma Restaurant (now located on Sheldon Street), where the Democrats met (and still meet) regularly for lunch and political strategy sessions.

In 1979 the doors of the church were locked, and the building faced the threat of demolition. Spurred by an appreciation of the spiritual and aesthetic wealth within St. Peter's, the congregation fought to restore the church to its original splendor. The people in St. Peter's congregation today are largely local elderly citizens and Puerto Rican newcomers. St. Peter's is affiliated with Center City Churches. Through this and other organizations St. Peter's is attempting vigorously to support and revive this neighborhood as well as other South End neighborhoods. St. Peter's can be viewed as a bridgework between old and new, English and Hispanic, in this densely populated community.

CHURCH OF THE GOOD SHEPERD

155 Wyllys
Colt Park
Parish House:
525-4289

Consecrated in 1869, this church was built by Mrs. Samuel Colt in memory of her husband and their three children who died in infancy. The architect was Edward Tuckerman Potter, who is described as "one of the athletes of Gothic revival, and one of those who did most to make even the Victorian phase of that revival rational and acceptable." Potter later designed the Caldwell Colt Memorial Parish House which stands nearby and the Mark Twain House on Farmington Avenue.

This is probably the only church in the world that is decorated with a revolver motif. The Armorer's Entrance is particularly interesting. If you look carefully you will find tucked among the crosses and the capitals of the columns a variety of gun parts: cylinders, stocks, gunsights, bullet molds, and set screws. Years ago a large iron cross surmounted the west end of the church. This finial, which looked more like a fleur-de-lis than a cross, was removed by the Bishop of Connecticut when a visiting prelate pointed out that the arms of this cross were also made of revolvers!

The interior of the church and the stained-glass windows are particularly elegant. A large memorial window in the west wall depicts two figures of equal size. One is Christ the Good Sheperd and the other is Joseph in Egypt during the seven "fat" years. It is said that Joseph's face is a representation of Samuel Colt himself, who also brought great prosperity to his countrymen. This was the first church in Hartford to be enhanced with a chime of bells.

In 1936 the church was badly damaged during the Great Flood. A small black marker above the main entrance shows how high the water rose. Over the ensuing years the steeple began to tilt so dangerously that the sanctuary could no longer be used and the parishioners were forced to hold services in the Parish House. Demolition of the church was seriously contemplated. However, in 1975 the Church of the Good Sheperd won a place in the National Register of Historic Places, making it eligible for federal funds to match those raised locally. The trustees raised the necessary monies, and the entire building was beautifully restored and refurbished.

Caldwell Hart Colt, the only surviving child of Elizabeth Hart Jarvis and Samuel Colt, died mysteriously at the age of 36 while cruising off Florida in his famous yacht, *Dauntless*. His reputation as a profligate bachelor equalled his renown as a sailor. Although acute tonsilitis was supposed to have been the cause of his early demise, the hearsay among Hartford historians is that Caldwell was shot to death by a jealous husband or fell overboard when intoxicated.

His bereaved mother turned to her old friend, Edward Tuckerman Potter, to design as a memorial to her son a parish house for the Church of the Good Shepherd, which she had created in memory of her husband and their children who had died as infants. Potter had been retired from the active practice of architecture for 20 years, but he responded to Mrs. Colt's request. This bizarre and completely unique memorial, dedicated in 1896, was his last building. Because Caldwell excelled at sports, particularly yachting, the architect emphasized sporting and marine motifs. There even was a mast which topped the structure, but this has disappeared. However, the main edifice, solidly constructed in brownstone, marble, and tile, has weathered the years and hard usage remarkably well. The sculptural details are particularly intriguing.

CALDWELL COLT MEMORIAL PARISH HOUSE

155 Wyllys Street
525-4289

CENTER CITY CHURCHES, INC.

170 Main Street
728-3201

Center City Churches, Inc., began in 1965 when eight downtown Hartford churches of various denominations met together to discuss their common ministry in the city. They were particularly concerned with the human problems of a large portion of Hartford's downtown population.

Through the Center City ministry, the churches pool their resources to provide social service, education, and health-care programs for the city's poor. Center City Churches is primarily concerned with meeting human needs for all ages. Sub-committees are involved with tutoring the young, working with youth, job training for those 14 to 21 years old, advocacy for families and adults, health screenings for the elderly and the indigent, emergency food for families and adults, breakfasts and noon meals for the poor, homeless, isolated, and elderly. Holiday dinners are open to all in the community.

The 10 member churches are Central Baptist Church, Center Church, Christ Church Cathedral, Church of the Good Shepherd, Emanuel Lutheran Church, First Presbyterian Church, Iglesia Bautista Hispana, Metropolitan Community Church, St. Peter's Roman Catholic Church, and United Methodist Church.

In colonial Connecticut the Congregational Church was the established, state-supported church. As a result all other religious denominations were frowned upon if not actively discouraged. The Episcopalians and Baptists were the first to protest this close alliance between church and state in Connecticut. In 1664 seven Episcopalians in Hartford and Windsor petitioned the General Assembly for permission to have their children baptized and to worship in their own way. The matter was referred to the Congregational Church so, of course, nothing came of it. By 1727, however, inspired by the Church of England's Society for the Propagation of the Gospel in Foreign Parts, the Episcopalians had grown strong enough to compel the Connecticut General Assembly to grant them the right to pay the church "rate" or tax to their own clergy rather than to the clergy of the established Congregational parish. The victory was won by a determined band of churchmen in Fairfield who chose to go to jail rather than to support the Congregationalists.

By the middle of the 18th century an Episcopal parish, St. Andrew's, in the "Scotland" district of the ancient town of Simsbury, was thriving. This is generally considered to be the "mother church" of Christ Church Cathedral, as the rector, Rev. William Gibbs, sometimes came to Hartford to pay encouraging visits. Unfortunately, his final visit during the Revolutionary War was extremely distressing to everyone concerned. (See Old St. Andrew's Church, Bloomfield.)

By 1762 Hartford Episcopalians had become sufficiently numerous to begin holding services in one another's homes and to form a parochial organization. They even held a public service in a local court house. Their pastor was Rev. Thomas Davies, a visiting missionary from Litchfield County. Inspired by his words, the Episcopalians on October 6 of that same year purchased a lot for an eventual church on Main Street (then called King Street). This lot was about 100 feet wide and extended westward to include half an acre. It comprised the eventual northwest corner of Main and Church streets, as the latter was not opened until 1794. Stones were gathered to build a foundation for the new edifice, but the efforts of the Episcopalians were frustrated by the outbreak of the American Revolution. Anti-English anti-Church of England feeling ran high in fiercely patriotic Connecticut, and the Episcopalians were roughly treated as

CHRIST CHURCH CATHEDRAL

45 Church Street
527-7231

potential traitors. Both their building lot and materials were illegally confiscated by a rabid Congregationalist and revolutionary named Samuel Talcott, so all the hopes and plans of their religious denomination were rudely dashed.

When the American Revolution was over, 10 of the 14 Episcopal clergymen in Connecticut met at Glebe House in Woodbury in March of 1783. Their purpose was to select a candidate for consecration as the first bishop of the newly organized Episcopal Church. Samuel Seabury, a native of Groton, was finally chosen. He immediately went to England to ask the English bishops to consecrate him. They, however, refused unless he would, as required by law, take an oath of allegiance to the King--which, as an American citizen, he could not do. So, he travelled up to Scotland to request the same of the Scottish bishops, who were more obliging. On November 14, 1784, Samuel Seabury was duly consecrated as Bishop of Connecticut, and the Diocese of Connecticut became the first Episcopal Diocese in the United States.

That same year the Episcopalians in Hartford went to court to recover their property that had been confiscated during the Revolution. They won their case and soon began to make plans for constructing a church. There is a tradition that in 1792, when the chief mason of the project, Prince Brewster, a loyal parish member, was laying the cornerstone for the new sanctuary, he said to the assembled citizens, "I lay this stone for the foundation of an Episcopal Church, and Sam Talcott and the gates of Hell cannot prevail against it!"

The church was a white frame structure, much like the Congregational churches in town. Most of the members, too, had been former Congregationalists, and many came from the best and most powerful families. Thus the Episcopal Church grew and prospered. The new church was not consecrated until November 11, 1801, when the Right Reverend Abraham Jarvis, second bishop of the diocese, performed the solemn ceremony in the presence of 15 other clergymen. At the same time Rev. Menzies Rayner was formally inducted as the first settled rector of the parish.

The Episcopalians continued to use this frame sanctuary until 1829, when the present church was constructed on the southwest corner of Church and Main streets. The architect was Ithiel Towne who, a few years later, would also become the architect of the new Wadsworth Atheneum. Then the Episcopalians sold their old church to the Roman Catholics, who moved it over to Talcott Street and changed its name to the Church of the Holy Trinity. This was the first Roman Catholic parish in Hartford, which later became St. Patrick's church. The building on Talcott Street was destroyed by fire in 1853.

On December 23, 1829, Bishop John Henry Hobart of New York performed the service of consecration for Christ Church's new stone sanctuary. It is interesting to note that the sentence of consecration was read by the Rev. William Jarvis of Trinity Church, Chatham (Portland). William Jarvis, brother of former Bishop Abraham Jarvis, became the father of Elizabeth Hart Jarvis, who eventually married Colonial Samuel Colt of Hartford. The Hart, Jarvis and Colt families, as well as the Morgans and Goodwins, played prominent roles in the growth of the Episcopal church in this part of the state.

On Trinity Sunday, June 15, 1919, Bishop Chauncy Bunce Brewster declared Christ Church to be the cathedral of the Diocese of Connecticut. The cathedral's first dean was the Very Reverend Samuel Rakestraw Collady. The cathedral today, as in the past, is an active spiritual and social force in the Greater Hartford community. At the present time the majority of the congregation lives in the suburbs. Like many churches in the downtown area, Christ Church Cathedral is a member of Center City Churches,Inc. and participates in their social service programs.

EMANUEL LUTHERAN CHURCH

311 Capitol Avenue
525-0894

Soon after the Civil War, Hartford's expanding manufacturing economy created a great demand for able machinists and tool makers. In response to these job opportunities, a number of Swedish people, largely Lutheran in religion, began arriving in this city. Because they were hard-working and ambitious and brought with them a variety of skills, the Yankees welcomed the Swedish newcomers with whom they had so much in common.

At first the Swedish Lutherans received only occasional pastoral visits from out of state, but by 1862 they held regular Lutheran worship services in a Congregational church on the corner of Market and Talcott streets. Four years later a Lutheran Church Society was formed. Finally on November 12, 1889, Emanuel Evangelical Lutheran Church was officially organized by 80 charter members who assembled at Asylum Hill Congregational Church for the occasion. They immediately organized a subscription drive to build their own church which soon stood on the corner of Russ and Babcock streets. It cost the fledgling congregation almost $10,000 and was dedicated on July 3, 1892. The first pastor was Carl L. Bengston.

Pastor Bengston was followed by equally able clergy-men, and the Lutherans prospered. In 1913, because the congregation had expanded substantially, the old building was sold, and a basement church was constructed on this present site. The architect was A. T. Simmons of Bloomington, Illinois, and the cost was $26,668. In 1922 Hartford architect Russell F. Barker was engaged to enlarge and improve the Simmons plans, and the congregation embarked on an $80,000 fund drive to complete the building. Two years later, on October 26th, this lovely Gothic sanctuary, one of the finest Swedish Lutheran churches in the eastern United States, was dedicated.

A new chapel and parish house, designed by Jeter and Cook and constructed by Carlson and Torell at a total cost of $335,000, was dedicated on April 22, 1956.

In 1971, along with a number of other Hartford congregations, the members of Emanuel Church, with the support of a Federal program, built Capitol Towers for senior citizens, an exceptionally successful and well-operated facility. The congregations believed that the contracts they signed for this housing would stand the test of time. Unfortunately this was not the case, and the churches were caught in a perplexing tax battle between the city and state.

Today 90% of Emanuel's congregation live in the suburbs. However they remain loyal to the mother church which was so vital to the spiritual and material survival of their immigrant ancestors and now inspires them and their children. A particularly joyous annual occasion is the Festival of St. Lucia celebrated every December 13.

Emanuel Lutheran Church is a member of the Center City Churches and participates in the activities of that organization for the betterment of the city of Hartford. Today this old Scandinavian neighborhood is largely Spanish-speaking.

FIRST PRESBYTERIAN CHURCH

136 Capitol Avenue
246-2224

On Sunday, November 10, 1850, a small group of Presbyterians met together for worship services at the old Washington Temperance Hall on the corner of Market and Temple streets. The following year this group met with the newly organized Presbyterians of Connecticut and took steps toward the formal organization of a church in Hartford. The Presbytery appointed Rev. James Ely to create interest in the project. From that day on services continued to be held, and the church's first pastor was appointed, the Rev. Thomas Spencer Childs of Springfield, Massachusetts, who had recently graduated from Princeton Seminary.

In July 1869 the cornerstone for the present church was laid. Renwick and Sands of New York were the architects. However, the Presbyterians' pastor, Rev. J. Aspinwall Hodge, actually supervised the daily building of this church. Constructed of gray Vermont granite with Portland brownstone trim, it is an attractive blending of Gothic and Romanesque architecture.

Today First Presbyterian is an active supporter of Center City Churches' various programs with youth, the elderly, and alcoholics. Six days a week a group of senior citizens meets here for recreation, personal counseling, and a wholesome mid-day luncheon.

OUR LADY OF FATIMA CHURCH

Fatima Square
236-1443

In recent years many people of Portuguese background have migrated to Hartford, attracted here by jobs and relatives. The Portuguese are especially active in local business enterprises.

In 1957 a Roman Catholic Portuguese parish was formed, and Father Jose Silva became the first priest. The first sanctuary, formerly owned by Grace Lutheran Church of Woodland Street, was located on the corner of Babcock and Russ streets. In 1986 the Portuguese community raised funds for the construction of a new church and rectory on Fatima Square near New Park Avenue, the first new church built in Hartford in the 20th century. The congregation consists of 700 families, most of whom live in nearby neighborhoods. Day care for the community is offered at this church.

Persons of African ancestry have lived in Hartford as long as those of English ancestry, chiefly because the white Yankee sea captains brought Africans here as slaves. (Legislation providing for the emancipation of all Negroes at the age of 25 was not passed in Connecticut until 1784.) It was customary in colonial days for everyone to attend the Congregational Church. Blacks, however, along with Indians and members of the servant class, were required to sit either in the back or in the gallery of the meeting house. Women, too, were initially segregated. Because pews were assigned on the basis of wealth and prestige in those days, the most affluent and powerful members of the community occupied the most desirable places.

In 1819 the black members of Hartford's First Congregational Church decided that they would like to worship by themselves so that they could create their own programs, organize their own meetings, and practice some real degree of self-determination. At first they assembled for the Sabbath in the conference room of the First Church under the leadership of their own black minister, Rev. Asa Goldsborough. The following year they formed a Sunday School exclusively for "people of color". In 1826 this developed into the African Religious Society of Hartford, and a meeting house was constructed on the corner of Market and Talcott streets. Three years later the blacks requested a separate public school for their children, and the school was located within the church.

In 1833 the church was reorganized and officially recognized by the Congregational Churches in Connecticut and the name was again changed to the First Hartford Colored Congregational Church. Later it was known as the 5th Congregational Church, then as the Talcott Street Congregational Church.

In 1835 Hartford experienced its first recorded race riot. Irish immigrants also lived in the Talcott and Market street neighborhood and, one Sunday, they taunted the black worshippers as they departed from their sanctuary. This infuriated the blacks, who fought back, and a fierce but short-lived battle ensued. Unfortunately, relations between the blacks and the Irish were not always as cordial as they might have been because both groups were poor and both competed for the same types of jobs.

In 1840 there were two public schools for blacks in this city, one at the Talcott Street Church and another in the black African Methodist Episcopal Church then located on Elm Street. One of the Talcott Street Church's most distinguished pastors was the Rev. Dr. James W.C. Pennington, the first black man to be given a doctorate by Heidelberg University in Germany. (See Pennington Plaque.) Dr. Pennington, a former slave, often exchanged pulpits with local white pastors and was twice elected president of the Hartford Central Association of Congregational Ministers. He was a strong proponent of education and urged the Hartford School Committee to improve the education of Hartford's black children. In 1852 they responded by erecting a proper school exclusively for black youngsters on Pearl Street right next to the A.M.E. Church which, by then, had moved to this part of town. Separate education for blacks continued in Hartford until 1868 when Connecticut passed a law requiring all children to attend school in their own district regardless of race.

During Dr. Pennington's pastorship, before the Civil War, both Talcott Street Church and the A.M.E. Church played active roles in the anti-slavery movement. When war broke out many young men signed up for service in the all-black 29th Regiment which distinguished itself during that tragic, fratricidal conflict. (There were also all-Irish and all-German regiments as it was customary for men of the same ethnic background to enlist in a particular military unit.)

Emancipation, however, did not substantially change the economic position of even the best-educated and most ambitious blacks in Hartford, although some acquired superior status as butlers, seamstresses, tailors, cooks, and domestics in powerful white families. A few like Holdridge Primus became more affluent; his son Nelson achieved notice as a painter. Charles Mitchell, who migrated to Boston, was selected by the Boston Republicans as the first black to run for the state legislature. For the most part, however, the blacks in Hartford continued to be relegated to less rewarding and more menial tasks in the community simply because of their race.

Hartford, along with other northern metropolises, experienced great population changes after the Civil War. Up to this time, three out of every four black citizens were natives of Connecticut. Ten years later 35% had come here from the South, and by the turn of the century the old black families were a distinct minority. The large in flux of southern blacks during World War I and World War II further diluted their numbers. In 1953 the Talcott Street Congregational Church merged with Mother Bethel Methodist Church, founded in 1916, to become the Faith Congregational Church. The following year they purchased their present sanctuary, which had been built in 1872 by the Windsor Avenue Congregational Church when this section of Main Street was called Windsor Avenue. Among the distinguished members of this white congregation were Mr. and Mrs. Appleton Hillyer, who founded Hillyer College, now the University of Hartford, and constructed the Horace Bushnell Memorial Hall in honor of Mrs. Hillyer's father. When this sanctuary was purchased by black Congregationalists, the former white congregation merged with the Fourth Church to form the present Horace Bushnell Congregational Church at Vine Street and Albany Avenue.

OLD CEMETERIES

Main Street

The first burial in Hartford's Old North Cemetery took place in 1807. Like the Ancient Burying Ground behind Center Church on Main Street, Old North is owned by the City of Hartford. It includes 17 acres of land and contains the graves of Horace Bushnell, Frederick Law Olmsted, Daniel Wadsworth, Samuel Colt's parents, and many other leading Hartford citizens of yesteryear.

Spring Grove Cemetery, located at 2035 Main Street, covers 33 acres and is still active. It is owned by a private association. The first burial took place here in 1845. As in Old North, many of the graves in Spring Grove are very interesting to historians.

METROPOLITAN A.M.E. ZION CHURCH

2084 Main Street
527-7087

In 1827 an African Religious Society was created in the Black Congregational church on the corner of Talcott and Market streets. Six years later this society split into the Colored Congregational Church and the Colored Methodist Episcopal Church. For a brief period of time both congregations continued to use the same place of worship. In 1842 the Colored Methodists moved to another building on what is now Elm Street and took the name African Methodist Episcopal Zion Society. They remained in this location until 1856, when all the land in the area was taken to create Bushnell Park. Then they moved into a building on the corner of Pearl and Ann streets. Forty-two years later they built a new sanctuary on the same site.

The Pearl Street church was sold to the city in 1924 to make way for the present firehouse. Because the AME Zion congregation lacked a permanent home, they held their services in the YWCA on Ann Street for two years. Then they moved into their present sanctuary.

Constructed in 1871, this was originally the North Methodist Church of Hartford. In 1919 the North Methodists moved to the corner of Albany Avenue and Woodland Street and sold this building to Emmanuel Synagogue. After the Jews sold the building to the AME Zion congregation, they moved into a new synagogue on Greenfield Street. Over the years the congregation of AME Zion has grown and prospered so that today the majority of the members and their families live in the suburbs. Even so, they continue to be loyal to this historic church of their forefathers in Hartford.

After the Civil War a group of freed blacks migrated to Hartford from Essex County, Virginia. These kindred souls, strangers in a new land, banded together for the worship of God and for mutual comfort and friendship. Initially they met in their various homes for prayer, song, and scripture. More friends continued to arrive from Essex County, so it soon became necessary to find some sort of a central place of worship. In 1871 this "central place" was a discarded box car on Spruce Street in downtown Hartford. Swinging their lanterns in the night, many of the members of this little church walked miles to homes as far away as Wethersfield and Windsor where they had found employment as domestic servants.

When the congregation grew larger, a new sanctuary, Hope Chapel, was founded on the corner of Albany Avenue and East Street. In 1881 a further increase in membership prompted a move to Wooster Street. Eight years later, however, the congregation divided into Shiloh Baptist Church and Union Baptist Church because of internal disagreements, so Union Baptist built a new brick church at 31 Mather Street in 1908.

Over the years the pastors of Union Baptist Church have all been strong leaders, but one of the best was Rev. Charles L. Fisher, a scholar and a man of letters who came to the pulpit in 1916. He stressed three principles to his congregation: save your money, get an education, and serve God. His wife, Rosa L. Fisher, was an equally dynamic individual. Another outstanding pastor was Rev. John C. Jackson who became the minister in 1922. At this time the congregation had outgrown the Mather Street church and was faced with either enlarging the structure or acquiring new quarters. Therefore, when the opportunity came to purchase the former St. Thomas Episcopal church at 1921 Main Street, the congregation moved to its present location in 1925. This church had been built by wealthy white Episcopalians in 1871 in memory of Thomas Church Brownwell, the third Episcopal Bishop of Connecticut and first president of Trinity College. The Union Baptists sold their Mather Street sanctuary to St. Monica's Episcopal Church, a black congregation.

Union Baptist Church grew and prospered under the leadership of the "Old Patriarch," as Rev. Dr. Jackson came to be known. During the Great Depression he served his people without salary, taking for himself only the offering collected on the last Sunday of each month. In 1938, when the Great Hurricane toppled the church's steeple, respect for Dr. Jackson brought many friends and admirers to the aid of his congregation, and the badly damaged sanctuary was soon rebuilt. Rev. Jackson gave 27 years of leadership to the New England Baptist Convention, and he worked unceasingly for civil rights and better employment opportunities for his people.

In 1943, traveling on a train through Alabama, Dr. Jackson was cruelly beaten by two white men while passing through a coach reserved for whites to join some friends. He never fully recovered from the effects of that assault. While the incident was widely reported in the press, he was unable to get a trial from the Department of Justice. However, local indignation resulted in the creation of a statewide Civil Rights Commission on June 29, 1943 ... the first in the nation. One of its original members was the Rev. Dr. Jackson. He died in 1953 at 86 years of age. A decade later a member of his former congregation, Mrs. Rachel Taylor Milton, pioneered the founding of the Urban League in Hartford. Her brother-in-law, the Rev. Cedric Mills, a member of St. Monica's parish, became the first black bishop of the Virgin Islands and a nephew, Spencer Shaw, became a professor at the University of Washington. The fantastic accomplishments of all members of the Taylor family alone ... nine girls and one boy ... demonstrate how this nation is finally profiting from the talents of its black citizens, talents that used to be so sadly wasted.

The Cathedral of St. Joseph, designed by Eggers and Higgins of New York City, was dedicated in 1962. It replaced the Portland brownstone original cathedral which had been consecrated in 1892 and destroyed by fire in 1956.

The focal point of this vast sanctuary is the gray-veined white marble altar. The aluminum baldachin which canopies the altar and the raredos, a gigantic ceramic mural of Christ in Glory, which soars behind it, are both the largest of their kind in the world. The stained-glass windows, made in France, are so large that the artist who designed and executed them had to rent a special studio in order to do the work. The great organ was made by the Austin Organ Company of Hartford.

There were very few Roman Catholics in colonial Connecticut. In fact, members of all Christian denominations other than Congregationalist were legally forbidden to worship in their own churches in Connecticut until the law was changed in 1706! During the American Revolution, when the French came to the assistance of the patriots, George Washington sternly reminded all his followers that the vital reinforcements they were receiving from abroad came "from a nation in which the Catholic faith is professed."

The presence of friendly French soldiers in Connecticut did relax the fiercely anti-Catholic biases of the Puritan Yankees. During the Comte de Rochambeau's historic conference with General Washington in Wethersfield, a portion of the French army was encamped in the South Meadows. There on July 26, 1781, Father Claude Pere Robin, chaplain of the troops, celebrated the first Roman Catholic Mass in Connecticut.

Many years later, in 1813, a Roman Catholic priest, Father Francis Matignon of Boston, passed through Hartford on his way to New York. Because Connecticut law forbade him to travel on the Lord's Day, he had to spend Sunday in Hartford. Learning of his presence the Rev. Nathan Strong, pastor of the First Congregational Church, invited Father Matignon to "occupy his pulpit", which he did, apparently to the delight of the female members of the congregation. The church's deacons, however, protested against Dr. Strong's liberality and asked him to meet with them. He answered defiantly and humorously, "Well, gen-

CATHEDRAL OF ST. JOSEPH

140 Farmington Ave
249-8431

133

tlemen, do your best and do your worst. Make the most of it. I have the ladies on my side!"

Three years later Laurent Clerc, a French Catholic, arrived in Hartford to assist Dr. Thomas Hopkins Gallaudet in establishing a school for deaf and dumb children. A few other Catholics, probably poor Irish, were living in Hartford by this time because in May of 1823 Bishop John Cheveros of Boston came here to offer a Catholic Mass in the Hall of Representatives of the Old State House. There he baptized a number of Catholic children, including Clerc's son. Because Hartford's sparse Roman Catholic population was viewed with suspicion by most of their neighbors, the Bishop counseled them, "Be sober, honest, and industrious. Serve faithfully those who employ you and show that a good Catholic is a good member of society, and that he feels grateful to those who are kind to strangers, and sincerely loves his brethren of all persuasions, though he strictly adheres to the doctrines of his own church. It is thus, my beloved friends, that you will silence prejudice and win the esteem and favor of all the inhabitants of this hospitable country."

The new Connecticut Constitution of 1818 disestablished the Congregational Church as the state-supported church, and thus gave a great boost to all other religious denominations. In June 1823, Hartford's first Roman Catholic church was "gathered" among the residents of Talcott Street. Six years later the city's Catholic population decided to buy their first church, a former Episcopalian sanctuary that stood on the northwest corner of Church and Main streets. The price for both building and organ was $900. On July 10 Bishop Benedict Joseph Fenwick, the second Bishop of Boston and the third American Roman Catholic Bishop, arrived in Hartford to complete the purchase. Episcopal Bishop Thomas Church Brownell, representing his denomination, commented, "Well, Bishop Fenwick, as we have a fine new church building, we will let you have the old one." To which Bishop Fenwick replied, "Yes, as you have a fine new religion, we will keep the old one!"

The former Episcopal church then was renamed Holy Trinity and moved over to Talcott Street. On August 26 Bishop Fenwick appointed the Rev. Bernard Cavanaugh first pastor of Hartford with missionary jurisdiction over the entire state of Connecticut.

On September 18, 1843, the Very Reverend William Tyler became the first Bishop of the See of Hartford, which had jurisdiction over the states of Connecticut and Rhode Island. Bishop Tyler's parents, of old Puritan stock, had both been converted to Catholicism. He was installed on April 14, 1844, in Hartford's Church of the Holy Trinity. At that time Connecticut had almost 8,000 Roman Catholic residents. Because there were even more Catholics in Rhode Island, however, the bishop made his home in Providence, so Hartford had no resident bishop.

Holy Trinity's modest sanctuary eventually became too small for Hartford's steadily expanding population. A second church, St. Patrick's, was constructed on Church and Ann Street in 1851. Soon after this Holy Trinity's wooden building was destroyed by fire. The following year the Sisters of Mercy were invited to come to Hartford to establish a parochial school and orphanage by the Hartford See's second bishop, the Very Reverend Bernard O'Reilly, also a resident of Providence. A third Roman Catholic Church, St. Peter's on Main Street, was consecrated in 1868. Four years later Rhode Island was finally divided from Connecticut as part of the Hartford See, so the bishop then required a residence and cathedral in Hartford.

In July 1872, the Hartford See's third bishop, the Very Reverend Francis P. MacFarland, purchased from James Goodwin for $70,000 a former farm and farmhouse known as "the old Morgan homestead." Two months later Hartford's fourth Catholic parish, the St. Joseph Cathedral Corporation, was legally established. This new parish was bounded on the north by Albany Avenue; on the east by Edwards Street, the railroad tracks, and Washington Street; on the south by Ward Street, and on the west by the New Britain town line. The Catholics planned to build here a cathedral; a bishop's house; a convent for their teaching nuns, the Sisters of Mercy; and a parochial school. Architect Patrick Keely of Brooklyn, New York, drew up suitable plans for these structures. (He had also designed Asylum Hill Congregational Church in 1866.)

Bishop MacFarland then decided his first priority was to construct the convent as a motherhouse for all the Sisters of Mercy in Connecticut, including those presently housed near St. Patrick's in Hartford. These devoted sisters are properly described as "a noble company of women without

whose sacrifice the parochial school system of the State was impossible." Founded in Dublin in 1827, and coming to Hartford in 1852, it is the oldest Roman Catholic religious community in the diocese. Mount St. Joseph Academy and St. Joseph College were also founded by the Sisters of Mercy.

Because St. Joseph had no cathedral, Mass was celebrated in the new convent. On April 29, 1877, the cornerstone for the Cathedral of St. Joseph was laid with much ceremony and rejoicing. More that 15,000 people attended, including 7,000 who came on special trains from all parts of Connecticut and from out of state. The basement chapel was dedicated February 10, 1878, and served as a cathedral for the bishop for 14 years. The following year the cathedral parochial school was opened under the leadership of the Rev. William A. Hartz. Finally, on May 8, 1892, St. Joseph's massive Portland brownstone cathedral, one of the most impressive sanctuaries in the United States, was formally consecrated, and "the ceremony of consecration was the most solemn and inspiring ever witnessed in the Catholic Church."

The Cathedral of St. Joseph is a member of the Asylum Hill Christian Community.

The cornerstone of this edifice, originally the Farmington Avenue Congregational Church, was laid July 2, 1898. The architect was Ernest Flagg of New York City.

Embarrassed by the fact that its appearance differed from traditional Congregational churches, the founders explained that "St.John at Poitiers in France, a small bapistry built during the fifth century, may be called the prototype of this small building, for it was the plan of that ancient church which prompted the design of this modern one."

Because portions of the exterior were decorated with shiny green and yellow tiles, Mark Twain jokingly dubbed it "The Church of the Holy Linoleum." Unfortunately, the church fathers, stung by such ridicule, finally scarified and plastered the tiles on the front of the building. However a few on the side remain as part of the architect's original plan.

The congregation stems from a variety of mergers which involved three old downtown churches: Pearl Street Congregational, Park Congregational on the corner of Asylum and High streets, and Horace Bushnell's Old North on the corner of Main and Talcott streets. All these buildings have been demolished. In 1914 Farmington Avenue Congregational Church's name was changed to Immanuel rather than Emanuel as this is the way the word is supposed to have been spelled traditionally in the Old Testament.

Today Immanuel Church is an active and creative member of the Asylum Hill Christian Community and deeply involved with the welfare of the neighborhood. The church is responsible for two major housing ventures ... Immanuel House on Woodland Street, which was opened in 1972 for moderate and fixed-income residents, and Immanuel Group Residence on Farmington Avenue for retarded adults.

IMMANUEL CONGREGATIONAL CHURCH

10 Woodland Street
527-8121

TRINITY EPISCOPAL CHURCH OF HARTFORD

120 Sigourney Street
527-8133

On September 12, 1859, twelve well-to-do Episcopalians who lived in the elegant new neighborhood of Hartford known as Asylum Hill, or Lork's Hill, gathered together to form a new parish called Trinity Church. As senior warden they elected Hezekiah Huntington, president of the Hartford Fire Insurance Company. In October they purchased land on Sigourney Street but, still without a building, they met regularly for Sunday services in the living rooms of their own commodious homes.

Being wealthy but thrifty Yankees, they then became aware of a very curious "bargain" that met their immediate need. In 1845 the Unitarians in Hartford had constructed a handsome, brownstone and brick Gothic church on the corner of Trumbull and Asylum streets. This extravagant building, however, soon proved much too large and expensive for their congregation to maintain, so in 1858 it was closed and offered for sale. The more affluent Episcopalians purchased the sanctuary, carefully demolished it, then proceeded to move it, piece by piece, to Sigourney Street. On October 2, 1860, Episcopal Bishop Thomas Church Brownell laid and blessed Trinity Church's cornerstone and, by the summer of 1861, the building was completely re-constructed! Trinity's first rector, Rev. Pelham Williams, a Harvard graduate, was formally installed on September 12, 1861.

In 1865 Trinity's third and most influential rector took over the leadership of the church. He was Rev. Francis Goodwin, son of James Goodwin, president of Connecticut Mutual Life Insurance Company. Francis Goodwin was the first cousin of J. Pierpont Morgan and most certainly the equal of his famous cousin in managerial talent, vision, intelligence, and energy. Francis Goodwin resigned his post at Trinity in 1871 because of a weak heart, but somehow managed to do the work of 10 healthy men for the rest of his long life. (He died in 1923.) He was particularly interested in the church and eventually became the first Episcopal Arch Deacon of Hartford. In 1892 he and Mrs. Goodwin, in memory of their daughter Lucy Morgan Goodwin, built Trinity Church's present parish house and chapel, Goodwin Hall.

Rev. Goodwin was passionately devoted to his native city of which his ancestor William Goodwin had been a founder back in 1636. He was, in fact, the one-man "city planner" of Hartford long before city planning came in vogue. The fact that the Goodwin family was one of the largest landowners in Hartford, of course, facilitated his endeavors. Moreover, he was closely related to other large landowners and enjoyed their confidence. For these reasons Rev. Goodwin in the 1890's became a major promoter of "more parks for Hartford." It was almost entirely because of his efforts that this city's unique and extensive park system was created. (See the chapter on Parks.) In the 1920's his son, Charles Goodwin, also a member of his church, personally spearheaded the creation of the Metropolitan District Commission which now gives the Hartford area such an abundance of pure water.

Another fine citizen and Trinity Church member was Elizabeth L. Knox, who served for 12 years on the City Council. Betty Knox gave tirelessly of herself to her native city and received numerous awards for her outstanding civic zeal as well as the deepest love of her fellow citizens, rich and poor, in Hartford. When she died in 1966 at the age of 57 she endowed the Knox Foundation which has continued her good works.

Trinity Episcopal Church is a member of the Asylum Hill Christian Community. The church is also involved with many other social service projects.

SACRED HEART CHURCH

26 Ely Street
Rectory: 527-6459

On August 26, 1872, Hartford's German Catholics organized informally under the leadership of the Rev. Joseph Schele, the poet-priest of New Haven, who came to this city regularly to offer Mass in the German language at St. Peter's School on Main Street. The cornerstone for this church was not laid until 1892, and a basement chapel was dedicated the following year. In 1917 the church was completed.

Today the congregation of Sacred Heart is largely Puerto Rican. The church is vigorously involved in trying to improve the standard of living of its congregation. The San Juan Tutorial Program and other educational opportunities are examples of Sacred Heart's commitment.

UNITED METHODIST CHURCH OF HARTFORD

571 Farmington Avenue

In 1820 the First Methodist Episcopal Church was founded in Hartford on the corner of Trumbull and Chapel streets. (See South Methodist Church for historical details.) Thirty-seven years later the congregation moved to Asylum Street. At the turn of the century the Methodists moved to their present location. This sanctuary was dedicated in 1905. The church's name evolved into First-St. Paul's because of mergers in 1939 and 1968 with other Methodist and Evangelical denominations. The church's present name was created in 1981 when the South Park Methodist Church of Main Street merged with this established congregation.

United Methodist Church is playing an active role in the preservation of the West End of Hartford from urban decay. The West End Civic Association meets here regularly and Beacon Day Care Center provides a valuable service for families in the community. Their newspaper, the *Westender*, is published every month.

ST. ANN'S CHURCH

8 Park Street
Rectory: 728-7445

St. Ann's is the oldest non-English speaking parish in Hartford. As early as 1888 French-speaking Catholics in this part of the city were gathered by Rev. M.A. St.Louis, and a parish was officially established the following year. The parishioners were largely French-Canadians who migrated here to work in local factories and in the construction business.

St. Ann's Church originally stood on the corner of Park and Putnam streets. The cornerstone of the present magnificent Italian Renaissance sanctuary was laid in 1924, and the building was dedicated two years later. Henry Ludorf of this city was the architect. When he died in 1977, he was buried from St. Ann's, which he considered his finest artistic achievement.

The French-Canadian population in this area is diminishing. Unlike nearby churches, which are now largely Puerto Rican, St. Ann's is not a territorial church, but exists chiefly to serve those who speak the French language.

140

Followers of the Russian Orthodox faith began arriving in Hartford around the turn of the 20th century. As they possessed very little education and few skills, they went to work in the city's many factories. Thanks to the vigorous efforts of the St. Peter and Paul brotherhood, the parish of All Saints was formally organized in 1914, and a church building on Broad Street acquired. By 1955 the Broad Street church was much too small for the congregation, so land for a new church was purchased on Scarborough Street the following year.

However, not until 1958 when the Very Reverend Michael Dirga was assigned as pastor were the monies raised to actually begin construction of the new sanctuary. Ground was broken in 1963, and the church completed and consecrated on June 14, 1964, the 50th anniversary of the Hartford parish.

The brilliance of this Orthodox Church is a fascinating addition to Hartford's great variety of ecclesiastical architecture. Most striking are the three golden onion domes. The equally colorful interior is adorned with lovely stained-glass windows, an ikonastasis which stands between the congregation and the altar, and numerous handsome candelabras. The architect was Peter Petrofishi.

The parish house next door was designed and built by Paul Uremko & Brothers, Inc. The colonial architecture of the parish house coupled with the Byzantine brilliance of the church symbolizes a healthy desire to retain the best of the old world culture while gracefully accepting that of the first American colonists.

ALL SAINTS RUSSIAN ORTHODOX CHURCH

205 Scarborough St
523-0344

Constructed in 1952 by the Hartford Ward (Congregation) of the Church of Jesus Christ of Latter Day Saints, this was the first Mormon chapel in New England. The strongly evangelical Mormons claim to be the "fastest growing church in the world."

In 1975 the Mormons built a new $1 million chapel in Bloomfield and sold this one to the Grace Tabernacle Church of God which had formerly been located at 76 Hebron Street in Hartford. Members of the congregation are largely West Indian in background.

GRACE TABERNACLE CHURCH OF GOD

1452 Asylum Avenue
242-9822

FIRST CHURCH OF CHRIST SCIENTIST

235 Scarborough St
236-4676

Christian Science in Hartford dates back to the year 1881, when its discoverer and founder, Mary Baker Eddy, sent two copies of her book, *Science and Health with Key to the Scriptures*, to the Watkinson Library of Reference.

On May 11, 1898, First Church of Christ Scientist, Hartford, was organized and incorporated. Services were held in various rented halls. In 1904 a lot on Farmington Avenue was purchased on which a chapel was erected, the first Christian Science Church to be built in the state of Connecticut.

As time went on the chapel became entirely inadequate to meet the needs of a growing organization. The Sunday School, committee activities, and officers of the church needed better facilities, including a larger auditorium. A lot at the southwest corner of Albany Avenue and Scarborough Street was purchased October 14, 1952. Construction started in August, 1955, and the first service was held in the new edifice on the first Sunday in June 1956. The architect was Wallace Dibble of Longmeadow, and his assistant was Norris Prentice of Glastonbury.

EPISCOPAL DIOCESAN HOUSE

1335 Asylum Ave
233-4481

When Mabel and Eleanor Johnson and their aunt, Elizabeth Stedman, returned to Hartford from a grand tour of Europe in 1911, they decided to build themselves a large home like the English manor houses they had so much admired. Their architects were E.K. Rossiter & Co. of New York City, who completed this mansion three years later.

Miss Mabel Johnson presented her home to the Episcopal Diocese of Connecticut in 1951. Twenty-two years later architect Richard Barllett of Bloomfield designed the addition to store the church archives.

142

As far back as 1659 it was noted in Hartford's town minutes that a few Jewish traders were starting to visit this area. They were Portuguese and Spanish Sephardic Jews who had migrated to America at this time to escape persecution in their former countries. Three years later Hartford's town fathers voted to allow "Jews then residing in town to have liberty to reside here seven months." One hundred and twenty-seven years later some of these Sephardic Jews became respected citizens of the community. In this "land of steady habits" the Puritan citizens were very loath to welcome newcomers of different religions.

During the 1840's a sizeable number of persecuted German Jews began to seek refuge in the United States, and many came to Hartford. In a short time enough Jews were residing in this city to be considered a distinct and separate religious group. A new Connecticut Constitution in 1818 had disestablished the tax-supported Congregational Church and had granted complete religious freedom to all Christians in the state. Jews, however, were not allowed the same kind of religious freedom until 1842. (It is interesting to compare that in 1763 a similar legislation was passed in Newport, Rhode Island, permitting Jews religious freedom.) The following year they organized the first Jewish congregation in Hartford and the first Reform Jewish congregation in New England ... Beth Israel (Home of Israel). At that time almost 200 Jews resided in this city. Their first religious headquarters was on Market Street. Later they moved to the corner of Wells and Main streets, then into a former Baptist Church which stood on the present site of the Richardson Building on Main Street. Renaming the old Baptist church Touro Hall, they used it as a neighborhood center for worship, public meetings, and civic and cultural events. This was their first building functioning as a synagogue.

The first rabbi of Beth Israel was Dr. Israel Meyer who served from 1856 to 1867. During this same period of time Dr. Meyer also was the drama critic of the *Hartford Times*. Dr. Solomon Deutsch became the Jews' second rabbi in 1874. Two years later, in 1876, under his leadership, a new Temple Beth Israel was built on Charter Oak Avenue.

The new temple was unique. It was the first building in Connecticut to be constructed as a place of worship for a Jewish congregation. Its architecture was most unusual for a Jewish temple because most tended to be built in the Moorish style of 10th and 11th century Islamic Spain. The Hartford temple, however, was contemporary high-Victorian ... a red brick building of Renaissance revival style with Byzantine influences. Inside are the original oak pews which can seat up to 800 people, two massive brass chandeliers, and the original woodwork. The temple was designed by Hartford architect George Keller and cost about $50,000. It was opened in 1876. In 1898 the temple was renovated and enlarged. It is assumed that Keller was in charge of these changes.

Although there were just 78 families in the congregation when the temple was first built, it drew wide community attention, particularly from the Congregationalists whose forbears had strong Old Testament leanings. According to an article that appeared in the *Hartford Courant* in 1875 on the day the cornerstone was laid, 12,000 people gathered to watch the history-making event. "The roofs of buildings in the vicinity were crowded, and many carriages filled the streets around the site." Adjoining the temple the Jews also built a religious school and offices.

Unlike many of the Roman Catholic newcomers to Hartford, the Jews preferred to use the public schools for educating their children. However, they placed a strong emphasis on regular religious school instruction to make sure that their children did not stray from the Jewish faith and heritage. Perhaps the public schools were attractive to the Jews because the Puritan founders favored the Old Testament portion of the Holy Bible. Both Jew and Puritan-Yankees, many of whom were merchants and businessmen, looked upon themselves as God's Chosen People. Because of this common Biblical background and daily life, their mores and values, if not their religions, were actually quite similar.

The German Jews were urban people and better educated than other immigrants, chiefly Irish, who were also arriving in Hartford at the same time. Thus, they immediately became active in useful activities like retailing, watch-repairing and tailoring. Stable Jewish families formed well-ordered communities. Settling along Front, State and Main streets, they worked hard, took care of their own, and disciplined their children who, in turn, studied hard in school. The integrity and prudence of these German Jewish businessmen was cited with approval a number of times in the *Hartford Courant*. One of their most successful was Gershon Fox who founded, on Main Street, the great department store that still bears his name ... G. Fox & Co.

The German Jews advanced rapidly in politics chiefly because of their ethnic cohesiveness. As early as 1860 two Jews, Alexander Rothschild and Marcus Herlitscheck, were members of Hartford's City Council. Like the Yankees, the Jews also stressed the learned professions, especially the law. As lawyers they were then well-equipped to extend their political influence both as legislators and as members the judiciary.

The old Temple Beth Israel was used by the German Jews until 1935, when a new temple and school were completed at 701 Farmington Avenue in West Hartford. This move was made under the leadership of Rabbi Abraham Feldman.

The second great influx of Jews into Hartford oc-curred at the turn of the 19th century. Fleeing persecution in Russia, Poland, Lithuania, the Ukraine, Hungary, Roma-nia and Galacia, these foreigners, all speaking strange languages, were not greeted enthusiastically by the German Jewish residents of the city. Like the Roman Catholic new-comers from many of the same European countries, these Jews established their own places of worship, religious schools and charitable societies. Congregating on Front and Main streets and Albany Avenue, the Eastern Europeans progressed in Hartford in much the same way as the earlier Jews. They banded together, helped one another, worked very hard, and put a great emphasis on religion, education, business and politics. Like those who came before them, these Jews also possessed many useful skills. Expert furriers like the Glotzers came from Russia. Fine cabinetmakers like the Margolis family came from Lithuania. The Ukran-ian Jews excelled at iron working, blacksmithing and even the so-called "junk" or scrap metals business. In one way or another the great majority proved to be orderly, productive citizens of the City of Hartford. By 1910 these newcomers outnumbered the German Jews five to one.

The Eastern European Jews brought with them a profound interest in Zionism, a movement that would culminate in the creation of a new nation, Israel, in the ancient Jewish homeland in the Middle East. By 1912 all the Jews in Hartford decided to join forces and over 30 of their independent charitable organizations were amalgamated to form United Jewish Charities. By this time, too, the national differences between the various Jewish communities in Hartford were less evident and a single "Jewish Community" evolved. As the Jews became more affluent they began moving away from their old neighborhoods into the north end of the city where they created a very middle-class community. They also gradually moved into West Hartford which by the 1970's had become one of the most popular suburbs for Jews in the Capitol Region.

Although names like Koppleman, Shatz, Schwolsky and Suisman became prominent in Hartford politics, the crowning glory came when the first Jew, Abraham Ribicoff, became Governor of the State of Connecticut in 1955. He went on to become a popular U.S. Senator.

When the Jewish congregation of Temple Beth Israel built a new temple in West Hartford in 1935, they sold their former house of worship to Calvary Temple, an evangelical, interdenominational Christian Church. Later the congregation of Calvary Temple also moved to West Hartford.

The abandoned old temple then became the property of Hartford's Redevelopment Agency. Neglected and unloved, the building slowly disintegrated and would have been demolished to make way for "urban renewal" had not a few citizens begun to take an interest in its unique architecture. The works of architect George Keller were attracting considerable attention ... particularly the Soldiers and Sailors Monument and the old Jewish Temple on Charter Oak Avenue. The Hartford Architecture Conservancy had been formed in 1973 with the express purpose of saving significant buildings like this temple from destruction. Leading Jewish citizens began to take a keen interest in the building.

In 1978 the Charter Oak Temple Restoration Association, COTRA, was formed. The association was encouraged by the fact that the temple had been placed on the National Register of Historic Places.

In 1982, COTRA became the permanent developer of the building. The roof was replaced, insulation was installed, and the original stencil decoration was discovered. The Hartford Foundation for Public Giving launched the second phase of the campaign with a challenge grant. The state and the Beatrice Fox Auerbach Foundation contributed. Many local Jewish foundations, funds, families and individuals made generous contributions as did local corporations, banks, other foundations and friends. Additional state and federal funds were eventually received.

By the end of 1984 over $600,000 had been raised and a full-time director employed. A new heating plant was installed, weatherproofing was completed, masonry was cleaned and repaired, a wrought-iron fence was restored, and the interior of the temple was greatly refurbished. Since June of 1985 the Charter Oak Temple has been open as a lively center for the visual and performing arts. Events such as chamber concerts, lectures, films, and art and historical exhibitions are now being hosted. Space is also available for social or organizational events.

**IGLESIA TEMPLO FE
(FAITH TEMPLE)**

1019 Broad Street
525-8080

In 1970 Templo Fe, a Spanish-speaking church with a Puerto Rican congregation, opened in an old warehouse at 93 Main Street. In 1977 the flourishing congregation purchased a former parochial school on Broad Street as their new sanctuary.

Faith Temple belongs to the Assemblies of God, the largest pentecostal and one of the largest evangelical denominations in the world. Faith Temple's chief purpose is to help people to help themselves by bringing them to Christ. Church members in good standing are required to be gainfully employed and are allowed to accept welfare only in dire emergencies. A strict emphasis is put on good personal habits and a strong family life. Male members of the church work chiefly in area nurseries, factories, and construction.

Although most of the congregation live in the neighborhood, buses are used to bring members in other parts of town to church services and regular weekly gatherings.

For 200 years the Connecticut River was Hartford's major transportation artery. Merchants and factory owners shipped goods of all kinds along the coast and abroad, and their mercantile success was reflected in many fine houses and the bustling activities at wharfside. By mid-19th century, the railroad began to overtake the river as the most efficient mode of transporting commercial goods. Merchants moved westward and their homes were converted to stores and multiple housing units. The housing was used by successive waves of immigrants coming to work in Hartford's booming factories. The eastside neighborhood developed a vitality of its own, born of the diverse cultures which inhabited it. In the late 1950s, the neighborhood was razed and its residents relocated in preparation for the building of Constitution Plaza.

CHENEY BUILDING

942 Main Street

This six-story structure of Portland brownstone and Berea limestone, designed by Henry Hobson Richardson, is generally considered to be the best example of his commercial architecture that still survives. In 1970 it was placed on the National Register of Historic Places. Richardson is revered today for being one of the great 19th century pioneers of contemporary architecture. Stanford White, who later became a noted architect himself, was clerk of the works when this building was being constructed. It was commissioned in 1875 by the Cheneys of Manchester, 19th century silk tycoons. The Cheney Building was originally a shopping mall containing many small shops and four floors of luxury apartments, all built around a central three-story court roofed with glass.

The president of Cheney Brothers silk mill and other members of his family had profited during the Civil War from an investment in the Spencer Repeating Rifle Company. This was the money they used to construct the Cheney Building. The rifle had been invented by one of their employees, Christopher Spencer. Spencer, born in Manchester in 1833, was a brilliant Yankee whose many inventions included an automatic silk spool winding machine, a four-wheeled, steam-drive buggy, and an automatic turret lather or screw machine that made him a fortune. He was a major force in the development of Hartford as a manufacturing center.

G. Fox & Company acquired the Cheney Building, also known as Brown-Thomson, in 1936. In one of the largest moving feats undertaken in Hartford, the new owners took the 8,000 ton building for a 110-foot ride. On a weekend the building was rolled over a series of rails without damaging the street or sidewalk. In 1977 G. Fox presented the historic structure to the city, which in turn leased it to developers. Over $7 million was spent for renovation into a three-story mall, offices and 120 luxury apartments overlooking the Connecticut River. Thus it has again become a mix of residential and commercial uses. It was renamed the Richardson Building.

Eventually, a glass-walled pedestrian skyway may link the Richardson, G. Fox, Sage-Allen and American Airlines with Constitution Plaza and the Civic Center. A mixmaster already connects G. Fox, Sage-Allen and the Richardson.

HARTFORD CLUB

46 Prospect Street
522-1271

For more than two centuries the merchants and politicians of Hartford were accustomed to gather together at local taverns and coffee houses to socialize and to discuss their mutual business and political interests. After the successful termination of the Civil War and the rapid expansion of the city's population to almost 40,000 residents, the prime "movers and shakers" of Hartford's thriving manufacturing and financial institutions and the city's most powerful political leaders began to crave more privacy. They decided, therefore, to establish a prestigious men's club . . . the Hartford Club . . . for the stated purpose of creating and "maintaining a library, reading room and gallery of art, and for the promotion of social intercourse by such means as shall be expedient and proper for that purpose."

The Hartford Club was organized October 13, 1873, and incorporated on July 2, 1874. The Club's first president was William James Hammersley, who had twice been mayor of Hartford, owned a local book store, and was the editor of *American Mercury Magazine*. The first clubhouse was located at 53 Prospect Street, on the southwest corner of Grove, in a former Trumbull home. Five years later the Club was moved to 54 Prospect Street. The Club's original incorporators were all distinguished citizens who have left their mark on Hartford in various ways. For example, General Joseph Hawley was an outstanding Civil War hero who became successively Governor of Connecticut, U.S. Congressman and U.S. Senator. A founder of the Connecticut Republican Party, and editor first of the *Evening Press* then of the *Hartford Courant*, General Hawley was correctly described as "a man inevitably in the limelight." He also became the second president of the Hartford Club. Another incorporator, Charles M. Pond, donated Elizabeth Park to the city. Others were Major General William B. Franklin, vice-president and general manager of Colt Patent Firearms; Colonel Frank W. Cheney of Manchester's Cheney Silk Mills; and Austin Dunham, founder of the Hartford Electric Light Company. There were many others, too numerous to mention, but all equally illustrious.

The Hartford Club, however, did have a few jarring moments. On October 11, 1877, the *Hartford Times* printed the following article entitled *An Indignant Lady* on Clubs:

"The Club? A success? To be sure it is.
Hartford would be nowhere without the Club.
It makes everything pleasant. Keeps men at
home evenings. Makes things cheerful for
wives. Promotes hospitality. Makes more
drunkards than all the saloons? No, indeed ...
Talk gossip? Men talk gossip? Never! Nobody
but women do that. It's so nice to have a Shaker
sort of place, where women don't call often, and
need not be invited. Less expense, and better
every way than the old style of opening up one's
house and having all the family trotted out to
show civility to strangers. There's only one
thing wanting, and that is a club house for
women. With that we shall be all right."

On January 19, 1882 the Club supplanted the Hartford
Theological Seminary as lessee of the Daniel Wadsworth
house that was located at 33 Prospect Street, on the present
site of Tower Square. Professor Henry Perkins, a club member, wrote the following charming description of the Prospect Street neighborhood in the 1800s:

"Whatever the eighties may have been elsewhere, in Hartford they were a placid era. The
nation was expanding and building railroad with
the help of Hartford's banks and insurance companies. Money was flowing into the city which
had begun to grow after a period of decline.
Everyone felt confident of the future when
Hartford would be larger and richer, but still the
same pleasant place we loved, without any radical alteration in its character or mode of living.
It would always be a city founded on New
England tradition and made up mainly of New
Englanders who would observe Sunday as generations of their Puritan ancestors had observed
it, would read the Courant every weekday morning and the Times, followed by a novel of
Dickens or Thackeray, in the evening. They
would continue to send their children to the
public schools and their sons to Yale. In the
summer they would take the Valley Railroad for
Fenwick or Watch Hill, and in the winter they

would race their cutters drawn by fast trotting horses on Washington Street. The future might hold more leisure, larger houses, more servants, better horses. There might be more expensive parties, more trips abroad, but life would all be cut from the same pattern, a pattern which made for contentment and a sense of security among the prosperous."

In 1887 the Hartford Club absorbed the membership of the Home Circle Club which had been started as a young men's temperance society, but had not been successful. Then, in 1901, the Colonial Club also merged with the Hartford Club. This increase in membership soon necessitated a much larger clubhouse. Therefore, the Hartford Club's president, Colonel William C. Skinner (who was also the president of Colt Patent Firearms Company), and his building committee, retained the Boston architectural firm of Andrews, Jacques and Rantoul to design a suitable new headquarters that would be located at 46 Prospect Street. Robert Porteus, a local builder, was then employed to carry out their plans.

On December 31, 1903 the *Hartford Times* ran a full-page story headlined: "Hartford Club's Beautiful New Home."

"The event begins a new epoch in the history of club life in Hartford. Never before has the city had such a handsome structure with such luxurious furnishings devoted to clubhouse purposes ... [which] all combine to make an interior of splendor and magnificence."

It is amusing to note that in building their new $200,000 clubhouse, the gentlemen did not forget their wives:

"Much consideration and good taste have been displayed in making provision for the ladies. They have an entrance of their own entirely apart from that of the men at the port-cochere at the north end ... a ladies' cafe and private dining room."

The wives of club members were allowed to continue to use these club facilities even if pre-deceased by their husbands.

On New Year's Day, 1904, the Club's 600 members were invited to a grand noon-time celebration. Everyone admired the handsome colonial design of the red brick and limestone clubhouse, the carved stone shields over the arches of the second story windows which were executed by local sculptor Albert Entress, and the fine landscaping of Hartford Park Superintendent Theodore Wirth as well as the large and luxurious interior of the building.

In 1912 club member Gov. Morgan G. Bulkeley inspired his fellows to construct a fine ballroom onto the back of the clubhouse. The ballroom was first used for Governor Bulkeley's daughter's coming out party. For over 50 years thereafter the Hartford Club ballroom was considered to be the best place in which to have a debutante dance or any other kind of large, formal party. In 1968, however, when the Travelers Insurance Companies decided to construct a new office building between Prospect Street and Columbus Boulevard, the facilities of the Hartford Club underwent major external and internal changes which included removal of the old ballroom. The architects for the project were Jeter and Cook of this city. During this period of reconstruction and renovation, club members used a temporary headquarters on Constitution Plaza.

World War I, the Great Depression, World War II, the Korean War, the Vietnam War, a staggering technological revolution an a corresponding civil rights revolution have all combined to radically alter the role of the Hartford Club ... as well as all other social institutions! Contrary to Professor Perkins' confident expectations. Hartford is no longer "a city founded on New England tradition and made up solely of New Englanders ..." In fact, the old New Englanders now comprise a minority in Greater Hartford's multicultural population. The Hartford Club's most recent membership rolls reflect the fact that today's "movers and shakers" come in every race, creed and color, and are female as well as male. When the completely renovated Hartford Club opened in 1972, *everyone* was allowed to use the front entrance to the building.!

In 1973 the City Club was absorbed by the Avon Country Club, so those members were extended the right to use the Hartford Club facilities.

Back in 1905 the Club's bylaws noted that "gentlemen residing more than five miles from the city and having no usual place of business in Hartford shall be considered strangers, and any member of the Club may extend the privileges of the Club to any stranger for a period not exceeding one day ..." The transportation and communication revolutions of the Space Age have changed all this. Members of similar clubs throughout the nation are now extended the same privileges of the strangers of yesteryear, and that list of clubs is growing. Because both business and politics are now international in scope, visiting strangers to the Club will soon represent the nations of the world. For the same reasons, Hartford's international tycoons will ... and do ... often find themselves in the equivalent of the Hartford Club in all portions of the world.

The *Hartford Weekly Times* was founded March 3, 1817 by Frederick D. Bolles, a printer, and John M. Niles, to champion the cause of what eventually became the new Connecticut Constitution of 1818. Editor Niles was a "Tolerationist" who favored disestablishment of the Congregational Church so that other religions would be free to flourish. He became a U.S. Senator and served as Postmaster General under President Martin Van Buren. A distinguished contributor to the *Times* was Gideon Welles of Glastonbury who later became President Abraham Lincoln's Secretary of Navy during the Civil War. For a short while the paper became the property of Samuel Bowles who later founded the *Springfield Republican.*

In 1838 twenty-three-year-old Alfred Edmund Burr (two of whose ancestors, Benjamin Burr and Thomas Olcott, had been founders of Hartford) purchased a half interest in the *Weekly Times.* Burr had been in the employ of the *Hartford Courant* for ten years. His employer made him an offer of partial ownership on condition that he become a Congregationalist and uphold the political faith of the Whigs! But Burr, being a member of the Unity Church and a Democrat, had refused. By January 1, 1841 he had managed to take full possession of the *Weekly Times* stock and had founded the *Hartford Daily Times.* For many, many years he published both papers, the latter in two parts ... one on Monday and the other on Thursday ... and their circulation was the largest in the state.

A contemporary wrote of Burr, "He made the *Times* a democratic newspaper of the most steadfast and rockbound quality ... and adhered firmly to his principles. He believed that the Civil War that broke out in 1860 had been needlessly forced upon the country and that it might have been averted by a wise spirit of conservatism and adherence to democratic principles.... From the time when Mr. Burr first made the *Times* influence felt as a political newspaper in Connecticut, his relation to the organization of theDemocratic Party has been an intimate one.... For many years no democratic platform was adopted in Connecticut which was not wholly or in part prepared by him..."

A close friend of Colonel Samuel Colt, also a Democrat, Alfred E. Burr promoted the growth of industry in Hartford and consistently advocated high wages for industrial workers. He also promoted public schools, public parks, the public reservoir, and a host of social service projects. In 1870 he became president of the Dime Savings Bank (a part-time job) which he had helped to found. Three years later he was invited to become chairman of the commission which built the new State Capitol. A fellow citizen approved of his efforts with the following remark: "Burr so directed the work that the cost came within the appropriations made."

Alfred E. Burr died in 1899 after serving the *Times* for 61 years. He was succeeded by his son, Willie Olcott Burr, who had joined the paper as a very young man. Willie lived in the present Day or Chamberlain House at Nook Farm. When Willie died in 1923 he had been with the *Times* for 60 years ... a father and son record probably unequaled among newspapers of the U.S.A. His sister was Ella Burr McManus who left money that ultimately purchased the huge *Stegosaurus* that now stands on Burr Mall.

The Hartford Times printing plant and office on the corner of Grove and Main Streets were moved to the new headquarters at 10 Prospect Street in October, 1920. The building was designed by Donn Barber of New York City. Barber was also the architect for Travelers Tower and the Connecticut State Library and Supreme Court. The striking portico of the *Times* has an interesting history. Presidents Truman, Eisenhower, Kennedy and Johnson have all addressed large Hartford crowds from its imposing steps. Oddly enough, this handsome facade with its terra cotta brick front and pillars was originally the front portion of the Madison Square Presbyterian Church in New York City. The church had been designed in 1905 by a famous New York architect, Stanford White, partner in the New York firm of McKim, Meade and White. In 1872 White had been clerk-of-the-works when Hartford's Cheney Building was constructed on Main Street. Once the Presbyterian Church's facade was moved to Hartford, however, White's original Corinthian columns were changed to a less ornate Ionic design, but the dancing gods and goddesses ornamenting the portico were retained. A charming as well as talented gentleman, Stanford White was murdered in 1906 just before the

Madison Square Church was completed by Harry K. Thaw during a dispute concerning the affections of a mutual lady friend. This titillating crime fascinated millions of newspaper readers.

In 1636 the land on which the *Times* building stands was assigned to the Rev. Thomas Hooker and the Rev. Samuel Stone for their homesites, so this must have been considered the most desirable location in newly established Puritan Hartford. The road in front of their homes, now Prospect Street, was then called Meeting House Alley because it led directly to the first settlers' church which stood on the present site of the Old State House. An early account of the area noted that Hooker "had a path from his home to the clean and beautiful river that flowed at the foot of the place." This stream has been known over the years as the Little, Park or Hog River and is now confined in underground culverts over which the highway has been constructed.

The *Hartford Times* ceased publication in October, 1976, victim of the altered reading habits of the general public. Many evening papers began to go out of business at this time because television, rather than a newspaper, became the preferred form of evening entertainment.

There is nothing more colorful, tempting or exciting than a large public market in the early hours of the morning. The bargain prices, the beauty and abundance of the fresh produce and flowers, are breathtaking. Since time immemorial one of the major functions of a proper town has been to provide such a market where farmers can display and sell their fruits, vegetables, poultry, meats, plants, flowers, and other perishables. So it is not surprising that this very modern public marketing facility has a long history!

As early as 1640 Hartford was required by the Connecticut Colony's General Court to provide a public market. The market was located at the southeast corner of what is now Thomas Hooker Square. Later there was an auxiliary market held regularly on the stone bridge on Main Street where that thoroughfare crosses the Little (Park) River. This used to be called the Market Bridge because stalls for produce were built on the span itself.

CONNECTICUT REGIONAL MARKET

101 Reserve Road
527-4047

Open Sunday-Saturday, 5-9:00 a.m. Tours: Make appointment for tours. Those wishing to buy should get to the market as early as possible. Remember that the early bird catches the worm!

In 1784 the Connecticut General Assembly granted the burgeoning Town of Hartford a charter to become a city. A few years later the city fathers decided they must have a suitable City Hall. Because the public market on the central square was becoming quite inadequate, they determined to combine these two public needs into one facility, and Samuel Belcher and William Hayden (see South Congregational Church) were selected as the architect-builders. Eager to provide their city with the very best, these two local artisans constructed a 58 by 110 foot building that looked like a massive Greek temple. Its elegantly columned portico faced east onto what soon became Market Street. To the south the building was bounded by Kinsley Street, to the north by Temple Street and to the west by a small police station. The public market was located on the ground floor; public officials' offices and the Council Chamber were on the second floor; and a large hall that could be used for all kinds of public functions on the third floor.

The new City Hall and Public Market were opened in June, 1829. Market stalls were rented to interested wholesalers and a clerk was appointed to collect revenues, keep the place clean, and maintain law and order. When Connecticut's new State Capitol was built in Bushnell Park in 1879, the Old State House became Hartford's new City Hall. Eighteen years later the Greek Temple was demolished and the public market moved to an area between Front Street and the Connecticut River. There it stayed until plans were made to build highway I-91 and Constitution Plaza, and this whole section of the city was torn up and transformed. Then the public market moved over to the only open land available, Colt Park.

Responding to an acute need for suitable public marketing facilities, the state created the Connecticut Regional Market Authority in 1939. After much deliberation and delay, this completely up-to-date Regional Market was constructed in 1952 on 33 acres of land in Hartford's South Meadows. It is state owned and operated, nonprofit and self-liquidating. At long last both farmers and national wholesalers had a convenient, central location where they could display and sell their produce. Transportation plays a big role in bringing fresh perishables from the producer to

the consumer ... especially these days when fruits and vegetables come by truck, rail and air 24 hours a day from all
parts of the world. Air shipments are received from Bradley,
Kennedy and Logan International Airports.

Within the market there are 15 major wholesalers of
produce, meat, butter, and poultry, one restaurant, one self-
service gas station one wholesale grocery store, and six
business offices. Over 100 local farmers and their trucks fill
the interior of the market every day during the growing
season from spring to fall. The Regional Market is adminis-
tered by the State Department of Agriculture but managed
by the Connecticut Marketing Authority which is composed
of seven members, all producers of agricultural products.

HARTFORD-BRAINARD AIRPORT

Airport Road

Hartford-Brainard Airport is the second oldest municipal airport in the nation. As the second busiest airport in
Connecticut today, Brainard provides excellent facilities for
general aviation and light aircraft. Only two miles from the
city's business district, Brainard is used by many corporate
planes. Charter and taxi services, sight-seeing flights and
flying lessons are available. The airport is under the management of the Connecticut Bureau of Aeronautics
headquartered here.

Hartford-Brainard Airport was created after two visiting Army airmen were killed when they used the golf course
at Goodwin Park for a landing field, no other facilities near
Hartford being available. Thus unfortunate accident was a
great blow to Hartford's civic pride and spurred city officials
to consider the establishment of an airport. A commission
was then appointed to select a site for a proper landing field
which was subsequently named in honor of Hartford's
Mayor Newton Case Brainard. The new airport was dedicated June 12, 1921.

The airfield's most historic moment was in 1927 when
a crowd of 25,000 people gathered at Brainard to greet
Charles A. Lindbergh after he returned from his sensational
solo flight across the Atlantic to Paris.

STACKPOLE, MOORE, TRYON

Corner of Asylum
and Trumbull Streets
522-0181

In 1980, the state's oldest men's store, Stackpole, Moore, Tryon, was listed in the National Register of Historic Places. Built in the 19th century, the store was "modernized" in 1896 when a cast iron facade was added by architect Isaac A. Allen, Jr. (architect of the Linden Building and additions to the Cheney Block). The store was known as Wells and Wilson until 1909 when T. Seymour Tryon, grandfather of the present president, William Tryon, bought the business with his two partners, J. S. Stackpole and H. B. Moore.

HARTFORD CIVIC CENTER

One Civic Center
Plaza

The Hartford Civic Center complex located in the middle of the downtown business district covers an excess of seven acres and contains 12 restaurants, 50 specialty shops and the Sheraton-Hartford Hotel. The 16,200 seat Coliseum is the finest facility of its kind in the Northeast and has showcased many of the top entertainers in the show business world.

The Veterans Memorial Coliseum is the home of the NHL Hartford Whalers and also hosts the Boston Celtics, UConn Huskies and the U of H Hawks. In addition to the torrid basketball schedule, the arena has hosted such stars as Bruce Springsteen, Prince, Kenny Rogers, Frank Sinatra and Neil Diamond. Family shows such as Ringling Bros. & Barnum and Bailey Circus, Sesame Street Live, the Harlem Globetrotters and Symphony On Ice round out the schedule.

The Assembly and Exhibition Halls, with a combined square footage of 70,000, accommodate various types of seminars, formal balls, national and regional conventions and tradeshows.

Transportation in and out of Hartford is quick and convenient with Bradley International Airport offering 165 flights daily, 57 direct, only 20 minutes away. Two blocks west of the Civic Center are two major bus terminals and the revitalized Amtrak Train Station.

GOODWIN BUILDING

Corner of Asylum
and Haynes streets

The Goodwin building, fronting on Asylum and Haynes streets, was built in 1881 by the Rev. Francis Goodwin and his brother James Junius Goodwin, both of whom had inherited large real estate holdings in the city from their father, a former president of Connecticut Mutual Life Insurance Company. Descended from William Goodwin, a founder of Hartford, the Goodwin family had always been deeply involved in the uses of local real estate.

Francis and James Goodwin were first cousins of J. Pierpont Morgan, who had been born in his family's home at 26 Asylum Street in 1837. The cousins grew up together and were intimate friends. They cooperated in a variety of local enterprises which included Connecticut Mutual and the Morgan Memorial sector of the Wadsworth Atheneum. Both Goodwins and Morgans are now buried at Cedar Hill, this city's most prestigious cemetery.

During his lifetime the Rev. Francis Goodwin was Hartford's most outstanding citizen. He personally was responsible for creating the city's magnificent park system as well as numerous other civic projects that greatly enhanced the quality of life in Hartford. Dr. Goodwin also excelled as an amateur architect, and designed Goodwin "Castle" on Woodland Street for his brother. When it was torn down to make way for a new insurance company, one whole room was saved and may be viewed at the Wadsworth Atheneum.

Although Dr. Goodwin no doubt greatly influenced the design of the red-brick Goodwin Building, the official architects were Kimball and Wisedell of New York City. Francis Kimball was the superintending architect of Trinity College in 1875. Nine years later he designed the present Day House at Nook Farm. The delightful exterior design of the Goodwin Building, with its moulded and cut-brick ornaments, decorated plaques and terra cotta copings are reminiscent of the elaborate carvings on the wooden mantle piece in the front hall of the Day House. It would seem that the same craftsman, probably German, must have created the birds on the exterior of the building and the squirrels on the mantle piece.

The Goodwin Building was intended as a mixed residential and commercial structure. The generous apartments with their high ceilings and large windows were particularly delightful and helped to fill an acute need downtown for middle and upper middle class housing. On March 26, 1976, the building was placed in the National Register of Historic Places. Despite the strong objections of preservationists in 1985 the Hartford Council approved the plans for Goodwin Square, a 30-story hotel and office complex, topped by a 50-foot clock tower. A "facadism" was executed, leaving only the shell of the building. The interior was removed, the exterior was propped up, and the void is being filled with new construction.

UNION STATION

Transportation Center,
Union Place
For Amtrak call
525-4580

The first Union Station to be located near the corner of Asylum and Spruce streets was constructed in 1849. An elaborate Portland brownstone structure "in the Italian style," it was designed so that trains ran through the building at ground level and crossed Asylum Street at grade. The crossing, protected by gates that were lowered when trains approached the station, was very inconvenient to traffic traveling east and west on the street.

Around 1886 Hartford's city fathers decided that the train tracks should be elevated as a safety measure to pass over Asylum Street. One of the architects applying for the job of designing a practical plan to achieve this objective was George Keller. He was on his way to Europe to work on another project, but managed to receive an assignment from the railroad to visit Hanover, Germany, to study a new railroad station there as a model for the Hartford station.

On March 15, 1887, the *Hartford Courant* published Keller's plans and drawings. They showed the viaduct arrangement carrying the tracks over the street traffic to the second floor of the station. The article stated: "The elevation of the building is Mr. Keller's study from the Hanover work and is designed as a general suggestion as to architectural effect ... details being in fact yet undetermined ... [It] represents a general arrangement, [the] relation of the depot to the crossing, [the] character of the approaches and the proportion of the parts."

In his *Reminiscences* George Keller stated that he had gone to Hanover with the presumption that, if his plans were chosen, he would be designated by the railroad as architect of the project. Therefore he was deeply troubled when the railroad simply used his plans without acknowledging him as the architect or paying him. So he sued the railroad and collected at least a token compensation for his labors. In all probability the final designing and building of the Union Station in 1889 was carried out by the railroad's in-house engineering staff.

On February 21, 1914 a large fire gutted the inside of Union Station. The building was a total wreck except for the brownstone walls that remained standing. Fortunately the station was well covered by insurance, so it was soon rebuilt more or less as it had been before the conflagration.

Like most rail facilities, Union Station lost passengers when people increasingly turned to automobiles and the highways built after World War II. The Station's original owner, the New York, New Haven and Hartford Railroad, sold it in 1965 to financier E. Clayton Gengras for $250,000. Gengras, a former owner of the Connecticut Company bus line, envisioned converting the historic structure into a modern transportation center and managed to interest the Greater Hartford Transit District in the project. In 1977 the Transit District won an essential $199,400 grant from the Urban Mass Transportation Administration of the U.S. Department of Transportation to begin making plans for the transformation. Completed in 1988, the reconstructed facility centralizes train, bus and taxi services and includes shops, restaurants, offices and ample parking. Hartford Design Group was the architect of the $17.3 million renovation project.

Union Place, a street that borders the east side of Union Station, is a short thoroughfare connecting Asylum with Church Street. Once a hangout for derelicts, Union Place is now a counter-culture showplace for Hartford's colorful storefronts, restaurants and bars.

There is a warm, friendly atmosphere here between store proprietors and then customers that is reminiscent of an old ethnic neighborhood. Outdoor flower planters, brightly painted trash cans, gay strings of criss-crossing lights, street musicians, an outdoor theater, and seasonal street festivals all combine to make this a unique section of the city.

An old four-story factory, the Gordon Building on the corner of Union Place and Church Street, was renovated into apartments for convenient downtown living by William B. Martin and Jean R. Belair Jr., two young real estate developers.

Many Union Place enthusiasts claim that this is the "coming" area of Hartford in all ways ... commercially, as a place of residence and as a modern transportation hub.

LEWIS STREET

Lewis Street was laid out as Wells Street in 1841 in honor of Dr. Horace Wells, the discoverer of anesthesia. In 1883 the street was renamed after Lewis Rowell, owner of much of the real estate and a resident in the area. Today only a few of the charming federal buildings that used to grace this little thoroughfare still remain, one of which is the University Club and another a restaurant. The ambiance of Lewis Street is threatened by a proposal to build a gigantic structure the entire length of the west side. Demolition has already begun.

The University Club has occupied 30 Lewis Street since 1908. In 1926 the Club constructed a five-story brick addition to the rear, overlooking the Ancient Burying Ground. W. F. Brooks was the architect.

In 1976 the Lewis Street Historic District was listed in the National Register. The parking garage on the corner of Lewis and Pearl Streets and 35-37 and 41 Lewis Street are not included in the district.

HARTFORD FIRE DEPARTMENT HEADQUARTERS

275 Pearl Street
722-8200

Make appointments for tours by calling the above number. This headquarters and all other engine houses in Hartford are open for tours Monday through Friday, 8:30 a.m. to 5:30 p.m.

In 1857 a school for black children that used to be located here next door to an old black Methodist church (now A.M.E. Zion Church) was removed to make way for a firehouse. In 1924 the church itself was forced to move when the firehouse was enlarged to encompass the entire southwest corner of Pearl and Ann Streets. The building was completed in 1926.

Until 1864 all fire departments in Hartford were staffed by volunteers. After a terrible fire destroyed a large portion of the Colt Armory that year, a full-time. professional fire department was established.

In 1764 Thomas Green, a member of a family that had been masters of the printing trade for generations, set up the first printing press in Hartford. On October 29th of that same year he published as an experiment the first number of the *Connecticut Courant*. The newspaper proved to be so popular that by December he began publishing it on a weekly basis and took into partnership an assistant named Ebenezer Watson. Because the *Courant* stood solidly on the side of American independence from England and against the hated Stamp Act and other forms of unjust taxation, the newspaper has been widely acknowledged as one of the forces that eventually led to the American Revolution and the successful separation of the colonies from the mother country.

In 1768 Thomas Green moved to New Haven and left the business in charge of Ebenezer Watson. Nine years later Watson died and for over a year his widow conducted the printing and publishing operation as perhaps the first female newspaper editor in America. In 1778 she took into partnership Barzillai Hudson whom she subsequently married. In 1815 George Goodwin & Sons, paper manufacturers, purchased a share of the firm which then became Hudson and Goodwin. In 1836 the weekly newspaper was sold to John L. Boswell who, the following year, also began publishing a *Daily Courant*. The firm dissolved at the death of Boswell in 1854, and the *Courant* was purchased by Thomas M. Day who took into partnership A. N. Clark, his bookkeeper.

On February 4, 1856 the new Republican Party of Connecticut was organized in Hartford in the law office of Joseph R. Hawley. Present were John Hooker (Isabella Beecher's husband), Gideon Welles and others who were firmly behind the anti-slavery cause of abolition. They joined forces with Francis Gillette, Charles Dudley Warner and fellow abolitionists to purchase the *Hartford Evening Press* as a vehicle for their views. In 1861 Hawley became the first man from Connecticut to enlist in the Union Army in which he eventually rose to the rank of major-general. The

THE HARTFORD COURANT

185 Broad Street
241-6200

Tours by appointment and only in the morning. Tour takes 90 minutes and includes a film.

Hartford Courant, which had espoused the Federalist and the Whig parties, was merged with the *Evening Press* in 1867 and became strongly Republican. Hawley was editor-in-chief, Warner literary editor, and William H. Goodrich became business manager. For a while the new ownership ran three Hartford papers ... the weekly *Connecticut Courant*, the daily morning *Courant* and the daily *Evening Press*! It is interesting to note the close relationship between the management of the *Courant* and the radical intellectuals who were residents of the Nook Farm community in the western part of the city. In later years Warner often served as editor-in-chief when Hawley was out of town. This was often the case as General Hawley was active in politics, first as governor of the State, then as U.S. Senator.

In 1880 the *Courant* completed a new five-story building at 64-68 State Street overlooking the Old State House. Charles Hopkins Clark, long a member of the editorial staff, became editor-in-chief in 1900. Much respected for his fine intellect, he unfortunately was a powerful opponent of Votes for Women. A benevolent and kindly man and a loving husband and father, Clark was quite certain that woman suffrage was a reform against nature. His attacks against the suffragettes were frequently quite bitter, and the ladies responded in kind. It was the custom in those days to have seasonal local fairs in Connecticut, so the suffragettes attended as many fairs as possible to give speeches favoring their cause. They were especially angered by a law which specifically denied the vote to "women, children, idiots and criminals." Therefore they regularly erected a voting booth at each fair on the top of which was a large sign stating: "Women, Children, Idiots and Criminals ... Vote Here. Our Candidate is Charles Hopkins Clark."

An excellent book, *Older Than the Nation*, by John Bard McNulty gives a detailed history of this unique newspaper which is now celebrated as "The Oldest Newspaper of Continuous Publication in America." The *Hartford Courant's* present headquarters were occupied in 1950, and three large additions to the plant have been made since that date. An ancient printing press, believed to have been used in printing early editions of the paper, may be viewed.

When the *Hartford Times* folded in October 1976, the *Courant* became this city's only daily newspaper. The daily circulation averages 225,000 and the Sunday paper 307,000. In 1989 the *Courant*, which is now owned by the Los Angeles Times Mirror Company, completed a four-story addition on Broad Street, with a new lobby and enlarged newsroom.

HARTFORD SQUARE

During the early 1980s, the Colt Park or Charter Oak region of Hartford began to be extensively redeveloped by Thomas K. Standish, founder and president of the Hartford Development Corporation. Like his ancestor, Thomas Standish, who settled in Wethersfield in 1635, he is a pioneer and visionary, his dream to transform this once elegant section of the city into a unique office environment that is both historic and ultra-modern.

HARTFORD SQUARE WEST

One Hartford Square

Hartford Square West is comprised of an extensively remodeled old factory and new two-story turrets. The factory, the Atlantic Screw Works, was built in 1902 and designed by the firm of Stuart and Davis who also designed the Municipal Building in Hartford. The turrets were added to create an entranceway to *L'Americain Restaurant*, a three-star French restaurant located at Two Hartford Square. Hartford Square West contains 83,200 square feet of Class A office space with a tenant list that includes Penn Mutual Life Insurance, Mohawk Data Sciences, the American Arbitration Association, Lehigh Portland Cement, and United States Fidelity and Guarantee Insurance.

HARTFORD SQUARE NORTH

10 Columbus Blvd

Hartford Square North contains 263,000 square feet of luxury office space in two connected wings of 11 and five stories in height, interlocked to form an L-shaped structure. Some of the special features are:

An exterior of alternating bands of glass and silver brushed panels dominated by curves, including two candy-cane shaped parts which will roll over the top of the building and are highlighted by bright red stripes;

Penthouse offices on the top floors, with curved walls, vaulted ceilings and adjoining rooftop gardens;

A lobby featuring Greek columns, green marble, exotic plants, reflecting pools and waterfalls;

An entry pavilion - done in neon, iridescent glass and steel - designed to resemble a Greek Temple;

THE SAMUEL COLT HOUSE

77 Huyshope Avenue

The Samuel Colt House is named in honor of Hartford's native son who invented the revolver. This entire Georgian-style structure is leased by the *Hartford Courant/Times Mirror Corporation* to serve as the paper's marketing center.

EQUATOR HOUSE

111 Charter Oak Avenue

Equator House, located directly behind the Church of the Good Shepherd, was originally a 19th century schoolhouse...Charter Oak Avenue School. Charmingly remodeled into a luxurious office facility, it now is the office of Equator Bank Ltd. Natural materials are used throughout the building...special wood finishes, Italian marble, black walnut trim and French tiles. The hand-some gazebo in front of *Equator House* doubles as a large elevator which transports automobiles down to a 20-car underground garage.

Bliss House is a delightfully eclectic structure that incorporates some of the high Victorian-Gothic features of the nearby Caldwell Colt Memorial (which was designed by Edward Potter who also designed Mark Twain's residence in Hartford). Although *Bliss House* looks as though it has stood here since the middle of the 19th century, the building in fact is entirely new. A veritable smorgasbord of visual delights, this three-story office building revives high standards of architectural craftsmanship. The campus-like layout makes possible five corner offices on each floor which offer spectacular views towards the city. The entire building is leased by Northeast Savings Bank for its executive staff.

BLISS HOUSE

147 Charter Oak Avenue

Congress Street was a major restoration project of the City of Hartford's Redevelopment Agency. This area was originally scheduled for demolition as part of a $15 million Charter Oak-South Green redevelopment project, but was saved by the City Council through the efforts of the Hartford Architecture Conservancy.

CONGRESS STREET RESTORATION

These charming homes began to be constructed in 1857. By the late 1860s there were 14 distinctive "Italianate" houses here, 11 of them lining the west side of the street. Seven were single houses; seven double houses, all were three stories, red brick with projecting flat roofs; and all had twin-columned porches set at the top of brownstone entrance steps, relieving the severity of the facades.

The great Italianate mansions on Wethersfield Avenue and Charter Oak Terrace were the homes of industrial and financial tycoons like the Colts, Days and Taylors, but Congress Street housed the enterprising machinists, businessmen, inventors and entrepreneurs who were on their way up the ladder of success. For example, Amos Whitney and Francis Pratt lived here when they founded Pratt and Whitney Machine Tool in the 1860s.

In the 20th century Congress Street, like other areas in this part of Hartford, declined when the more affluent moved westward and these fine homes gradually degenerated into shabby boarding houses.

Today, under the banner of historic preservation aided by the economic imperative to create within the city an employable resident work force of all races, creeds and colors for post-industrial Hartford, Congress Street has been spiritually reborn and physically restored. The major part of the restoration consists of 53 structures with 292 dwelling units. Housing types include efficiency through three-bedroom apartments with rentals in the middle to upper income range. The $20 million in private financing for the project was provided by local banks and insurance companies with CIGNA taking the lead role. Construction began in 1978 and was completed in 1984.

In addition to the structures on Congress Street, other buildings have been selected for individual restoration and redevelopers have been named. The upgrading of the South Green part of the city has been stimulated by the fact that buildings on seven streets in the area have been nominated for inclusion in the National Register of Historic Places.

SOUTH GREEN

South End of
Main Street

The South Green, also known as Henry Barnard Park in honor of the great educator, has served the south side of Hartford for centuries as a kind of town common.

In early colonial days the South Green was reportedly the site of a witches' gathering. Puritan Hartford, on May 26, 1647, earned the dubious honor of conducting the first recorded hanging of a person convicted of witchcraft in New England -- Alse Young of Windsor. The Connecticut Colony's gallows were located on the northeast corner of what are now Albany Avenue and Garden Street. The next victim of witchcraft superstition was Mary Johnson, who was executed June 6, 1650. A son was born to Mary Johnson while she was imprisoned at Hartford. Nathaniel Ruscoe, the jailer's son, took pity on her and agreed to raise and educate the child. In 1651 John and Joan Carrington of Wethersfield were executed on the Hartford gallows, and in 1654 Lydia Gilbert of Windsor followed them.

Eight years later Rebecca Greensmith, described as a "lewd and considerably aged woman," along with her husband and seven disreputable friends, reportedly "had a

merry making" one spring night by dancing noisily around
a tree on the South Green and drinking large quantities of
"sack" (sherry). They allegedly held other nocturnal gatherings that excited considerable community annoyance and
suspicion. Arrest and a short period of imprisonment would
probably have been their fate had it not been for the sudden
death of the daughter of John Kelley, a local resident. Before
she died, the girl accused the Greensmiths of bewitching
her. They were immediately arrested and then carefully
examined for "familiarity with the Devil" by local ministers
and the minister from Farmington. In the process Rebecca
Greensmith implicated all seven of their merry-making
associates. Some of them fled town, while others were imprisoned. The Greensmiths, however, were the only ones found
guilty of witchcraft. They were hanged on January 25, 1663.
This was the last time any individual was executed in
Connecticut on a charge of witchcraft, 30 years before the
witchcraft hysteria gripped Salem, Massachusetts.

In 1816 the town voted to fence the South Green and
26 years later appropriated money to grade it so as to be suitable for military encampments. In 1869 the present iron
fence and curb around the green were constructed. The
green was often rented to circuses, caravans and other public entertainments for $25 a day. For example, in 1880 it
was the site of Hartford's first encounter with aeronautical
technology. At that time a young man named John Graham
came here with some "captive" balloons described by the
Hartford Courant as "vertical air coaches" and "archimedial
phaetons." Graham delighted astonished citizens by taking
them on rides in his balloons. There is no record of how many
Hartfordites accepted this opportunity to ascend into the air
or if Graham's profits were more than the rent he had to pay
for the use of the green.

In 1898 during the great park-building era in Hartford,
the South Green was renamed Barnard Park in honor of
Henry Barnard, the great educator, whose home on Main
Street overlooks this area.

COLT PARK

Wethersfield Avenue

Historically Colt Park is of great interest, for it was once the camping ground of the Saukiog Indians. Some of their names, Sequassen, Wawarme, Masseek, Weehasset, Nepauquash, are memorialized in the names of the streets. Years ago it was also Dutchman's land. To the north of the armory where the pumping station of the Connecticut Natural Gas Company now stands was the Dutch fort, House of Good Hope. Huyshope Avenue recalls this old fort and fur-trading post, and Van Block Avenue and Hendricxsen Street are so called in memory of the first Dutch explorers.

In 1905 the Hartford Electric Light Company installed here the world's first central station steam turbine.

Along the south edge of the park you may see some odd looking houses. This is the remainder of Potsdam Village, another of Sam Colt's enterprises. When Colt built his dikes to keep out the spring floods of the river, he reinforced them by planting willow trees in the earthworks. The trees thrived and soon Colt was troubled by the fact that the willow shoots, valuable for making furniture, were going to waste. Learning that the best makers of willow furniture were to be found in Potsdam, Germany, he decided to import a few. But the willow-workers would not accept his proposals. They lived in communal villages and never moved singly! Naturally Sam Colt offered to import the entire village. But this was not satisfactory unless he would agree to build them homes similar to those in Potsdam. They also demanded plenty of German beer and ample leisure time for playing musical instruments. Thrifty Colt, determined not to waste his willow shoots, complied with all their needs, and they finally moved to Hartford. Soon Colt was the most important manufacturer of willow furniture in America. He did a brisk trade in the West Indies and South America where the light, cool furniture was much appreciated.

Rocco D. Pallotti, a colorful and controversial politician, was born on Windsor Street and championed the citizens of the Old Second Ward. Although a Democrat, his arch enemy was the John Bailey-Tony Zazzaro machine that ruled most of the city. However, Pallotti was so beloved by his own constituents who always gave him a solid vote, that the machine was never able to defeat him.

In the old days ground-level railroad crossings, all within a 1000-foot radius, endangered people and vehicles using Windsor, Avon, Canton and Russell streets. Local residents, especially children, were often killed at these crossings by passing trains. In 1927 Rocco Pallotti, who represented his neighborhood as an alderman on the Hartford City Council, introduced a strong resolution to create an underpass that would enable the street traffic, both pedestrian and vehicular, to go safely and swiftly under the tracks at these four intersections. Finally in 1937, the Pallotti Underpass was completed. The event was celebrated with the biggest carnival and fiesta ever held on the East Side...a three-day community thanksgiving graced by the presence of Connecticut's Governor "Uncle Toby" Cross!

Alderman Pallotti also sponsored the building of Connecticut's first public swimming pool in nearby Riverside Park. This too was a great reform because East Side children frequently drowned while swimming in the Connecticut River.

MAIN STREET STONE BRIDGE OVER THE PARK RIVER

Until 1955, the Park River formed a natural barrier between the northern and southern portions of the city of Hartford. Commercial development occurred primarily north of the Park River in today's downtown area. In 1833, the Old Stone Bridge was built over the Park River replacing an earlier wooden bridge. The span of the bridge was 104 feet. It was thought at the time of construction to be the longest span in the country for a single arch bridge. Many people distrusted its strength. Farmers coming into town often left their teams and wagons south of the bridge and walked into the business area.

The Park River, a fast flowing river, provided the power for dozens of mills. By the mid-19th century, steam power was widely recognized as more efficient than water power. Mills no longer needed river locations, and the Park River was soon lined with tenements housing thousands of factory workers and their families. The visually unattractive nature of the neighborhood and the fact that the Park River frequently flooded resulted in burial of the river. After the 1936 flood, the river was encased in a conduit and the Whitehead Highway was built on top. When the Hartford Public Library was built in 1955-57, this view of the bridge was obscured. One iron railing was taken down and an identical iron railing remains in place on the other side of the stone bridge.

From the earliest days the enthusiasm of Hartford's leaders for practical philanthropy was founded on their Puritan heritage. Most of them were merchants, businessmen, or hard-working farmers who aspired to be economically successful. But they also were devoted to the welfare of the entire community, taking seriously the Biblical admonition "...from everyone to whom much has been given, much shall be required...." Diligence in one's calling, thrift, and a concern for the unfortunate were among the most highly regarded virtues of the founders, and they persevered during the long process of secularization, as Puritans changed to Yankees.

Those in Connecticut who acquired wealth during the early days of the republic were almost certain to be faithful Congregationalists, staunch Federalists (or conservatives) and members of the Standing Order--the power structure of that period. Even more to the point, those engaging in philanthropy were in many instances descended from clergymen. Religion supplied the spiritual motivation and vision, while business experience made them no-nonsense do-gooders. And the concentration of wealth in Hartford, thanks to its economic diversity, provided the wherewithal to share it for the common good.

Inevitably, as the city grew, philanthropy became more institutionalized. Especially after the Great Depression and the introduction of federal and state welfare programs, good works no longer depended solely on churches or individual movers and shakers like the Wadsworths and Goodwins. Yet modern examples of generous family philanthropy have been set by such well-known business leaders as Beatrice Auerbach, Clayton Gengras, and Robert C. Knox, whose capital gifts have benefited scores of institutions like St. Joseph College, the Science Museum of Connecticut, the Institute of Living, the University of Hartford, the Y.M.C.A. and the Boys' Club. Robert Knox's sister Betty, a Hartford city councilwoman, established in her will the Knox Foundation, best known for the mini-parks around the city and the carousel in Bushnell Park.

Fund-raising for a variety of social purposes and the distribution of grants by corporations and foundations are still major activities. In fact, Hartford has a well-earned national reputation for being a caring city. As in the past, local businessmen and women are actively involved with City Hall and the Board of Education in ameliorating the city's transition from an industrial economy to one of high technology and service through intensive job recruitment and training programs. At the forefront of this effort is the Greater Hartford Chamber of Commerce. The 10 largest companies all have departments of community affairs that together invest millions of dollars in a multitude of projects. Additional support is provided by several local foundations. Organized in 1925, the Hartford Foundation for Public Giving is the seventh largest public foundation in the United States, with accumulated assets of nearly $100 million. Between 1936 and 1985 it distributed $49 million to education, hospitals, social service agencies, and the arts.

HARTFORD HOSPITAL

80 Seymour Street
Public Information
524-2521

On March 2, 1854, a boiler explosion leveled the Fales and Gray Railroad Car Works in Hartford, leaving 21 dead and 50 injured. Care for the injured could be provided only in private homes or in doctors' offices, since at that time there was no general hospital in the city. Community leaders called a meeting soon after, out of which came a proposal for a hospital. This proposal was taken to the General Assembly in May 1854 and a charter was granted for the Hartford Hospital.

From 1855 until 1860 the new hospital used a house at the apex of Maple and Retreat avenues, where care was provided for up to five patients at a time by a husband and wife who resided there. In 1860 the first building was completed and opened on the triangular site bordered by South Hudson and Jefferson streets and by Retreat Avenue. With its porticoed main entrance on South Hudson Street, it consisted of a main building and a two-ward North wing. The combined bed capacity of this new structure was 44.

From these small beginnings, Hartford Hospital has grown to what it is today: an 885-bed regional, referral, teaching hospital with special emphasis on heart disease, trauma, pediatrics, and cancer. It is a renowned organ transplant center and has extensive education and research programs. Hartford Hospital is the largest in the Northeast in terms of patients cared for, and is in the upper 10% of the nation's largest general hospitals. It operates the largest food and laundry services in the state and is the eighth largest employer in Greater Hartford, with more than 5,000 employees working either full- or part-time.

Hartford Hospital was the first hospital in Connecticut to provide a freestanding medical office building for its medical staff. In 1987, about 25 years after its first building was erected, the hospital built a new medical office building at 85 Seymour Street for more than 500 physicians.

Since 1985 Hartford Hospital has provided an air ambulance service with its LIFE STAR helicopter. During its first two years, LIFE STAR transported 1,095 patients, which included the transfer of patients from 78 hospitals in seven states and Canada to 40 receiving hospitals in seven states. It has been directly and indirectly responsible for the survival of a number of patients who otherwise would have died or been severely disabled.

Jefferson House was established by Hartford Hospital in 1884, adjacent to the hospital on Jefferson Street, as a facility to care for those elderly poor who were well enough not to require hospitalization, but who had no home to which to go. Today Jefferson House is a short-term rehabilitative care facility for those over age 60 and is located in Newington.

In January 1986 Hartford Hospital and Meriden-Wallingford Hospital affiliated to form the Connecticut Health System.

From its founding, Hartford Hospital has received dedicated and generous support from both individual and corporate members of the Greater Hartford community. In its turn, the hospital's goal has been and is to provide the highest quality health care to a community that has broadened in scope to include patients from all over New England.

In 1822 the Hartford Retreat, now the Institute of Living, was organized to assist "the distracted, the despondent, the tempted and the broken in heart." It is the oldest hospital in Connecticut and the third oldest in the nation. The new institution, backed by Dr. Eli Todd of Farmington and the Connecticut Medical Society, pioneered the radical concept that emotional disorders, like physical disorders, could often be cured.

Dr. Todd, an eloquent spokesman for the project, decried the fact that the mentally ill were often subject to cruel and immoral harassment by their ignorant associates. After a successful fund drive, a 15-acre campus was purchased and a hospital for 40-50 patients was constructed. Today this original structure is the Center Building of the Institute. Dr. Todd became the new hospital's first superintendent at the munificent salary of $1,000 a year. In the latter part of the 19th century when the campus was enlarged to 35 acres, Hartford's nationally renowned landscape architect, Frederick Law Olmsted, laid out the grounds. Some of the buildings now standing on this attractive campus were erected in 1822-24, others in 1845, and still others when the campus was renovated by Olmsted. Additional units were erected in the 1930s and 1960s. A new patient building is now being planned.

The Institute of Living today is one of the most respected private, non-profit psychiatric hospitals in the world. It is devoted to the care and treatment of all forms of psychiatric illnesses occurring in the age groups of 16 years and above.

The hospital provides a complete range of psychiatric treatment programs including psychotherapy, psychopharmacology, group and family therapy, somatic therapy such as electroshock, and a wide range of avocational, recreational, and social therapeutic programs.

The Institute has in-patient facilities, an Outpatient Department for adults, an Outpatient Department for children, and a Day Treatment Center. These Outpatient Clinics are operated as charitable services for those unable to obtain private psychiatric care through their own resources. The staff of the Institute serves in consultative and educational roles to many state and local educational, social, and welfare agencies.

The hospital also operates a high school approved by

INSTITUTE OF LIVING

400 Washington St
Public Relations
241-6909

the Connecticut Department of Education and the New England Association of Colleges and Secondary Schools.

Because the Institute of Living is a teaching institution as well as a hospital, it is involved with the education of psychiatrists, psychologists, social workers, nurses, occupational therapists, and others in the field of mental health. The Institute's Research Department conducts many projects in the treatment and prevention of psychiatric disorder and psychological conditions.

The Institute of Living and its neighbors, the Hartford Hospital and Trinity College, have cooperated in employing a neighborhood out-reach representative who takes an active part in assisting area residents to improve the quality of life in this section of the city.

PERCIVAL C. SMITH TOWER

80 Charter Oak Ave

Percival C. Smith Tower, under the management of the Hartford Housing Authority, was completed in 1970 and named for the man in charge of the Authority at the time. Designed by Hartford architect Louis Drakos, the Tower has 200 living units for people who must be over 65 years of age or disabled.

SHELDON-CHARTER OAK COMMUNITY

Charter Oak Ave

Sponsored by the Greater Hartford Council of Churches and completed in 1968, this co-operative housing project contains 91 units of low and moderate income housing and is privately managed.

The Polish National Home, a superb example of Art-Deco architecture, was designed by Henry Ludorf of Hartford. The exterior of the Home still has its bas-relief decoration, bronze grill work, light fixtures, and bronze doors that are typical of the geometricized "art moderne" style that was very popular when it was constructed.

The building, which houses a ballroom and community club, was completed in 1930 by the Polish community despite the financial problems precipitated by the "crash" and the Great Depression. Although most of the residents of this old ethnic community have now moved to other portions of Hartford or to the suburbs, 1,800 persons are still members of the club, which is open seven days a week. Every October an annual Pulaski Day celebration is held here, followed by a grand parade. In the days when many factories were located in this part of the city, the Polish National Home was a favorite place for union meetings.

POLISH NATIONAL HOME

60 Charter Oak Ave
247-1784

On March 16, 1918, a group of dedicated citizens, incorporated under the name of the Abraham Jacoby Hospital, began to make plans for the creation of a third general hospital in Hartford. Four years later they purchased a large pre-Civil War mansion, the former home of Judge Charles H. Brainard at 119 Capitol Avenue, and renamed their new institution Mount Sinai Hospital. On May 7, 1923, the hospital was officially opened with 65 beds.

In 1925 Mount Sinai's trustees purchased an old mansion on Buckingham Street, a handsome brownstone structure, and converted it into a school for nurses which was in full operation until 1936. Eight years later the present site on Blue Hills Avenue was acquired. However, it was not until March 23, 1950, that a new 115-bed Mount Sinai Hospital opened its doors. Nine years later the Auerbach wing added 74 more beds at a cost of $2 million.

MOUNT SINAI HOSPITAL

500 Blue Hills Ave
Public Information
242-4431

During the 1960s the hospitals in Hartford experienced considerable pressure to enlarge and improve their facilities. As a result a completely modern 385 bed Mount Sinai Hospital, including the new Samuel S. Suisman Building, was constructed. The architects were E. Todd Wheeler and the Perkins and Will Partnership.

Mount Sinai today offers a broad spectrum of medical and surgical services and runs a School of Radiologic Technology. Annually 19,000 patients are admitted, and 45,000 emergency room visits made. Mount Sinai is affiliated with the University of Connecticut School of Medicine.

ST. FRANCIS HOSPITAL AND MEDICAL CENTER

114 Woodland St.
Public Information
548-4190

St. Francis Hospital was founded in 1897 by a tiny band of Sisters of St. Joseph of Chambery, a teaching and nursing community of religious women. Mother Ann Valencia, the brilliant and dedicated first administrator, was the only religious of the "founding five" who was a trained nurse and familiar with hospital organization. A native of France, she spoke little English. Her confident response to all crises, large or small, was "I fix!", which she did very efficiently until her death in 1936.

St. Francis initially occupied a small brick building that had been the bishop's residence on the corner of Woodland and Collins streets. It had accommodations for 30 ward patients and two private cases and, during its first year, 314 patients were admitted. Within the next six years two new buildings were completed, which increased the hospital's bed capacity to 172.

St. Francis Hospital has added "and Medical Center" to its title, an accurate reflection of its expanded services and facilities and continued sophistication.

Today St. Francis is the largest Roman Catholic hospital in New England and the third largest hospital in the state of Connecticut. Its School of Nursing offers the only three-year program in the Greater Hartford area.

When Asylum Hill was first being developed back in the middle of the 19th century, the large plot of land that is now 1000 Asylum Avenue was a swamp. It was purchased by William Collins, a retired Hartford merchant and brother of Erastus Collins, who also owned land on the Hill. Both were communicants of Asylum Hill Congregational Church. Brother William, inspired by the building of Bushnell Park in which he had participated, determined to turn this swampy area into a park-like estate. Therefore he spent his remaining years improving and planting the land with a great variety of trees and shrubs, many of which may still be admired. He also built his own home on the corner of Woodland Street and Asylum Avenue.

Samuel G. Dunham, second president of the Hartford Electric Light Co., eventually married William Collins's daughter, Alice. For many years the Dunhams and their five daughters lived here. When the girls married, Dunham built them and their husbands homes on this family compound so that he could continue to enjoy their company and the eventual company of many grandchildren.

In the 1930s the National Fire Insurance Company, founded in Hartford in 1871, was anxious to move its headquarters out of the congested center city in order to construct a more up-to-date building. So the company purchased the Dunham estate and employed the architectural firm of Eggers and Higgins in New York City to create for them an appropriate structure. Great care, however, was taken to disturb as little as possible the beautiful trees and shrubs planted by William Collins. The company moved into its new home office the day after the bombing of Pearl Harbor in 1941.

In 1946 National Fire was purchased by Continental Insurance Companies of Chicago. Nine years later this building became the headquarters of the Security Insurance Company of New Haven which had been founded in 1841. The name of the company was changed to the Security Insurance Company of Hartford when the administrative offices were moved to this city in 1965. E. Clayton Gengras was president of the new company which, through the next few years, expanded its operations and holdings considerably.

**E. CLAYTON
GENGRAS
AMBULATORY
CARE CENTER**

1000 Asylum Avenue
Public Information
548-4190

In November 1976 the 1000 Asylum Avenue building was sold to St. Francis Hospital and transformed into the E. Clayton Gengras Ambulatory Care Center. The Center now houses the hospital's outpatient clinics, excellent accommodations for patients and staff, and more than 60 physicians' offices. Rental from the building's offices is paid to a hospital-owned subsidiary company.

HARTFORD REGION YWCA CENTER

135 Broad Street
525-1163

This is the major program and residential center of the YWCA of the Capitol Region. There are seven other program centers and a camp in other parts of Greater Hartford that comprise the total regional organization.

Founded in 1867, Hartford's YW was the first in the nation to include a dormitory component. This new eight-story tower, designed by architects Moore and Salsbury, and built by the Charter Oak Construction Company, was opened in 1974. A residence for women only, the YW offers the most modern facilities for city living; beds for 101 permanent or transient guests, all except one single rooms, with or without baths; kitchen facilities and individual food lockers on each floor; an extensive women's physical fitness center; ample parking; convenient mass transportation; nearby shopping areas; and the best job market for women in the entire Capitol Region.

The YW's programs are designed to be very flexible and responsive to the changing needs of women and girls. The Rape Crisis Service is one example. Classes range from financial management to pottery. The Hartford Region YWCA in every way provides a setting in which diverse women and girls of the metropolitan urban/suburban area can meet and work together.

The YWCA is also the headquarters of the Junior League of Hartford.

Since the YMCA first opened its doors in downtown Hartford in 1852, it has played an important role in the life of Hartford and surrounding towns.

At the time of its founding Hartford was experiencing a major influx of young men who were seeking employment in its factories and businesses. The YMCA was organized specifically "to seek and assist young men who came to reside in the city." The YMCA not only provided housing, it also provided cultural, educational, recreational, and spiritual opportunities.

In 1892 the Hartford Y built a magnificent new headquarters at the corner of Pearl and Jewell streets. The architects were Fuller and Wheeler of Albany, New York, and the brownstone, turreted building they created was an excellent artistic compliment to the nearby brownstone arch designed by George Keller in memory of the veterans of the Civil War. Construction of the Y involved the active cooperation of many local business leaders who were very impressed by the fact that their own employees and the city-at-large were benefiting greatly from the agency's programs. In those days, it was not customary for corporations to contribute to any type of charitable enterprise, including building funds for social services. Philanthropic individuals were thus the only means of support for such endeavors. Governor Morgan G. Bulkeley, president of Aetna Life Insurance Company as well as Connecticut's top political mogul, took a particular interest in the Y's building program. In order to circumvent prevailing customs at the same time that he assisted the fund drive, he called together a meeting of his own employees. After enthusiastically outlining to them the potential benefits of a new YMCA facility, he urged each individual to make a personal contribution. He also promised that if they would do so, the company would then give every one of them a handsome personal bonus that matched their gift to the Y! Needless to say, with such remarkable Yankee ingenuity at work, the YMCA's fund drive went "over the top"!

YMCA OF METROPOLITAN HARTFORD

160 Jewell Street
522-4183

In 1892 manual and academic training was extended through Hillyer Institute, which became Hillyer Junior College, an independent school after 1947 and now the University of Hartford. A separate Hartford County YMCA was founded in 1918 and together the two organizations served the 28 towns of Connecticut's capital region for the next 50 years. In 1972 the two merged to form the present YMCA.

Over the years many activities have been provided. In 1939 an Industrial Management Club was begun in order to provide industrial workers an opportunity to develop leadership and management potentials. With the cooperation of industry and business, classes were held, seminars conducted, and visits made to Hartford plants.

Another innovative program called Friends of Boys, organized young shoeshine and newspaper boys into territories in order to reduce the problem of bullying competition and street fighting. In 1943 educational testing, job referrals, and family counseling were introduced.

In 1972 the downtown headquarters was torn down and replaced by a much larger, more up-to-date facility designed by Hartford architects Malmfeld Associates.

In terms of physical education the YMCA's new Hartford headquarters are among the finest and most complete in the world. The Y has become a leader in the development of cardio-vascular training programs...life-restoring alternatives to heart attacks and other daily pressures of modern living. The modern building has live-in facilities for 220 persons, male or female, and food service for residents and members.

In recent years the Hartford Association has been more active than ever in helping meet the needs of people in today's environment. Responding to current social needs, the YMCA developed parent-child clubs called Indian Guides and Indian Princesses, established before-school and after-school child-care centers called Latch Key, and is helping encourage achievement of potential among minority teenagers with a Black and Hispanic Achievers Program. A collaborative effort with the City of Hartford and the United Way provides a comprehensive community center program under YMCA management at the Stowe Village Housing Project.

Health enhancement programs, including early calisthenics classes, then sports such as basketball, volleyball, gymnastics, and swimming, as well as today's corporate fitness and cardiovascular health programs, all have been YMCA innovations. Today's wellness movement can also be traced to the YMCA.

Camping programs led to the founding of Camp Jewell in 1901, Camp Woodstock in 1922, and Camp Holiday Ridge in 1954. In 1955 the first comprehensive, year-round outdoor center in the country was opened by the YMCA in Colebrook.

Besides these three camps, the YMCA operates nine community-based branches: Farmington Valley, Glastonbury, Hartford Central (with an extension at Stowe Village), Indian Valley, South Regional, Tobacco Valley, Wheeler Regional, East Hartford, and West Hartford, the latter two located in buildings constructed by both the YMCA and YWCA.

The Y's Metropolitan Hartford membership rolls indicate an overwhelmingly enthusiastic response to the usefulness of the organization. The total membership in the Y's twelve branches numbers 33,000 boys, girls, men, and women. In addition, 20,000 participate as non-members. More than 11,000 young people use Y camping programs every year.

In 1972 Asylum Hill Inc. was created by Aetna Life & Casualty, Connecticut Mutual Life Insurance, Hartford Insurance Group, and Society for Savings to improve the quality of life on the Hill. Three grass-roots neighborhood civic associations, numerous local property owners and small businessmen, and the Asylum Hill Christian Community have joined AHI's neighborhood improvement team. The Hartford Police Department has also been very cooperative. AHI issues a newspaper every other week and sponsors various programs including an annual Octoberfest to draw the total community together.

Both Aetna Life & Casualty and Connecticut Mutual have demonstrated their commitment to the neighborhood by offering area employees special financial incentives to live as well as work on the Hill. Society for Savings has pioneered by making a conscientious effort to explore and implement new concepts and policies in neighborhood reinvestment. This type of corporate citizenship is essential to the economic and political resurgence of post-industrial Hartford.

Housing and architectural organizations conduct tours and open-house events highlighting the residential, cultural, and recreational attractions of the center city.

ASYLUM HILL INC.

121 Sigourney Street
522-4241

SAND

45 Canton Street
278-8460

The South Arsenal Neighborhood Development Corporation was first organized in 1967, stimulated by the creation of Model Cities by the federal government. Since then funds for the organization have come from HUD, community block grants to the City of Hartford, Hartford Process Inc., the local business community, and local foundations. SAND contains units of low- and middle-income housing and includes the Everywhere School. The architect for the housing units was Jack Dollard of Hartford and the designer of the school and grounds was Milton Howard Associates of Hartford.

Community involvement has been and is absolutely essential to the creation and maintenance of this new community. Unlike most low- and moderate-income ventures, SAND fosters the concept of "helping people to help themselves" coupled with strong community control and responsibility.

One of the most unique components of SAND is the Everywhere School, which occupies 10 separate buildings-- eight learning centers, each with pupils, a gymnasium, and an administration building. The basic educational philosophy of the Everywhere School is that young people do not learn just in the classroom. They learn everywhere...at home, in church, in the community at large, and from all types of community leaders. Thus parents, families and friends of the students take a very creative part in the total educational experience of these young people. SAND also supports an after-school art studio with two resident artists to increase the community's cultural awareness. Neighborhood social services are available at SAND. These include a Senior Citizens Center, recreational programs for all ages, youth counseling for education and employment, and a tenant program to educate tenants in effective home management.

The SAND neighborhood is one of the essential building-blocks of a healthy post-industrial Hartford in which all citizens may enjoy a wholesome quality of life no matter what their race, creed, color, sex, or economic status.

Photo courtesy of C. Reich.

TRINITY
COLLEGE

Summit Street
527-3151

*Tours: Call the college for
information on tours.*

Until the turn of the 19th century the only college in
Connecticut was New Haven's Yale, a staunch bastion of
Congregationalism founded by clergymen in 1701. Individuals affiliated with other religious denominations, especially
the growing numbers of Episcopalians, fiercely resented the
fact that teaching positions at Yale were strictly limited to
members of the Congregational Church which, until 1818,
was the established church of the State of Connecticut. Eager
to have an institution of higher learning which would reflect
their own religious values and traditions, the Episcopalians
in 1824 petitioned the General Assembly for a charter to
create a new college which they artfully named for President
George Washington, whom Connecticut's predominantly
Federalist legislators greatly admired.

The petition of the Episcopalians was granted, and the
new college came into being with all of nine students. Fledgling Washington College was located on the present site of
the State Capitol. The new educational institution took pride
in the fact that it was the first in the world ever to specifically state in its charter that no one must ever be excluded as
either a student or teacher because of religious affiliation ...
even Congregationalists! Finally in 1845 the new Episcopal
college felt sufficiently secure to change its name to the more
traditional one of Trinity College.

In 1872 the college was forced to make way for the
new State Capitol. The campus was moved to Gallows Hill
where public executions had been held for many years.
Even so, all agreed this was a lovely site, and the college
trustees employed prestigious English architect William
Burges to design for them the first Gothic structures ever
to be built on an American campus. The resident architect
who supervised the work was Francis Kimball of New York
City. The model for Trinity in Hartford was Trinity College
of Oxford University in England. The new campus was
completed in 1878.

Since that time there have been numerous additions.
The exquisite Gothic Chapel completed in 1932 was the
most ambitious. The 1960s saw a tremendous expansion of
the old campus, and a number of new residence halls and
other fine facilities were constructed. Perhaps best known
to the general public is the *Austin Art Center* designed
by O'Connor and Kilham of New York and dedicated in 1965
in memory of A. Everett Austin. "Chick" Austin was a former

professor of fine arts at Trinity and one of the most original and distinguished directors of the Wadsworth Atheneum. During his term of office the Atheneum gained a national reputation for the unusually high quality of its art collection. His wife, Helen Goodwin Austin, was a granddaughter of Rev. Francis Goodwin, another of this city's great benefactors. Austin Art Center's art exhibits and dramatic, musical, and lecture programs are much enjoyed by the general public. Call 527-8062 for information.

Cinestudio is a theatre showing foreign, art, and vintage, as well as contemporary films, during evenings only. 527-38ll.

Female students were first accepted by Trinity College in 1969. Today the college has nearly 2,000 undergraduate students, evenly divided between male and female. More than 200 graduate students are enrolled.

Trinity has a fine library of close to 710,000 volumes. Reference privileges are extended to qualified users outside the college. The Watkinson Library section may also be used by the public. The Watkinson is a major research library, principally in the humanities, with many rare and out-of-print volumes. The Watkinson's greatest treasures are four elephant folios of hand-colored prints taken from the original sketches of John James Audubon. Drawn in 1827, they are considered to be some of the finest in existence.

Trinity College, through its Director of Community Education and its programs in urban and environmental studies, is vitally concerned with improving the quality of life in post-industrial Hartford. It houses the Southside Institutions Neighborhood Alliance (SINA), a partnership among the College, the Institute of Living, and Hartford Hospital. SINA's efforts have assisted Broad-Park Development Corporation, helped revitalize Park Street, and played major roles in the founding of the *Southside News* and the Hartford Street Youth Gang Project.

Since its founding Trinity has been closely linked with the city. The college hosts the Upward Bound Program for high school students, it operates a sports camp for 500 children during the summer, and it offers free courses to city employees. Trinity undergraduates are active volunteers, working in food drives, soup kitchens, and convalescent homes, in addition to tutoring and acting as Big Brothers and Sisters. Trinity's Child Care Center provides bi-lingual day care to 70 area families.

TRINITY COLLEGE CHAPEL

Summit Street
527-3151

For tours of the chapel call the college. During the summer months the carillon concerts are followed by chapel tours.

In 1874 William G. Mather, who later achieved wealth and power as an industrialist in Cleveland, Ohio, was fined $1 while a student at Trinity for "defacing the woodwork" of the college chapel. Fifty-four years later, this same gentleman, grown wiser and considerably more affluent, indicated to former president Remsen B. Ogilby that he would like to give his alma mater a new chapel. Dr. Ogilby was delighted and determined that everything would be of the highest quality.

Frohman, Ross and Little, architects of the Washington Cathedral, designed the elegant Gothic limestone sanctuary. Ground was broken in December of 1928, and the cornerstone was laid on Sunday morning, June 15, 1930. Every work day began with prayers by Dr. Ogilby, and each worker was inspired to special pride in his craftsmanship by the president's keen interest in every detail and desire for perfection. In fact, the entire building process was more reminiscent of medieval than modern times. The chapel was consecrated on June 18, 1932, and the workmen still return annually to inspect their handiwork at a regular meeting of the Chapel Builders' Alumni Association.

In 1940 J. Gregory Wiggins of Pomfret, Connecticut, undertook to decorate the chapel with wood carvings. Mr. Wiggins was a close friend of Dr. Ogilby, an enthusiastic medieval scholar, and a devout Episcopalian. He combined his interest in the Middle Ages with a hobby he had taken up as a boy in Chattanooga, Tennessee. A whittler like so many youths, he drifted into wood carving, teaching himself the craft. In time he achieved a wide reputation. In 1951 the Boston Athenaeum had an excellent exhibition of his wood carvings and printed a special catalogue in his honor. His work in Trinity College Chapel is no doubt his masterpiece. Unfortunately he died in 1957 before he was quite finished. John C. E. Taylor, professor of fine arts at the college, took up the chisel and completed the task.

In 1955, responding to a local need for engineers, scientists, and managers, Rensselaer Polytechnic Institute of Troy, New York, established a branch graduate center in South Windsor. The center became a separate corporation named "R.P.I. of Connecticut" in 1961. Ten years later this $7 million building in downtown Hartford was completed. The architects were Jeter, Cook and Jepson, and the contractors were Standard Builders of Hartford. In 1976 the new facility was officially renamed the Hartford Graduate Center.

Hartford Graduate Center is unique among institutions of higher learning in Connecticut in that it serves the educational needs of working professionals by giving them the opportunity to earn advanced degrees on a part-time basis without taking time from their jobs.

In recent years HGC's mission has been greatly expanded to include a wide range of special studies not included in the degree curriculum, but still fitted to the particular requirements of employees in area businesses. Although United Technologies Corporation was the original sponsor of the graduate center, many types of industries including banking, insurance, health, safety, and environmental, now use this educational facility as the development of modern technologies, especially the computer, has revolutionized almost every facet of the state's economy.

Today, HGC enrolls 2,200 post-graduate students for master's degrees in computer science, electrical and mechanical engineering, metallurgy, business administration and management, and bio-medical engineering and management. The programs are offered in the evening.

HARTFORD GRADUATE CENTER

275 Windsor Street
548-2400

In 1933 Hartford College for Women was created as a local branch of Mt. Holyoke College to make available to Hartford area girls the first two years of a top-quality college education. Six years later it became an independent institution and, in 1958, moved to the present campus. At that time the college was under the leadership of President Laura Johnson, who served from 1943 to 1976.

HCW is an outstanding private, liberal arts college with a faculty-student ratio of one to ten. Almost all of the students, upon completing their associate in arts degree, have

HARTFORD COLLEGE FOR WOMEN

1265 Asylum Avenue
236-1215

Call for appointment.

199

transferred to four-year colleges where they have completed work in more than 50 major fields. The student body includes both on-campus residents and older women from the surrounding communities. The college is a member of the Greater Hartford Consortium for Higher Education.

The Hartford Counseling Center on the campus serves adult women of the community as well as enrolled students. It offers a variety of career-counseling services including vocational interest testing and a placement service, career seminars, skills courses, and legal assistant training.

HCW's 14-acre campus is particularly attractive. The main building was formerly the home of Mr. and Mrs. Charles F. T. Seaverns. Their handsome Georgian home was designed by the New York architectural firm of Goodwin, Bullard and Woolsey. Porteus, Walker Company of Hartford was the builder. Philip Goodwin was a native of Hartford and the brother of James Lippincott Goodwin, whose home he designed on Woodside Circle. He also designed other residences on Woodside Circle, and the Museum of Modern Art in New York City.

Olmsted Associates of Boston landscaped the grounds of the new Seaverns estate. Frederick Law Olmsted, Jr., was still a member of the firm at the time. Early in the 1920s, however, the landscaping was turned over to Robert Marshall of Wethersfield, who put in most of the unique and lovely planting that is still extant. Marshall was a specialist in rare trees and shrubs.

When the Seaverns estate was acquired by Hartford College for Women, it was remodeled for institutional use by Hartford architect John W. Huntington. (It is interesting to note that Mrs. Seaverns's parents endowed Hillyer College, which is now part of the University of Hartford.) The house is now named Paul Butterworth Hall. Huntington also designed or remodeled other campus buildings and nearby residences. The Laura Johnson House was originally the home of Mr. and Mrs. John Trumbull Robinson and was designed by Mrs. Robinson's brother-in-law, Louis Weeks.

The University of Hartford is a privately supported co-educational, non-denominational university offering undergraduate and graduate educational programs in liberal arts and sciences, fine arts, business and public administration, education, engineering, music, and electronic technology.

The University was formed in 1957 through an association of three established degree-granting institutions: Hartford Art School, founded in 1877 (the third in the nation); Hartt College of Music, founded in 1920; and Hillyer College, founded in 1879.

Through the Alfred C. Fuller Music Center, the Mildred P. Allen Memorial Library, the Auerbach Auditorium, the Gengras Student Union, the Joseloff Art Gallery, William H. Mortensen Library, and the Stanley Sculpture Court, the University sponsors for both students and Greater Hartford a rich variety of lectures, concerts, art exhibitions, and special symposia. Moore and Salsbury of Avon, Connecticut, were architects for the original campus and designed the first buildings.

With a 215-acre campus, eight schools and colleges, and student housing for 3,000, the University in only 30 years has risen to the top rank of higher institutions in the Northeast offering both liberal arts and career programs of study. Among its newer facilities are a modern computer center, engineering and science laboratories, and the 700-seat Lincoln Theater. In 1989 it completed a $21 million conference center named after Harry J. Gray, former chairman of United Technologies. Some 4,200 full-time and 3,200 part-time students are currently enrolled, approximately 58 percent from Connecticut.

Joseloff Gallery: changing exhibitions of work by area and other artists. 243-4393.

Lincoln Theatre: site of theatre, music, dance performances by university and other arts organizations. 243-4228 box office.

Millard Auditorium: located in Hartt School of Music. A musical performance hall for Hartt faculty, students, and visiting artists. 243-4454.

THE UNIVERSITY OF HARTFORD

200 Bloomfield Avenue
West Hartford
243-4100

Tours by appointment.

201

GREATER HARTFORD CONSORTIUM

201 Bloomfield Ave.
West Hartford
233-1553

The Greater Hartford Consortium was founded in 1972. By pooling resources and coordinating some activities, neighboring colleges are able to offer more and better programs at lower cost than the colleges would expect to achieve separately.

Member colleges are:
Hartford College for Women - two-year undergraduate
Hartford Graduate Center - graduate
St. Joseph College - graduate and undergraduate
St. Thomas Seminary - two-year undergraduate
Trinity College - undergraduate and graduate
University of Hartford - undergraduate and graduate
Connecticut Public Television is an Associate Member.

The major activity of the Consortium is a cross registration program under which full-time undergraduates, graduate students and employees may enroll at other colleges in courses not offered at their own college. This program has the effect of extending significantly the breadth and depth of the curriculum of each institution. Cross registration is supported by a free shuttle bus and mail service and by standard reciprocal library privileges for students and faculty of all member colleges. The cross registration program may, by mutual agreement, include completion at another college of a major not offered at one's own college.

Formerly the residence of actress Katharine Hepburn and her family, the house was presented to the University of Hartford in 1972. The architect was Milton Hayman and the builder Robert Swain. The house was constructed in 1927.

UNIVERSITY OF CONNECTICUT SCHOOL OF LAW

55 Elizabeth Street
241-4638

The School of Law now occupies most of the Gothic buildings vacated by the Hartford Seminary when it moved to new quarters nearby in 1981. The School has an enrollment of nearly 500 full-time day students and approximately 200 evening students. MacKenzie Hall serves as the Attorney General's office for the State of Connecticut.

In 1833 a group of conservative Congregational ministers, upset by the "new liberalism" being espoused by the professors of Yale College, founded the Pastoral Union of Connecticut. They opened their new school for training ministers the following year at East Windsor, near the birthplace of Connecticut's famed theologian, Jonathan Edwards. In 1865, discouraged by the "lack of social and literary atmosphere" in that charming country town, they moved to Prospect Street in Hartford. Fourteen years later they relocated on Broad Street.

In 1913 the Seminary, Hartford School of Religious Education and Kennedy School of Missions became a single corporation named The Hartford Seminary Foundation, an "inter-denominational university of religion" which offered at least seven advance degree programs.

Again in need of new facilities, the trustees of the Seminary purchased a large portion of land from James J. Goodwin and retained the celebrated Boston architect, Charles Collens (1873 - 1956) to design five handsome Gothic structures for their new campus. Collens was also the architect for the Union Theological Seminary and Riverside Church in New York City. Although the new buildings were not officially dedicated until May 17-18, 1927, the Seminary actually began moving into its new home in 1924.

In 1972, in response to financial, ecclesiastical and theological pressures for change, the Seminary voted to restrict its offerings and commit its considerable resources to two unique programs, both of which continue the thrust of its history and concerns: one focuses upon the practice of the ministry as it is performed by communities of believers, both clergy and lay, throughout New England and eastern New York State; the other upon Christian-Muslim relations and the study of Islam in a world-wide context. It offers the Doctor of Ministry degree, and the Master of Arts and Doctor of

HARTFORD SEMINARY

77 Sherman Street
232-4451

Photo courtesy of Laurie Johnson.

Philosophy degrees in Islamic studies under a joint program
with McGill University. It currently enrolls approximately
one thousand clergy and lay persons each year in courses
that range form semester-length to two-to-four year programs.

In 1981 the Seminary moved into a new modern structure designed by Richard Meier and located diagonally
across the street. Its former buildings, too large for its purposes, were sold to the University of Connecticut School of
Law. The radical architecture, which Ada Louise Huxtable of
the New York Times praised as "a dazzling structure on the
leading edge of the building art," symbolizes the institution's
transformation from undergraduate ministerial training to
post-graduate programs.

THEATRE,

HARTFORD.

On Monday Evening, September 2d, 1799, will be presented the favorite
COMEDY, called,

Wives as they were,

AND

Maids as they are.

*Written by Mrs. Inchbald, author of Such things are ; I'll tell you what ; Every one has his
fault, &c. &c. and performed in London upwards of 100 nights successively to overflowing houses.*

Sir William Dorillon,	Mr. Hodgkinson,
Lord Priory,	Mr. Jefferson,
Sir George Evelyn,	Mr. Hogg,
Oliver,	Mr. Hallam,
Mr. Norberry,	Mr. Perkins,
Nabson,	Mr. Cromwell,
Servants,	Mess. Lee, Stowell, & Roberts,
And, Bronzely,	Mr. Hallam, jun.
Lady Priory,	Mrs. Hodgkinson,
Lady Mary Raffle,	Miss Brett,
And, Miss Dorillon,	Mrs. Hallam.

To which will be added the celebrated MUSICAL ENTERTAINMENT of

The PRIZE;

OR,

2, 5, 3, 8.

Doctor Lenetive,	Mr. Jefferson,
Label,	Mr. Perkins,
Mr. Heartwell,	Mr. Hallam, jun.
Mr. Caddy,	Mr. Hogg,
And, Juba, *(a black boy)*	Miss Harding.
Mrs. Caddy,	Mrs. King,
And, Caroline,	Mrs. Hodgkinson.

☞ Tickets, and places for the Boxes to be had as usual, and of Mess. Hudson & Goodwin—BOX 4/6, PIT 3/, GALLERY 1/6.
. Performance to begin precisely at a quarter past seven.
The Ladies and Gentlemen of East-Hartford, East-Windsor, Glastenbury, &c. are respectfully informed the FERRYMEN have con-
tracted to attend regularly every Evening after the performance is concluded.

WADSWORTH ATHENEUM

600 Main Street
Museum: 278-2670

For up-to-date information about museum activities and exhibitions dial 247-9111.
Museum Hours:
Tuesday through Sunday 11 a.m.-5 p.m.
Office Hours:
Monday through Friday, 9 a.m.-5 p.m.
The museum is closed Mondays and major holidays.
General admission for adults is $3. Students and senior citizens, $1.50. Children under 13 and members of the Atheneum get in free. Free admission on Thursday all day and Saturday from 11 a.m. to 1 p.m.
Museum Cafe hours:
Tuesday through Sunday 11:30 a.m-2:30 p.m. For reservations call 728-5989.
Library hours:
Tuesday, Thursday, and Saturday, 11 a.m.-5 p.m.
Museum Shop hours:
Tuesday through Sunday, 11 a.m.-4:30 p.m.
General tours of the museum are offered on Thursdays, Saturdays, and Sundays at 1 p.m. Tours begin in the Main Lobby. Special tours can be arranged through the Education Office, ext. 322.

The Wadsworth Atheneum, founded by Daniel Wadsworth in 1842, is America's oldest continuously operated public art museum. Its collections span more than 5,000 years of art history, from ancient Greek and Roman bronzes to Renaissance and Baroque paintings, Meissen porcelain, the Wallace Nutting Collection of 17th-century American furniture and decorative arts, 19th-century American landscapes and 20th-century masterpieces.

Commissioned in 1842 and opened in 1844, the original Gothic structure was designed by Towne and Davis, New York architects. (Ithiel Towne was also the architect for Hartford's Christ Church Cathedral.) The moving spirit behind the building of the Atheneum and its chief benefactor was Daniel Wadsworth, son of merchant-patriot Jeremiah Wadsworth who had served as George Washington's commissary general during the American Revolution. Colonel Wadsworth was an extremely able businessman who managed to accumulate a large personal fortune which he devoted not only to the welfare of his own family but to the improvement of his home town. His son, Daniel, was equally public spirited. The Puritan mores of the time mandated that well-to-do citizens volunteer both personal attention and private funds to the public good, and the Wadsworths were all very conscientious citizens. Their family mansion was originally located where the Atheneum now stands. Many were entertained in the large Wadsworth homestead, including, on several occasions, George Washington. Young Daniel decided to move the Wadsworth family home to a site on Buckingham Street and to erect in its place a handsome tri-partite structure to house an art gallery, the Young Men's Institute, and The Connecticut Historical Society. The Institute became the Hartford Public Library in 1893 and moved to its present location, further south on Main Street in 1957. The Historical Society moved to its current Elizabeth Street home in 1950. Two other important Hartford institutions have been connected with the Atheneum during its history: The Watkinson Library, which was incorporated in 1858 and moved to Trinity College in 1952, and the Hartford Art School, founded in 1886 and relocated as part of the University of Hartford in 1964.

Today the Wadsworth Atheneum is considered as one of the best art museums in the country. Its wealth of treasures includes works of art from ancient times to the present. When the museum opened its doors for the first time, five historical scenes of the American Revolution by John Trumbull were on display. Wadsworth had married Trumbull's niece, Faith, and when the painter died at the age of 87, he bequeathed five more of his paintings to the museum.

Frederick Edwin Church, a personal friend of Wadsworth, was born in Hartford in 1826. Church became a prominent 19th-century artist and was connected with the Hudson River school of painting. Some of his paintings hang in the Atheneum. His extraordinary home on the Hudson now is a national shrine.

The early years of the present century saw two major additions to the museum, both created by or for famous Hartford sons. The Morgan Memorial was presented by J. P. Morgan in memory of his father, Junius Spencer Morgan. The Colt Memorial was presented by Elizabeth Hart Jarvis Colt. Benjamin Wistar Morris was the architect for both these additions. The two Memorials contain, in part, fascinating personal collections of the Morgan family and unique Colt artifacts as well as Colt firearms.

Completed in 1934, the Avery Memorial was built to honor philanthropist and collector Samuel Putnam Avery, Jr. The architects were Morris and O'Connor of New York. This building contains a theater which saw the world premiere of the Gertrude Stein/Virgil Thomson opera "Four Saints in Three Acts." It also houses the Lions Gallery of the Senses, which emphasizes sensory exploration of artworks or environments for the sighted and the visually impaired. The Lions Gallery, which first opened its doors in 1972, was the culmination of a project begun by the Ladies Visiting Committee of the Connecticut Institute for the Blind in 1967. Research for the facility was conducted by Mary Pope Cheney, and financial support came from the Lions International District 23B, the Howard and Bush Foundation and the Concordia Foundation.

In March of 1968 the Atheneum began an extensive renovation program which was completed the following year. Hartford's Huntington, Darbee and Dollard were the architects. The exteriors of the old buildings were carefully retained. This was extremely difficult, and an expensive process in the case of the original Gothic structure of 1842. Each stone was numbered and the entire building dismantled, then reassembled exactly as it had been on the outside, yet completely new on the inside.

The Auerbach Library is located in the original Atheneum building in the space formerly occupied by the Young Men's Institute. This space was renovated through the generosity of the late Beatrice Fox Auerbach in honor of her two daughters and furnished with the original woodwork from the Watkinson Library. Mrs. Auerbach was the owner of G. Fox & Company, founded by her grandfather, Gershon Fox. A very successful businesswoman, Mrs. Auerbach, in true Hartford tradition, was always more than willing to do her best for her native city.

In recent years the museum was thoroughly renovated and much more of its vast collection was put on view.

The MATRIX gallery features changing exhibits of works by contemporary artists.

In 1774 a group of Hartford citizens formed a private club to purchase "a collection of useful and religious books for the benefit of themselves and families, and the promotion of virtue and useful knowledge." This club, originally known as the Hartford Library Company, was incorporated by the state legislature in 1792.

In 1838 the Hartford Young Men's Institute was organized. One of its purposes was to make books available to the young men of the community for an annual subscription fee. The following year the Hartford Library Company merged with the Institute. In 1844 the Institute moved into the newly constructed Wadsworth Atheneum, where it remained for the next 113 years. In January of 1878 the Institute's name was changed to the Hartford Library Association. Five years later a special act of the General Assembly authorized the City of Hartford to give the library some financial support. Therefore, on May 9, 1893, its name was changed again to the Hartford Public Library, although the library is to this day a private corporation.

The present headquarters of the Hartford Public Library was designed by Hartford architect Sage Goodwin and opened to the public on January 2, 1957. The structure is unique in that it spans a four-lane highway. It sits astride a former Hartford landmark, a stone bridge constructed over the Park or Little River in 1834. At the time this was considered one of America's engineering marvels as it was one of the first keystone bridges in the country. This bridge is still visible if you drive along the highway under the library. But the Little River is no longer to be seen as it now flows through a conduit under the road on its way to the Connecticut River!

Today the main library and its eight branches contain more than 400,000 volumes, 3,000 phonograph records and thousands of mounted pictures. The Hartford Collection of books by and about Hartford and its residents is especially interesting.

HARTFORD PUBLIC LIBRARY

500 Main Street
525-9121

9 a.m.-9 p.m. Mon.-Thurs.
9 a.m.-5 p.m. Friday &
Saturday (October through
May, Sundays 1 p.m.-5 p.m.)

CONNECTICUT HISTORICAL COMMISSION (BULL HOUSE)

59 South Prospect Street
566-3005

Office open Monday through Friday, 8:30 a.m. to 4:30 p.m. Closed holidays.

The historic brick townhouse, headquarters of the Connecticut Historical Commission, was built by Amos Bull in 1785. The Connecticut Historical Commission, a state agency established in 1955, is responsible for implementing programs designed to preserve in perpetuity the cultural heritage of Connecticut. In order to meet the goals and needs of historic preservation in Connecticut, the Commission administers and makes available to all a program of services in all geographic areas of the state.

The Bulls were a very prominent and numerous Connecticut family. Amos was born in Enfield, but lived in Farmington, Wethersfield, and New York City as well as Hartford. Like most Yankees, he was a versatile fellow. As a school teacher and choir master he apparently did well. But he also tried his hand successfully as a merchant. While residing in New York City during the American Revolution he was arrested for allegedly selling goods to the British whose warships were anchored off New York harbor. But he pleaded innocent to all charges and was exonerated.

Amos Bull had five wives. Two died while married to him, two he divorced, and one outlived him by fifteen years. Wife #1, Lucy Norton, produced one daughter in 1769 and died two years later. Wife #2, Catherine Lush, with whom he lived in the Silas Deane House in Wethersfield, turned out to be ten years older than her unsuspecting husband and was also childless. Bull's first divorce involved this spouse. When he petitioned the Connecticut General Assembly for a divorce in 1787, he accused Catherine of numerous vices: "Intemperance, Inchastity, Fals(e)hood, Profane Cursing and Swearing, as well as the most intolerable Brawling and Contention." A practical and ambitious fellow, Bull pointed out to the Yankee legislators that a man in his position required a wife "who might render him happy in the conjugal bed and be useful to him in the way of business." Sympathetic with Bull's plight, the legislators granted him a divorce and he immediately married his next-door neighbor, Abigail Webb, whose former Wethersfield home, like the Silas Deane House, is now preserved as a museum.

Abigail became the first Mrs. Bull to occupy the brick townhouse that her husband built on South Main Street on a narrow lot that he had purchased from his uncle. In 1788 when Bull constructed his new home there were only 250 houses in Hartford and most of these were made of wood. According to tradition, the bricks came from nearby Windsor and the brownstone from down-river quarries at Portland. The fact that the townhouse was built of such sturdy materials is no doubt one reason why it has managed to survive the ravages of Hartford's various urban revolutions.

Abigail Webb Bull was a "good" wife in that she bore her husband two children. Unfortunately they both died in infancy. The front portion of their new home was arranged as a store. No doubt Abigail assisted her spouse by minding the store in which they sold linens, hardware and household items. One of their most noteworthy sales were made in 1798 to the State of Connecticut when Bull provided the locks, hooks and brass nails for the new State House in Hartford...now the Old State House! Just down the street from the Bulls, Dr. Daniel Butler built his new home. (See Butler-McCook Homestead).

Amos Bull, as choirmaster, also frequented the South Congregational Church (not the present building) although he himself had joined the Episcopal Christ Church that had been constructed on Main Street in 1792.

In 1801, for some unrecorded reason, Bull divorced his third wife. Soon after he married Charlotte Tryon and began making plans for opening a school in his home. He advertised, "(The) Reading Academy is open at present for a few scholars; females are preferred. None need apply but such as are well disposed to learn and improve. There is nothing in common education so much mistaken or neglected as ing...In this school are taught SPELLING, READING, GRAMMAR, GEOGRAPHY and other things useful and necessary. The school is small, the terms are moderate, and the utmost attention is paid to every pupil."

The school was successful. Since Hartford in those days was an active publishing center of school books, Amos Bull's advice and endorsement were frequently sought by local book publishers. Unfortunately wife #4 died in 1809. She left her husband with five children, some of whom were probably adopted since she and her spouse were both in their fifties at the turn of the century. The following year he married Elizabeth Spencer, who shared his pedagogic enthusiasm. They soon opened an evening school as well as the Reading Academy. Elizabeth continued to be Bull's faithful helpmate until his death in 1825.

Four years before his death, Amos Bull sold his brick townhouse to two men named Burr and Robins who were listed in the deed as "partners in trade." They may have used the place as a combination home and store. Until the end of the first quarter of the 20th century the place, passed through the hands of 13 owners, being used sometimes as a home, a store, or both. The old Bull house finally became the property of Capitol Motors from 1939-1957. This company bought the property to display cars and decided to remove the old townhouse. Then they found that it would be less expensive to move it into the back portion of the Main Street lot and to remodel the place for offices rather than build a new office headquarters. The second floor was rented to the Resolute Insurance Company. For a few years after Capitol

Motors sold the property, the Bull House was occupied by a Greek restaurant, the Apollo. Finally, in 1966 thanks to the interest, intervention and direction of Mayor Ann Uccello, this historic Hartford landmark was purchased with federal and private funds. Frances A. McCook donated a portion of her home lot as a site for the place which the Senate planned to use as headquarters for its newly formed Connecticut Historical Commission. Thus for a second time the Bull House was moved, this time to a hopefully permanent location about 400 feet from the lot on which it was first built. How appropriate that two of Hartford's remaining 18th-century homes should now stand together as adjoining museums!

The commission allows free admission for scheduled groups with advanced reservations to visit the Commission's historic sites and museums.

The great educator Henry Barnard was born in this lovely Greek Revival town house in 1811. Because his father was a wealthy merchant, young Barnard did not immediately go to work after his graduation from Yale in 1830. Instead he took an extended trip to Europe. Being particularly interested in the field of education, he availed himself of this opportunity to make the acquaintance of the most noted European educators of that time and visited various new types of schools like the Pestalozzi schools in Switzerland.

Although he had intended to practice law on his return to Hartford, Barnard entered politics instead and was elected at age 26 to the Connecticut General Assembly, in which he served for three terms. While in the legislature he was appointed secretary of the Connecticut Board of Education. It was during his political career that he determined to dedicate his life to the cause of public education. His goal was to create public schools that would be "good enough for the best, but cheap enough for the poorest."

HENRY BARNARD HOUSE

118 Main Street

A National Historic Landmark. Henry Barnard's birthplace is now St. Elizabeth House, operated by Mercy Housing and Shelter Corporation, a social service organization.
246-5643

His first achievement was the introduction and passage of a bill "to provide for the better supervision of the common schools." Henry Barnard recognized the fact that the state itself must assume responsibility for the education of the people. Thus he pioneered three very revolutionary projects: first, to raise the status of teaching by making it a permanent, well-paid profession open only to trained individuals; second, to make the school house comfortable, well-equipped and conveniently located; third, to install libraries in the schools or at least in every town. This, of course, required money which the Connecticut taxpayers were, at first, unwilling to appropriate.

When his political party, the Whigs, was defeated in 1842, Barnard's opportunities to work in Connecticut were temporarily ended. So he simply transferred his efforts to Rhode Island, where, in time, he organized the Rhode Island Institute of Instruction, the oldest state teachers' association in the United States. He also established town libraries in 29 of the state's 32 towns and inaugurated traveling model class rooms which he took from place to place as examples of what the public schools should be!

Under his direction the normal school in New Britain, Connecticut, opened its doors to 35 students on May 15, 1850. The following year Barnard became the principal of this school as well as secretary of the Connecticut State Board of Education. This same year he published a book, *School Architecture*, the first book ever written on the subject in this country. Shortly thereafter he also published a two-volume work on *Normal Schools* which was used well into the 20th century. In 1855 he began a truly monumental project which for 26 years consumed much of his time and most of his private fortune, *The American Journal of Education*. Consisting of 32 large volumes, this opus has been described by a leading modern educator as "the greatest possible contribution to education." It examines every phase of education from the earliest schools of antiquity to Barnard's day. Presenting a survey of the educational systems of every country, it discusses the problems of the delinquent, the sub-normal, the criminal, and the physically handicapped. It treats of vocational and trade schools, military and naval academies, in short, every aspect and detail of teaching mankind.

Barnard received many invitations to serve as the head of various colleges, and he accepted two: one as Chancellor of the University of Wisconsin, and one as president of St. John's College, Annapolis. However, his health failed and he did not stay long at either institution.

One of Barnard's great dreams was to create a national bureau of education for the collection and dissemination of educational information. When, at long last, the U.S. Congress created such a department in 1867, Henry Barnard was invited to become the first U.S. Commissioner of Education, a position he held for three years.

The final 30 years of his life he spent in semi-retirement in his Hartford home, writing his *American Journal of Education* and keeping up his fight for public schools with undiminished enthusiasm. Today his remarkable personal collection of school books may be found at the Watkinson Library at Trinity College. His fellow Hartfordite, J. P. Morgan, purchased the collection and donated it to the library in his honor. In 1900 Henry Barnard died in the house of his birth at the age of eighty-nine, still full of vision and enthusiasm.

After his death Barnard's home was purchased by the Roman Catholic Daughters of the Holy Spirit. They named the place St. Elizabeth Guest House, built a large addition to the rear, and used it as a home for working girls. St. Elizabeth's mission is to reach the hungry and homeless in Hartford.

The Henry Barnard House became a National Historic Landmark in 1966.

THE GREATER HARTFORD ARCHITECTURE CONSERVANCY

278 Farmington Ave.
525-0279

The Greater Hartford Architecture Conservancy held its first general meeting on December 12, 1973, at The Connecticut Historical Society. Since then GHAC has grown by leaps and bounds to a membership of more than 1,000 individuals and almost 30 corporations. The Conservancy has greatly increased local appreciation of the remaining Victorian architecture in Hartford and has popularized the concept of "recycling" rather than destroying old buildings in the name of "urban renewal." Both professionals and volunteers at GHAC have done an excellent job of researching and documenting downtown structures of architectural or historical merit.

Since 1976 GHAC has raised money for a revolving fund for historic preservation. The fund is used to purchase threatened and significant buildings that will then be sold to buyers who will restore them. Proceeds from the sales of properties are returned to the fund to make future purchases. The James Colt House and the Day-Taylor House are both fine examples of what can be done to refurbish formerly abandoned buildings. This type of housing is essential to Hartford's long-range goal of making the city an attractive place of residence for those who work here.

In its first 15 years GHAC directly assisted in $23 million worth of projects that created more than 300 housing units, two-thirds of them for low- and moderate-income families. Not only does the agency promote historic rehabilitations and affordable housing, it creates new jobs and acts as a catalyst for new developments in all of Hartford County.

The Conservancy sponsors educational programs, technical assistance programs, lectures, walking tours, and annual rehabs.

In 1856 this Italianate style home was constructed for James B. Colt, brother of the great gunmaker, Colonel Samuel Colt. Later it became the home of General William Buel Franklin, vice-president and general manager of Colt's, then the home of Mr. and Mrs. George H. Day and their five lively children. George Day was president and treasurer of the Pope Manufacturing Company, and general manager of the Association of Licensed Automobile Manufacturers of America. Mrs. Day and their daughter, Josephine, were pioneer Connecticut suffragettes. George, Jr., became a much respected judge.

By 1920 this section of Hartford began to decline as well-to-do families moved westward, and large homes like this were soon turned into boarding houses. The most recent owner ran it as an apartment house with 13 units. In 1974 a fire broke out on the back stairway and caused considerable smoke damage, so the house was abandoned.

Even so, Howard Nannen, a city planner with the Greater Hartford Community Development Corporation, decided that the house could be saved and recycled. He joined forces with Thomas Giardini, a local builder, and formed the Hartford Heritage Corporation to manage the building. With the assistance of local banks, the Greater Hartford Architecture Conservancy and 11 limited partners, they purchased the old James Colt house for $35,000. By September of 1976 they had charmingly remodeled the place into eight very attractive living units which were immediately rented to eager tenants who appreciated this type of quality housing within the city limits. Now the house is a model of what can be done to bring old city mansions back to life.

JAMES B. COLT HOUSE

154 Wethersfield Ave.

ARMSMEAR

80 Wethersfield Ave
246-4025

This was originally the home of Samuel Colt, inventor and manufacturer of the revolver. It was registered as a National Historic Landmark in 1966 and is now a home for the widows and daughters of Episcopal clergymen. Visitors are welcome.

Colonel Samuel Colt, this country's first great industrial tycoon, was born in Hartford in 1814. He was the son of a local businessman, Christopher Colt, and the grandson of John Caldwell, a much respected merchant and the first president of the Hartford Bank. However the Colts and the Caldwells suffered severe financial losses during the War of 1812. So, although young Sam was born with a silver spoon in his mouth, it was soon snatched away from him.

The official motto of the Colt family was "Vincit Qui Patitur" ... "He Conquers Who Suffers." But young Sam humorously claimed that the real family motto he learned as a child at his mother's knee was, "It is better to be the head of a louse than the tail of a lion!"

No scholar, but even as a youth an ardent inventor, Colt was expelled from a private school in Massachusetts for setting off an experimental underwater explosion. His father then sent him off to sea as a midshipman. During the voyage he whiled away his idle hours by whittling a wooden model of the revolver which would later make him rich and famous. He was 16 years old.

Before the gun business occupied the major part of his time, he invented the nation's first successful electrically discharged submarine mine, conducted a telegraph business that utilized the first cable ever laid underwater, and developed the first waterproof ammunition.

Courtesy of The Colt Collection, The Hartford Public Library.

Sam was a master showman. Unable to persuade anyone to invest in his new revolver, he traveled all around New England and down the Mississippi River staging demonstrations of the ludicrous effects of "laughing gas" on human subjects. He billed himself as "Dr. Coult," and his shows were a great success. With the money he earned from them he was able to start manufacturing revolvers.

His first gun factory in New Jersey failed for lack of orders. U.S. Army officials were unimpressed by Colt's new-fangled pistol with its strange, many-chambered revolving breech. Colt countered by either giving or selling below cost his guns to lesser army men who were actually in the front lines of the country's battles. Colt revolvers were thus successfully used during the war with the Seminole Indians in 1837 and by Texas Rangers in the war between Texas and Mexico. When war broke out between the United States and Mexico in 1846, Colonel Zachary Taylor, who had already tested Colt's new gun when fighting against the Seminoles, was put in charge of a large body of American troops. Taylor absolutely insisted that the U.S. government supply him and his men with a thousand Colt revolvers. The guns were enthusiastically received by the soldiers, resulting in more orders. American pioneers, streaming westward, also prized the new weapon that, in those rough and tumble days, was accurately dubbed the "Peacemaker" or "Judge Colt."

Colt's business grew at a phenomenal pace. Almost overnight he became one of the wealthiest men in the country. Those who worked for him prospered too. Long before Henry Ford instituted his $5 a day, Sam Colt recognized both the human and financial validity of paying industrial workers a liberal wage and creating for them a decent environment. He astonished Yankee Hartford by paying his factory manager, E. K. Root, the highest salary ever paid a man in Root's position. But Root earned every penny of it, as did all Colt's employees, for he drove them as hard as he drove himself.

Colt was the first American manufacturer to have an overseas plant. When the British army refused to buy any foreign-made guns, he set up a factory in England!

Colonel Colt at age 42 turned his thoughts to love and domesticity. The object of his affection was Elizabeth Hart Jarvis of Middletown. A young woman of impeccable social standing, her father was Rev. William Jarvis and an uncle had been Episcopal bishop of Connecticut. The wedding took place on June 5, 1856, in Middletown. The groom and his friends arrived from Hartford that morning on a private yacht. They were accompanied by the Colt Band, which

*"Armsmear" the home of Colonel
& Mrs. Colt, as it appeared in it's
heyday.*

entertained them during their voyage down the Connecticut River. After the ceremony the newlyweds departed on a four-month tour abroad which included a visit to Russia, where they were personally received by Czar Alexander II, one of Colt's first enthusiastic customers.

When the Colts returned to Hartford from their honeymoon, they settled down at Armsmear, the handsome Italianate villa the Colonel had built for his bride. Armsmear, the design of which has been attributed to architect Octavius Jordan, was frequently renovated and enlarged with "Gothic piazzas", additional towers, new rooms, and a glorious glass conservatory. "A long irregular front lies parallel with Wethersfield Avenue," Mrs. Colt described her home, "its lines well broken by the covered arch entrance into the grounds, the retreating facade of the dining-room, the oriel window and the corner tower...suggesting at once the elegance and the refinement, the comfort and the privacy of such a home. It is of massive stone, spacious, towered, domed, with large halls for state occasions and crowds, as well as cozy cabinets with boudoirs for household comfort and genuine sociability..."

Behind Armsmear the Colts built an enormous greenhouse, 2,632 feet in length, in which their gardeners grew a vast array of flowering plants and luscious fruits. Their "grapery" yielded over a ton of grapes each year; the fig house produced almost 2,000 figs, and nearly 7,000 peaches and nectarines were gathered annually. They even grew bananas and pineapples under glass. The grounds around Armsmear were magnificent and included a deer park and a lake complete with swans.

The Colts' marriage was brief but happy, marred by the tragic early deaths of three of their four children. The Colonel himself died when he was only 48 years of age, worn out by a life as tempestuous as it was creative. His widow carried on as the Grande Dame of Hartford, busying herself with a variety of good works and charities until her death in 1905. Guided by the ubiquitous Francis Goodwin, she willed her estate to the city to be used as a public park. Armsmear, radically altered, became a home for the widows and daughters of Episcopal clergymen. The drawing room, however, does contain some interesting Colt memorabilia, and there are pictures of how Armsmear looked at the height of its glory.

HARTFORD STAGE COMPANY

Church Street
between Main and
Trumbull streets
Box Office: 525-4258
Administrative Office:
525-5601

Formerly located at 65 Kinsley Street, The Hartford Stage Company, a repertory theater founded in 1964, is celebrating its 25th season in 1989. It brings to this Capitol Region the best in new, contemporary, and classical dramas and comedies. This long-awaited three-story building of the Stage Company was opened October 14, 1977. Designed by Robert Venturi, it can accommodate audiences of 350 and has room to expand to a capacity of 467. The theater's striking facade of red and grey-black brick arranged in a herringbone pattern is intended to resemble the patterned masonry of the Mark Twain House at Nook Farm in this city.

In the 1870s Mark Twain dealt a sharp blow to local Puritanical prejudices against the theater by encouraging the theatrical ambitions of his young Nook Farm neighbor, William Gillette. When Will went to New York City, ostensibly to "study," he actually had a part in Mark Twain's dramatization of *The Gilded Age*, a book Twain wrote in collaboration with Gillette's brother-in-law, Charles Dudley Warner. In 1875, when Will and *The Gilded Age* company appeared at Hartford's Allyn Theater, the residents of Nook Farm shocked the city fathers by turning out in force to cheer his performance!

Hartford's theatrical history has been truly remarkable. Puritan attitudes prevented theater production in Connecticut until the late 18th century. The American Revolution ushered in an era of more broad-minded attitudes toward popular entertainment for a professional touring company. In 1794 a theater was constructed in the center of town and the street on which it stood was named Theater Street. Aware of the prejudices of their audiences, the actors stressed the idea that their plays were "educational" and "morally uplifting." But the city fathers were not favorably impressed. The *Connecticut Courant* sternly observed that the theater had been injurious to public morality...a majority opinion. Not only was the theater closed, but it was turned into a Sunday school! Theater Street became Temple Street, and a bill was passed in the Connecticut General Assembly in 1800 banning all dramatic productions throughout the entire state!

For 50 years this dramatic drought continued, until finally, in 1852 the Legislature decided to allow towns to make their own decisions concerning theatrical performances. So in 1853 George Wyatt started a Dramatic Lyceum in Hartford, which failed. In 1869 Roberts' Opera House opened on Main Street. Although cramped and dingy, this theater proved a success. It was joined by the Allyn Theater, located within the Allyn House, where the Civic Center now stands. Despite Will Gillette's pioneering performance, serious lovers of the drama were not satisfied until the opening of Parsons' Theater on the corner of Central Row and Prospect Street in 1896, a major event in Hartford's theatrical life. Then the best shows came to the city, some to open and some on tour. In 1920 the Schuberts took over the theater and ran it with distinction. Financially weakened by the Great Depression of the 1930s, Parsons' went downhill and finally was torn down to make way for the huge Constitution Plaza complex.

In 1951 the New Parsons' Theater opened on Main Street and died after three tormented seasons. The Hartford Stage Company, happily, is obviously here to stay.

Hartford is the hometown of numerous stage, screen, and TV personalities. They include not only Will Gillette but also Otis Skinner, Katharine Hepburn, Sophie Tucker, Ed Begley, Tom Tryon, Katharine Houghton, Mike Yellin, Marietta Canty, Linda Evans, Ann Corio, Gary Merrill, Charles Nelson Reilly, Totie Fields, Louis Nye, Rita Gann Morley, and Norman Lear.

**BUSHNELL
MEMORIAL HALL**

166 Capitol Avenue

Primary performance hall for:

Connecticut Opera: presents four major opera productions each season, featuring both internationally known
opera stars and regional American talent. 527-0713

Hartford Ballet: one of the country's foremost regional
dance ensembles, presenting four company productions as
well as visiting companies each season. 527-0713

Hartford Symphony Orchestra: noted professional
symphony orchestra presenting several annual series with
outstanding visiting artists. 246-6807

The Bushnell's own programs include Broadway and
other touring productions, visiting orchestras and artists, lecture and travel series, and performances by various local arts
organizations. 246-6807 box office, 527-3123 general office.

Clergyman and civic reformer Horace Bushnell of
Hartford was at one time almost tried for religious heresy
by his fellow Congregational ministers. Ultimately they
honored him as Hartford's leading intellectual. As one of
his associates commented, "He lived always in two worlds,
his head among the stars and his feet firmly planted on the
solid earth, moving along the ways of common life."

Born in 1802 in Bantam in the rugged Litchfield Hills,
Bushnell graduated from Yale University in 1827 and became
first a teacher, then a lawyer. In 1833, however, he gave up
what had promised to be a brilliant legal career and was
ordained a minister in the North Church that used to stand
on Main Street in Hartford. That same year he married
Mary Apthorp of New Haven.

During his Hartford ministry, Bushnell wrote and published a number of books, including his classic *Christian
Nurture.* Twice he was invited, but refused, to become the
president of a college, first of Middlebury, then the University of California. Although ill health compelled him to live
for a while in the more congenial climate of California, during which period he assisted a fellow Connecticut Yankee,

Collis P. Huntington, to lay out the Central Pacific Railroad
through the Sierras, he always ultimately returned to his
theological, literary, and civic endeavors in Hartford.
Besides spearheading the creation of the city's first public
park, he also brought about the building of Hartford's first
public reservoir. It was located on Lord's Hill, the present
site of the Hartford Insurance Group.

In a book about her father, Mary Bushnell Cheney
(Mrs. Frank Woodbridge Cheney of Manchester) took note
of Bushnell's uniquely determined spirit. Even when "wor-
ried, wearied, and hindered" in his effort to bring about
some civic improvement he counseled that a reformer "must
never sleep, never be beaten, never desist. And if, by many
years of toil, he gets his work on far enough to...take care of
itself, he does well."

For many years another daughter, Dotha Bushnell
Hillyer, wife of banker Appleton R. Hillyer, cherished the
idea of constructing a great Memorial to her father in Hartford. Mrs. Hillyer herself was a devoted and active citizen
of the city. As early as 1919 Mrs. Hillyer, with the assistance
of her daughter and son-in-law, Mr. and Mrs. Charles F. T.
Seaverns, and a small group of incorporators began to make
plans for the building. It was their hope to erect an auditorium that would be not only a beautiful addition to the
architecture of the city but a vital and continuing force in
the cultural life of the community.

Architects Corbett, Harrison and MacMurray of New
York City drew up plans for the project which was Colonial
in spirit, but not in a strictly architectural sense, because of
its great size. The builder was R. F. Jones and Company of
Hartford. The cornerstone was laid by Mrs. Seaverns on
October 16, 1928, and the completed building dedicated by
her on January 13, 1930, just two years before her mother's
death. The huge organ, one of the largest concert instruments of its kind in the country, was especially
manufactured by the Austin Organ Company of this city.

The Hall has undergone two major renovations. In
1973 Yale's expert theater technician George Izenour collab-
orated with architects Venturi and Rauch of Philadelphia to
modernize the facility. The Hall's acoustics were improved,

a promenade lobby was added to the rear of the orchestra level, new sound and lighting equipment was installed, and the organ was rebuilt.

The most ambitious renovation in the Hall's history was completed in 1984. To improve sight lines to the stage, the floors of the mezzanine and balcony were resloped and their seats restaggered. Seventy-one new seats were added, increasing the Hall's total capacity to 2,799. The refurbishment of the theater's upper levels also called for the overhaul of out-dated ventilation systems and the addition of two new bars and a lounge.

The most visible changes resulted from the complete redecoration and refurnishing of the Main Foyer, Founder's Lobby, Promenade Gallery, and Colonial Room. In these public spaces, new lighting and signage were introduced.

Behind the scenes, the green room was completely renovated and two meeting rooms, a service kitchen, and a new administrative office suite were created.

Significant exterior projects focused on the Hall's West entrance. A marquee canopy was installed as well as a set of electric eye doors which will improve access for the handicapped.

Stecker, LeBau & Arneill of Hartford provided all architectural and design services for this $1.6 million project.

The Bushnell Memorial has presented to the citizens of Hartford an impressive array of the world's most celebrated leaders and talented artists in the fields of music, drama, film, politics, entertainment, and culture.

NOOK FARM COMPLEX

77 Forest Street
525-9317

Nook Farm Complex consists of two juxtaposed organizations. The Mark Twain Memorial owns and operates the Mark Twain House while the Stowe-Day Foundation owns and operates the Harriet Beecher Stowe House and the Stowe-Day Library. Both organizations jointly operate the Visitors Center, where all tours start. For information about hours and admission rates, including group tours, telephone 525-9317. Both houses open year-round: Sept. - May, Tues. - Sat., 9:30 - 4:00 p.m.; Sun., 1 - 4, closed Monday and major holidays. June - Aug., open daily, 10 a.m. - 4:30 p.m. All tours are with guides and take approximately 1 hr. 30 mins.

for both houses. The Museum Shop at the Visitors Center offers a wide selection of books and gifts appropriate to the Victorian era and Nook Farm notables.

Nook Farm was well known to the literary world of the 19th century because it harbored such a remarkable number of intellectuals and authors. Most prominent were Mark Twain and Harriet Beecher Stowe. Also well known were Charles Dudley Warner, editor of the *Hartford Courant* and a popular author; Isabella Beecher Hooker, wife of John, sister of Harriet and a leader of the Connecticut suffrage movement; Francis Gillette, U. S. Senator and abolitionist; and his son, William Gillette, the popular actor whose romantic "castle" on the Connecticut River is now open to the public.

One of the chief reasons Mark Twain and the other *literati* of Nook Farm decided to make Hartford their home was the fact that the city was in their time a great center of the publishing business. In 1783, largely through the efforts of Hartford native Noah Webster (see Noah Webster House in West Hartford), the U.S. Congress framed a federal law "for the Encouragement of Literature and Genius." Thanks to the protection offered by this law, Hartford became a thriving center of publishing soon after the American Revolution. By 1820 the city had 20 publishing houses. The idea of selling magazines by subscription was pioneered in Hartford, the first American children's magazine brought out in 1789, and the first American cookbook in 1796. Hartford's *Cottage Bible* was a best seller for many decades. Until the turn of the 20th century the city was the home of this country's leading publishers of school books. It was no accident that West Hartford's Noah Webster pioneered the first American spellers, grammars and dictionaries.

When selling new books, Hartford's book peddlers used the "sample" technique. They showed the customer a nicely bound dummy with the first few chapters of the proposed volume. Then they took orders for the complete book. In this way local publishers avoided the pitfall of over-printing. These old peddlers' dummies are now collector's items. In the old days Hartford's literary wares were distributed door-to-door all over the nation. So it is not surprising that the Fuller Brush Man was also spawned in Hartford.

In 1879 David M. Smyth of this city invented and patented the first successful book sewing machine. Today Smyth Manufacturing Company makes several complete lines of machinery for manufacturing hard-bound books, and Smyth equipment is used in almost every book bindery throughout the world.

Mark Twain's investment in the Paige Typesetter was not such a success. This complicated machine that eventually bankrupted the famous author may now be seen in the basement of the Mark Twain Memorial.

Soon after the American Revolution the Hartford Wits enjoyed a national reputation for their literary works. Noah Webster was their friend and admirer. (See Noah Webster's House.)

During the first half of the 19th century Hartford's most celebrated author was Lydia Huntley Sigourney known throughout the United States as "The Sweet Singer of Hartford." Sigourney Street was named in her honor. After the Civil War the production of books in this city rose sharply. In 1884 the runaway bestseller was General U. S. Grant's *Personal Memoirs*, published by Mark Twain. Twain wanted to aid Grant, who was by then an old man, mortally ill, and almost bankrupt. More than 300,000 copies of the book were sold, and General Grant received the largest royalty check ever given to an author up to that time...half a million dollars!

In modern times the authors of Greater Hartford who have achieved renown are Wallace Stevens, the poet-insurance executive who won the Pulitzer prize for poetry in 1955, and Elizabeth G. Speare, who has twice won the Newberry Award for the best children's book of the year. Other well-known local authors of children's books are Oliver Butterworth and Jane Quigg. Tom Tryon has also achieved wide recognition as a novelist as well as an actor.

Early in the 20th century Hartford's preeminence as a publishing center began to decline. However, there are still some strong local printing establishments.

In 1959 a group of public spirited citizens created a non-profit corporation called Connecticut Educational Television. The following year the State Board of Education authorized this group to activate educational channels and agreed to cooperate in their endeavor. When Channel 24 began operating October 1, 1962, it was one of only three public television stations in New England.

CPTV provides the public with a constructive alternative in television programming in the areas of information, instruction, and entertainment. The station does not sell advertising. Funds for its maintenance are provided by individuals, service organizations, corporations, foundations, and the government--local, state, and federal. The annual CPTV auction is a particularly enjoyable and well-supported event.

CONNECTICUT PUBLIC TELEVISION

24 Summit Street
278-5310

For tours call the Public Relations Department.

Harriet Beecher Stowe lived in this charming Victorian "cottage" from 1873 until her death in 1896. The architect and builder of the house are unknown, but the design suggests the country homes created by Andrew J. Downing and Calvin Vaux. Beautifully restored, authentically furnished and refurbished with Stowe possessions and memorabilia, the home is a delightful "period piece."

Mrs. Stowe's most famous novel, *Uncle Tom's Cabin*, was no doubt the most influential anti-slavery novel published prior to the Civil War. Less well-known are her other excellent novels concerning life in New England. Mrs. Stowe was also very interested in interior decorating and gardening and, during the warm months of the year, the gardens surrounding her old home are exceptionally attractive. She and her sister Catherine Beecher wrote *The American Women's Home* which became very popular among the ladies because it suggested advanced ideas concerning home decor and household economy. Many of their concepts are exemplified in this house, which now is owned and maintained by the Stowe-Day Foundation.

HARRIET BEECHER STOWE HOUSE

73 Forest Street

(See Nook Farm Complex for information about hours and group rates; 525-9317 for 24 hr. recorded information)

Portrait of Harriet Beecher Stowe c. 1853 by Artist Alanson Fisher (1807-1884). Photo courtesy The Stowe-Day Foundation.

MARK TWAIN MEMORIAL

351 Farmington Ave.

(See Nook Farm Complex for information about hours and group rates; 525-9317 for 24 hr. recorded information)

When Mark Twain (Samuel Clemens) built this house in 1874, the *Hartford Times* commented, "The novelty displayed in the architecture of the building, the oddity of its internal arrangements, and the fame of its owner will all conspire to make it a house of note for a long time to come."

In 1896 Samuel Clemens himself wrote: "To us our house was not insentient matter; it had a heart and a soul and eyes to see us with and approvals and solicitudes and deep sympathies; it was of us, and we were in its confidence and lived in its grace and in the peace of its benediction."

The house was constructed when the great author was at the peak of financial prosperity which enabled him to indulge every whim or extravagance. His architect, Edward Tuckerman Potter, provided him with designs which were a radical departure from boxier examples of traditional American architecture. In fact this house, with its elaborate brick work, sweeping cornices and romantic gables, is more European in origin than American. German building magazines of the period show several examples of very picturesque "villas" that closely resemble this work of Potter.

The elaborately stenciled interior of Twain's home is equally flamboyant. In 1881 it was extensively redecorated by Louis Comfort Tiffany and the Associated Artists. This stenciling has now been beautifully restored. The decor of the interior is further enhanced by the remarkable furnishings and art objects the Clemens family collected on their many trips abroad. The over-all effect is one of magnificence, clutter, and genuine warmth which express the exuberance of Mark Twain's unique personality. The building was registered as an historic landmark in 1963.

During the time he resided here (1874-1891), Twain wrote and published seven of his major works including *The Adventures of Tom Sawyer, Adventures of Huckleberry Finn,* and *A Connecticut Yankee in King Arthur's Court.*

The ill-fated Paige typesetting machine, which may be viewed in the basement of the house, was designated an historic engineering landmark in 1976. Named for its inventor, James W. Paige, the intricate machine was intended to revolutionize the printing business. Unfortunately it only succeeded in making its investors $2 million poorer. Twain himself lost almost $300,000. This loss, coupled with the failure of his New York publishing firm, forced him to close his Hartford home and set out on a lecture tour to pay his debts.

The residence of Mark Twain, Farmington Avenue, Hartford.

The library is housed in a fine Victorian mansion built in 1884 and designed by Francis Kimball of New York City. Kimball was the "architect on the job" for the "long walk" section of the Trinity College campus under the famous English architect William Burges. Kimball designed this handsome home for Franklin Chamberlin, a local attorney. Later it was purchased by Willie O. Burr, owner of the *Hartford Times*. Burr's sister, Ella Burr McManus, donated the funds that were eventually used to purchase the giant *Stegosaurus* created by Alexander Calder that now stands on the Burr Mall in front of the *Hartford Times* building in the center city. Later Burr's mansion was renamed the Day House in honor of Katharine Day, benefactress of the Stowe-Day Foundation.

In 1973 the Stowe-Day Foundation completed an underground stack area for the library as well as renovations to the Chamberlin-Burr-Day House itself. The Stowe-Day Library is non-circulating. Certain books, exclusive of first editions and inscribed copies, may be borrowed through inter-library loan.

STOWE-DAY LIBRARY

77 Forest Street

(Open year-round to qualified researchers and students, Monday through Friday, 9 a.m. to 4:30 p.m., 522-9258). This fully catalogued research library contains 15,000 volumes, 4,000 pamphlets, and 150,000 manuscript items that deal with architecture, the decorative arts, history, and literature of the 19th century, with emphasis on Nook Farm residents and the abolitionist and woman suffrage movements. It includes as well extensive photographic collections on Harriet Beecher Stowe, her family, friends, and Hartford neighbors. The books and papers of the Mark Twain Memorial are also housed in this library.

THE CONNECTICUT HISTORICAL SOCIETY

1 Elizabeth Street
at Asylum Avenue
236-5621

*The **library** is open 9 a.m. to 5 p.m. Tuesday-Saturday (closed Saturdays from Memorial Day through Labor Day). Admission is free.*
*The **museum** is open 12 to 5 p.m. Tuesday-Sunday (Closed Saturdays from Memorial Day through Labor Day). Admission is free to CHS members; admission for non-members is $2 for adults, $1 for children 3-12, free to children under 3. Admission is free to the public the first Sunday of each month.*
*The **library** and **museum** are closed on Mondays year-round (except for tours scheduled in advance), and on major holidays.*
***Group and School Tour Visits**: Special arrangements should be made for guided group visits to the museum and/or library by advance reservation. Information can be obtained by calling 236-562l.*

The Connecticut Historical Society is one of the nation's oldest and most vigorous historical organizations. It was established in 1825 for the broad purpose of "discovering, procuring and preserving whatever may relate to the civil, ecclesiastical and natural history of Connecticut."

The Society was housed in the Wadsworth Atheneum in Hartford from 1843 until 1950, when it moved to its present location. The heart of the current building was originally constructed in 1928 as the home of Curtis H. Veeder. Architects were William F. Brooks, F. A. W. Glazier, and C. D. Adams of Hartford. Mr. Veeder won fame and fortune in 1894 by inventing the American cyclometer, forerunner of modern-day counting devices. Today Veeder Root Inc. of Hartford, a member of Veeder Industries Inc., leads the world in "numerics," which is the manufacture of counting and controlling instruments, such as the price meter on gasoline pumps, patented by the company in 1933. Hartford also pioneered the making of bicycles. It was while riding a Hartford- made Columbia bicycle that Mr. Veeder conceived the idea of a meter to measure how fast and far he was traveling.

Bookstacks were added to the original Veeder home in 1951, and the 250-seat Hoadley Auditorium was added in 1956 under the direction of Schutz and Goodwin, architects. Jeter & Cook were architects for a 30,000-square-foot addition in 1971 which brought the Society's physical plant to its current size of 63,000 square feet, set on eight beautifully landscaped acres in Hartford's west end.

The Society's museum collections of more than 100,000 objects are particularly strong in 17th- and 18th-century Connecticut furniture. The choice Seymour and Barbour furniture collections represent some of the finest examples of the colonial and early Republic periods, and are on permanent display. Individual pieces of earlier and later design which extend the range of the Society's holdings have been donated or purchased.

The collection of more than 600 paintings, ranging from the 17th century to the present, features the works of many American masters. Equally impressive are the Society's very large collections of early engravings, lithographs, and photographs. The extensive Morgan B. Brainard collection of 18th- and early-19th-century painted tavern signs is on permanent display in the auditorium.

Because the Society's collections are so varied and extensive, only a small portion of them can be displayed at any one time in the museum's nine galleries. Regularly changing exhibitions on a variety of topics, from the Charter Oak legend to Irish immigration to women's history to the state's role as an industrial pioneer, explore many important and intriguing historic themes.

The research library boasts a modern, superbly equipped reading room, in which amateur and professional researchers alike are welcome to consult the Society's remarkably rich collection of 100,000 books and two and a half million manuscripts. Among the library's many important special collections are manuscript and printed Connecticut and New England genealogical materials, titles printed in Connecticut from the introduction of printing in the state in 1709 down to the 20th century, and one of the nation's largest collections of early American children's books.

ISHAM-TERRY HOUSE

Built in 1854, the Isham-Terry House is a fine example of the Italianate style so popular before the Civil War. The house was purchased by Dr. Oliver Isham in 1896 and it remained the family home for 80 years until it was bequeathed to the Society by his sisters. The house is an imposing landmark with its distinctive tower, porches, and wide bracketed overhangs. Its rooms are filled with eclectic 19th-century furnishings in many design styles. Many original features, such as the gas lighting fixtures and decorative painted ceilings, are still in place.

Operated by the Antiquarian & Landmarks Society, Inc.
394 Main Street
247-8996

Open Sunday 12-4 p.m. (May 15-October 15)

THE HISTORICAL MUSEUM OF MEDICINE AND DENTISTRY

230 Scarborough St.
236-5613

*The **Museum** is open daily from 10 a.m. to 4 p.m. There is no admission charge; group tours can be arranged. Literature is regularly produced in the form of newsletters as well as research articles on artifacts in the collection.*

The Historical Museum of Medicine and Dentistry is a component of the Hartford Medical and Dental Societies. The Museum opened in 1973 with a collection of items left to the Societies over the years; since then, because of an active acquisition program, with the exception of the Smithsonian in Washington, the Museum is second to none throughout the United States.

The collection dates from the Revolutionary War to the first quarter of the 20th century with extensive collections in most of the medical specialty areas, such as obstetrics, urology, ophthalmology, and surgery. A large collection of historic equipment may be seen, including arm and leg splints, and blood-letting and trepanning instruments. The microscope collection dates to 1790. Dental instruments date to the colonial period.

One room of the Museum is devoted to a dental office of the 1920 era, and another room to Horace Wells, a Hartford dentist, who is credited with the discovery of general anesthesia.

Elsewhere in the Museum larger furnishings may be seen, such as medical examining tables from the Victorian period, electrical devices from the mid-19th century, and the more recent electro-cautery and diathermy units. A collection of basal metabolic units of the 1930s to '50s are also on display, as well as a large collection of physicians' hand bags from 1870 to 1950. The pharmacy collection is also not to be overlooked.

GREATER HARTFORD ARTS COUNCIL

The Hartford Courant
Arts Center
214 Farmington Ave
525-8629

Through the Greater Hartford Arts Council local businesses contribute substantially on an annual basis to a variety of arts organizations. The major beneficiaries are the Hartford Symphony, Hartford Ballet, Connecticut Opera Association, Wadsworth Atheneum, Bushnell Memorial Hall, and Hartford Stage Company. In 1987 the Hartford Courant Foundation provided the lead grant for an Arts Center, located at 226-228 Farmington Avenue, which has brought together under one roof the staffs of the performing arts organizations. Rehearsal space makes the Center a lively place.

In addition, several large corporations have their own

programs for promoting the arts. United Technologies has become one of the country's major arts supporters, contributing as much as $3 million annually to museums, libraries, and performing groups nationally and abroad. The Hartford Insurance Group makes its Wallace Stevens Theater and Tower Suite available to non-profit community groups for lectures and performances. For 20 years the Producing Guild has presented critically-acclaimed dramas and musicals on the stage of the Stevens Theater. Connecticut Bank & Trust Company's main office provides an attractive setting for its own art collection. Its latest contribution to public art is a series of 12 baked-enamel panels depicting railroad heralds by Robert Cottingham that are on permanent display at Union Station. Aetna Life & Casualty exhibits the works of Connecticut artists at the Aetna Institute Gallery, which produces six exhibits every year. Located at 205 Farmington Avenue, the Institute is open to the public. A large selection of art owned by Aetna is displayed throughout its corporate headquarters.

PUMP HOUSE GALLERY

Bushnell Park

The Pump House Gallery is a renovated space located in the pumping station in Bushnell Park. The gallery was established in 1985 through the efforts of the City of Hartford and the Bushnell Park Foundation and operates under the city's Office of Cultural Affairs. The gallery serves as a public exhibition space with special emphasis on Greater Hartford area artists and shows of local interest.

Built in 1949, the pumping station was originally constructed as part of a flood control project and was used to redistribute excess water back into the park's river. For years the 750-square-foot gallery section of the pump house stood idle, used only as storage space for the city's Parks and Recreation Department.

The Pump House Gallery hosts a series of outdoor lunch-time performances. Throughout the summer the gallery courtyard provides afternoon entertainment, attracting corporate brown-baggers as well as members of the local arts community. The "Good Tuesdays, Good Thursdays" program brings dancers, musicians, and poets to the courtyard for hour-long performances.

REAL ART WAYS

56 Arbor Street
232-1006

Real Art Ways (RAW) is a nationally-recognized contemporary arts center located in downtown Hartford. Its purpose is to provide leadership in the field by offering emerging and established artists of the highest quality the resources needed to create and present work, while serving the region as a showcase for, and advocate of, art at the forefront of current disciplines.

Founded in 1975 as a non-profit study, work, and living space for a few young artists, Real Art Ways has grown to become the largest interdisciplinary presenter of new and experimental art in central New England, with a paid staff of eight and an operating budget in excess of $450,000. With program activity ongoing in five areas-- Music, Gallery, Performance, Media (Video and Audio), and Urban Artists Colony (Residencies and Commissions)--RAW offers more than 100 public performance, lectures, and other events per year.

Maple Grove, Riverside Park.

HARTFORD PARK SYSTEM

Major Parks 2,150.93 acres in total

Batterson Park		714.84 acres
Farmington	465.43 acres	
New Britain	14.94 acres	
Plainville	4.50 acres	
West Hartford	55.92 acres	
Park Lakes	174.05 acres	
Bushnell Park		36.99 acres
Colt Park		114.00 acres
Elizabeth Park		101.45 acres
Hartford	19.60 acres	
West Hartford	81.85 acres	
Goodwin Park		237.00 acres
Hartford	152.00 acres	
Wethersfield	85.00 acres	
Hyland Park		39.75 acres
		(Zion Street area)
Keney Park		693.64 acres
Hartford	583.64 acres	
Windsor	110.00 acres	
Old North Cemetery		20.00 acres
Pope Park		75.27 acres
Riverside Park		51.00 acres
Soldiers Field (all in Wilson)		20.00 acres
Zion Hill		27.50 acres

Aaron Fein Square	.04 acres	**MINI PARKS**
Ancient Cemetery	1.34 acres	
Barnard Park (South Green)	1.70 acres	
Brookfield Triangle	.25 acres	
Buckingham Square	.03 acres	
Burr Mall	1.70 acres	
Campfield Green	.63 acres	
Chandler Street Triangle	.12 acres	
Charter Oak Memorial	.06 acres	
Columbus Green	.63 acres	
Franklin Square	.02 acres	
Freeman Street Triangle	.05 acres	
Gallaudet Triangle	.41 acres	
Keney Memorial	1.51 acres	
Lafayette Circle	.01 acres	
McManus Memorial	.05 acres	
New Britain Avenue Triangle	.08 acres	
Newbury Street Triangle	.01 acres	
Old South Cemetery	2.70 acres	
Porter Memorial Park	.04 acres	
Pulaski Mall	1.75 acres	
Sigourney Square	2.85 acres	
Washington Street Triangle	.02 acres	
White Street Triangle	.10 acres	

BUSHNELL PARK

In the mid-19th century, Trinity College stood on "College Hill," the present site of the State Capitol. Down the hill to the west, north, and east flowed a river, variously called the Mill, Little, or Hog River, that eventually emptied into the Connecticut River at Dutch Point. Later it was renamed the Park River. In 1939 it was channeled into underground conduits for flood control purposes. Before 1850 this river provided water power for a variety of mills, factories, tanneries, and a soap works that clustered along its southern bank. Along the northern bank were grouped eight or ten ramshackle tenements, exposed outhouses, a dozen pig sties, the city dump, and a little African Methodist Chapel.

Rev. Horace Bushnell, a local Congregational minister and civic leader, was deeply disturbed by this unsightly slum which was the first view to greet travelers as they arrived on the train from New York. Bushnell envisioned instead a lovely park that would be the focal point for the rapidly expanding city ... a public park much in the spirit of the old New England town common. Being a practical idealist, he went to Hartford's Court of Common Council (City Council) and persuaded the aldermen to include in Hartford's charter a new provision that would enable the city to take land by eminent domain for park purposes. Then he presented the political leaders with proposed plans for a new park. In his own words, "The stress of my endeavors was to raise an imagination of the picture it would make, so different from the filthy picture it then was, knowing well that if the imagination was carried, the judgment would be too."

Dr. Horace Bushnell.

At first some of the city fathers, skeptical of Bushnell's radical proposals, were slow to cooperate. One night an old grist mill in the area mysteriously burned to the ground, and some of Bushnell's opponents muttered darkly of arson. Nonetheless, Bushnell persisted, and finally, on January 5, 1854, Hartford citizens voted 1,005 to 682 to purchase the necessary land. This was the first public park in the world to be voted and paid for by a city.

Unfortunately, ill health forced Dr. Bushnell to be absent from Hartford for two years following the successful vote. When he returned home he was horrified to find that nothing had been done since his departure, and that there were some who even wished to sell the land for private development. Bushnell then vigorously attacked the problem

Bushnell Park Drive, Bridge over Park River opposite Union Place c. 1910.

anew and persuaded the City Council to sponsor a competition for a park plan. When the proposals came in they all proved to be very expensive, so Bushnell and City Engineer Seth Marsh attempted to do the job themselves. The results were not satisfactory.

Many people believed that Hartford's famous son, landscape architect Frederick Law Olmsted, became the park's architect, but this was not the case. In 1860 the Court of Common Council appointed five park commissioners, headed by George Beach, who then employed Jacob Weidenmann for $600 a year to lay out the park. Weidenmann was a native of Switzerland who had come to this country in 1856 and was associated with Eugene Haumann, a national leader in the field. After persuading the city to purchase even more land, Weidenmann designed and completed Hartford's central park. He went on to design Hartford's Cedar Hill Cemetery. In 1872, after Frederick Law Olmsted had achieved fame as the architect of New York City's Central Park as well as other prestigious urban parks, he and Weidenmann became professional associates. Not until 1896, however, did Hartford's Board of Park Commissioners secure the services of Hartford-born Olmsted to advise them on all matters relating to Hartford's expanding park system. He was particularly involved with the creation of Riverside, Goodwin, and Pope parks. He also was the architect for the new Trinity College campus and the grounds of the Institute of Living.

The cost of the ground originally taken for Hartford's new Central Park was $130,000; the cost of the additional land, $27,800. The cost of improvements made up to January 1, 1868, came to $150,200 ... a grand total of $308,000. Years later Horace Bushnell wrote, "now the Park is universally popular. I do not know that it has an enemy. And I hear of it as being said, every few days, by one or another of the old economic gentlemen that opposed it with most feeling: 'After all, the best investment our city has ever made is the Park.' This one thing is now clear to us all, that everything in the outward look of our city has been improving since the Park was made."

On February 14, 1876, just two days before Dr. Bushnell's death, the City Council voted to change the name from Central Park to Bushnell Park, in honor of the great man who was the moving spirit behind its creation.

CAROUSEL

Bushnell Park
728-3089

April 15--May 15, weekends only
May 15--August 31, Tuesday
through Sunday 11 a.m.--5 p.m.
September, weekends only
25 cents

This old-fashioned carousel was created in 1914 by Stein and Goldstein of Brooklyn, New York, the same firm that made the Central Park carousel in New York City. The carousel was purchased for $55,000 by the Knox Foundation in 1974 from an amusement park in Canton, Ohio. It was dismantled and shipped to Hartford where the horses, chipped and cracked after years of neglect, were restored in painstaking detail under the guidance of artist Tracy Cameron. A Wurlitzer band organ was located and meticulously rebuilt by Gavin McDonough.

The pavilion that encloses the carousel was designed by Hartford architect Jack Dollard. It is a unique building in that it has no foundation, but rests upon 24 concrete piers. The Champlin Company of Hartford prefabricated the frame, the walls, and the roof. Hartford Builders Finish was the contractor. The 96 stained-glass windows that grace the structure portray the changing seasons. They were designed by Tracy Cameron and created by Jerry Alexander of the Avon Craft Center.

FOX MEMORIAL ENTRANCE

Bushnell Park

This entrance to Bushnell Park was erected in 1952 as a memorial to Frederick K. Fox, who bequeathed the City of Hartford $10,000 to be used for "some enduring work of art."

HOADLEY MEMORIAL ENTRANCE

Bushnell Park

This sandstone entrance to Bushnell Park was erected by Horace E. Hoadley as a memorial to his grandfather, Jeremy Hoadley, a former mayor of Hartford, and presented to the city in 1909.

KENEY PARK

North Hartford, CT

Francis Goodwin.

The general store and homestead of Henry and Walter Keney, donors of the Keney Clock Tower, were located on the present tower site on Albany Avenue. Henry was a bachelor, and Walter and his wife had no children. Walter's wife, a Goodwin, was closely related to Rev. Francis Goodwin, creator of Hartford's remarkable system of public parks. Since the Walter Keneys had no children of their own they and Henry Keney looked upon young Francis Goodwin as their proper heir. As both brothers were very wealthy, the potential inheritance involved a considerable estate.

In later years Dr. Goodwin recalled that when Henry Keney "...was making his will leaving a large sum of money to the Hartford Hospital, he was planning to leave the balance of his estate to my brother and me. I said to him, 'Henry, you know James and I have sufficient. You are a childless man and when you are gone your name will be gone. Why don't you leave this money to build a large country park in the north part of the city where you drive every day? By so doing you will not be forgotten, for your name will be spoken by someone every day in the years to come.' Mr. Keney gave the matter due consideration, and then in a few days called me in and said, 'Francis, you are right. I will do as you suggest and leave the balance of my estate to build a park.'"

Thus Henry Keney in his will appointed Rev. Francis Goodwin and three other men trustees of his estate, authorizing and directing them "whenever they shall find it expedient and practicable to purchase a suitable tract of land" in the northerly part of town, to lay it out for a public park, and when completed to convey it to the city of Hartford.

A year after Mr. Keney's death the duly incorporated Keney Park Trustees, guided by landscape architects Olmsted, Olmsted and Eliot, began to purchase land for a new park. Frederick Law Olmsted, designer of Central Park in New York City, was respected nationwide for his professional expertise. He was a native of Hartford and a personal friend of Rev. Dr. Goodwin who, although an amateur, had a keen knowledge of landscaping. For nearly 10 years Rev. Dr. Goodwin, working with park superintendent George A. Parker, devoted a good portion of every day to carrying out, and frequently modifying, Omsted's plans. One hundred and ten acres of Keney Park extended into Windsor. This land had been owned by Dr. Goodwin, but was deeded to the city along with the acreage purchased and improved with Keney funds. It is interesting to note that in constructing the 693.64 acre park, more than half a million yards of earth were moved, over a million trees and shrubs were planted, more than 50 miles of drain pipes were laid, and 10 miles of gravel roads and 9 miles of paths were created.

Keney Park was formally turned over to the city by the trustees on November 15, 1924. It was accepted by Dr. George C.F. Williams, president of the Park Board, "to hold as a trust for the people of this city." Dr. Williams observed, "Now Keney Park rounds out the system of parks projected long ago, and Keney Park is supremely the achievement of the Reverend Francis Goodwin."

True to his Yankee heritage, Rev. Dr. Goodwin had invested the Keney funds so astutely that when he had paid for all the landscaping he still was able to present the city with the full amount of the original bequest.

RIVERFRONT RECAPTURE, INC.

1 Hartford
Square West
293-0131

For nearly 50 years Hartford's historic waterfront has been isolated from the city by a dike, an interstate highway, and downtown development. Now that the river's water quality has improved nearly 80%, the existence and potential of the state's greatest natural resource have been rediscovered. Organized in 1981, with Travelers Insurance Company taking the leading role, Riverfront Recapture has developed a $20 million master plan for bringing people back to the river in both Hartford and East Hartford.

On the Hartford side the main features being implemented are a 6-mile walkway stretching from Wethersfield to Windsor, a pier and gazebo at the southern end called Charter Oak Park, the restoration of Riverside Park at the northern end, a pedestrian bridge across Founders Bridge, and a new entrance to Charter Oak Park on Van Dyke Avenue near Colt's. On the East Hartford side Great River Park will have a riverwalk, boat launch, marina, and floating restaurant, in addition to new office buildings and the Riverpoint condominiums financed by Phoenix Mutual. At the confluence of the Connecticut and Hockanum rivers the Science Museum of Connecticut plans to build a four-story, $20 million museum which will have a planetarium and an IMAX movie theater.

The State has approved funding of $12.5 million for these improvements. When the new Charter Oak Bridge is completed, Charter Oak Park will be extended south to include a public boat launch and another dock area. Still pending is the centerpiece of Riverfront's plans--a plaza over I-91 that would connect Constitution Plaza with the riverfront.

In June of 1989 the five acres of Charter Oak Park were opened to the public. There are picnic tables and lighted paths for walkers, joggers, and cyclists. From the boat landing the *Lady Fenwick* offers seasonal cruises on the river.

Hartford has 46 parks and public squares covering more than 2,150.93 acres, the largest park system of any city in the Northeast.

Two individuals are largely responsible for the remarkable amount of open space in this city. First was Rev. Horace Bushnell who pioneered the whole park idea in 1854. Of equal importance was Rev. Francis Goodwin, a relative and admirer of Bushnell. Upon becoming chairman of the Park Commission in the 1890s, Rev. Goodwin envisioned a connecting ring of parks around the urban core. He loved nature, was an ardent amateur landscape architect, and was also independently wealthy, his family having been very active in local businesses. Financier J.P. Morgan was his first cousin. Like Morgan, he had a sharp head for finance and a keen eye for beauty. At this period of history, Hartford contained a surprisingly large number of childless, wealthy citizens. These individuals received Rev. Dr. Goodwin's special attention, as did the local politicians. In less than two decades, Rev. Dr. Goodwin had maneuvered money, land, and people in such an artful and creative fashion that his native city was, indeed, surrounded by a lovely ring of parks. In many other areas, too, Hartford was and is blessed by this voluntary city planner who had such excellent taste and indefatigable civic energy.

Elizabeth Park was once the estate of Charles N. Pond, whose family had a large interest in the New Haven Railroad. At one time Pond served as treasurer of the State of Connecticut and as an officer of the Hartford Trust Company. During the evening hours, however, he often drank heavily and terrorized his neighbors by using either his living room fireplace or backyard as a shooting gallery. A morose man who fancied spiritualism as well as spirits, Mr. Pond brooded over the notion that he himself would die at the same age as his father, and he eventually did. A widower with no children, he planned to leave his large estate as a refuge for inebriates. Fortunately for Hartford, Rev. Francis Goodwin persuaded him to leave it instead as a garden park in memory of his wife, Elizabeth. Relatives contested the will, and a compromise was finally reached which gave the land but only $100,000 for development to Hartford.

Elizabeth Park was designed and laid out by Theodore Wirth, who became superintendent of Hartford's parks on March 1, 1896. He had had extensive experience supervising

ELIZABETH PARK

Prospect and
Asylum avenues

Elizabeth Park Rose Garden.

the parks in New York City and was an authority on roses.
Mr. Wirth horrified the Hartford Park Commissioners by
coolly ordering twice the amount of manure they authorized
when creating the rose beds, for which wisdom future generations owe him many thanks. Elizabeth Park is the oldest
municipal rose garden in the nation. Almost 900 varieties
of roses and over 14,000 rose bushes may be seen here.
The best rose time is from mid-June to July 4, although a
great many roses bloom until frost. Elizabeth Park also has
beautiful displays of annuals and perennials. The peony
exhibit of over 100 varieties is the only public collection in
the nation. The park's greenhouse is open all year round
and contains lovely exhibits. The spring show at Eastertime
and the chrysanthemum show in the fall are outstanding.

Sponsored by the Knox Parks Foundation, the Horticultural Center of Hartford is now permanently head-quartered in this former caretaker's cottage in Elizabeth Park. The Center is a place where residents of Greater Hartford may be trained so they can take their knowledge about how to grow things in a city back to their neighborhoods. Previously the Parks Foundation worked with residents to provide outreach efforts to city neighborhoods, but now they have a focal point for their programs in the Park.

This project of the Knox Foundation joins the Bushnell Park Carousel and other urban enterprises in an effort to improve the quality of life in Greater Hartford.

HORTICULTURAL CENTER OF HARTFORD

Elizabeth Park
Hartford
232-7956

Elizabeth Park Rose Garden.

HARTFORD CIVIC CENTER

1 Civic Center Plaza
Administration:
249-6333
Box Office:
727-8080
Chargeline:
727-8010

The Hartford Civic Center, New England's largest sports and entertainment complex, features a 16,000 seat arena, 95,000 foot exhibition area, attached shopping mall with 49 shops and 13 restaurants, as well as the 400 room Sheraton-Hartford Hotel. Opened on January 9, 1975, the facility was the culmination of a joint effort led primarily by the City of Hartford, Aetna Life & Casualty, ITT, and the Greater Hartford Chamber of Commerce.

The original 10,000 seat coliseum was temporarily out of business for two years when the roof collapsed under the weight of snow and ice from a storm in 1978. But the city rallied and a sparkling new, "bigger and better" arena opened in February of 1980.

The new Civic Center Coliseum hosts many types of events, including the NHL Hartford Whalers, college basketball, concerts, family shows, and a wide variety of other special events.

Photo courtesy of The Hartford Courant.

New monument of The Founders of Hartford in The Ancient Burying Ground. Photo courtesy of Garen Photography.

THOMAS HOOKER
Frances Wadsworth (1910-1978)
1948
bronze
Main Street, in front of Old State House

Frances Wadsworth was a resident of Granby, Connecticut and a descendent of Captain Joseph Wadsworth of Charter Oak fame.

The Society of the Descendents of the Founders of Hartford commissioned this work in 1940. Hooker, a great Puritan divine, led the first settlers from Massachusetts Bay Colony to Hartford. As no paintings, drawings or written descriptions of Hooker's appearance existed, Wadsworth created an imaginary portrait based upon her interpretation of his character as a powerful and convincing preacher. Hooker holds in his right hand a scroll. This is a reference to his sermon of 1638 in which he set forth the principle of self-government under constitutional limitations created and preserved by the people.

The statue, which measure eight feet in height, was sculpted in a highly stylized manner. Wadsworth sculpted in terms of representational forms and had each article of clothing carefully researched and approved by historians. However, the forms are abstracted from nature by the very roughness of surface revealing the evidence of modelling in clay. This creates a discrepancy between the optical fact of her interpretation and the historical accuracy of costume the sculptor so carefully sought.

Robert H. Schutz designed the pedestal, which is inscribed with a quotation from Hooker's constitutional sermon: "The foundation of authority is laid firstly in the free consent of the people."

ROCHAMBEAU BOULDER
Thomas Hooker Square

A plaque on his boulder reads: "This tablet commemorates the historic first meeting of General George Washington and Comte de Rochambeau, Commander-in-Chief of the French Army in America, which took place September 20, 1780.

"On that occasion, and in a subsequent meeting the following May, was developed the strategy which resulted, at Yorktown, in victory and independence for the American Colonies.

"Erected by the City of Hartford, September 20, 1946, in grateful remembrance. Upon their appearance in the city, they were received with imposing ceremonies. The Governor's guards, and a company of artillery, were on duty upon the occasion."

Two other plaques on this boulder commemorate the 175th and 200th anniversaries of the First Company of the Governor's Footguard. Founded in 1771 and still flourishing, the Footguard is the oldest military unit in continuous service in the U.S.A. According to tradition the Footguard's distinctive uniform was modeled after the uniform of the British Coldstream Guards, Britain's oldest regiment founded in 1651 by the Puritan general George Monk. Two Warwick patentees, founders of Connecticut, Colonel George Fenwick and Sir Arthur Haselrige, contributed units to the original Coldstream Guards! The Footguard uniform consists of a scarlet coat, the tails of which are faced with buff, and a black velvet front crossed with silver braid. The vest and breeches are of buff, and the leggings are black velvet. The hat, or busby as it is known, is of bear skin with shield in front bearing the State coat of arms and supports a red and black feather plume on the side.

PUTNAM STONE
Thomas Hooker Square

On February 1, 1958, the "grateful fellow citizens" of William H. Putnam unveiled this plaque in recognition of Mr. Putnam's ". . . lasting contribution toward a better life

for the people of Connecticut, especially those of Greater
Hartford." They noted that Mr. Putnam ". . . with ability, courage, devotion and vision . . . served his city and his state in
business, education, politics, religion and the arts. His efforts
and achievements in the fields of hospitals, flood control,
housing development, bridge building and other splendid
civic projects place him among our greatest leaders." Putnam
Bridge which spans the Connecticut River from Wethersfield
to Glastonbury is named in honor of this able and public
spirited man, a direct descendant of General Israel Putnam
of Revolutionary War fame.

PLAQUE MEMORIALIZING THE ROYAL
CHARTER THEFT
corner of Main Street and Tower Square

This plaque was placed here in 1964. It reads: "A.D.
1687 - Sir Edmunds Andros, Governor of All New England,
under King James II, came before the General Court which
as tradition records was sitting in a tavern on this site and
demanded the surrender of the Royal Charter granted by
King Charles II, A.D. 1662, giving the power of self-government to the Colony of Connecticut. During a stormy debate
the lights were extinguished and the Charter spirited away to
be hidden in an oak tree. A.D. 1689 — following the acces-
sion of William and Mary, government under the Royal
Charter was resumed. The Travelers Insurance Company
and the Connecticut Society of the Colonial Dames of
America here honors the memory of this act of patriotism."

COLONIAL MEETING HOUSE YARD PLAQUE
on outside wall of Putnam, Coffin & Burr Division of
Advest, Inc., 6 Central Row

This plaque is a detailed map of how Thomas Hooker
Square looked when it was called Meeting House Square in
the 17th century.

HORACE WELLS PLAQUE
Enoch Smith Woods
1894
bronze
Corner of Main and Asylum streets, opposite the Old State
House

The bronze plaque dedicated to Horace Wells (1815-1848) is situated to the right of the entrance of the Hartford National Bank on the Corning Building. It was presented to the City of Hartford by the Connecticut State Dental Association, and unveiled December 10, 1894. The tablet commemorates Wells who discovered and demonstrated the use of anesthesia on this spot in 1844.

Woods designed this 3' x 1'6" relief one year after he was commissioned to do the Colonel Thomas Knowlton statue, and two years after the presentation of the Nathan Hale statue to the Wadsworth Atheneum. Due to a misreading of the inscriptions, the Fine Arts Commission only tentatively attributed the plaque to Woods and misdated it. The attribution to Woods and the date can be affirmed by a careful reading of the plaque and a corroborating published account in the *Hartford Times*.

SAFE ARRIVAL
Frances Wadsworth (1910-1978)
bronze
Travelers Plaza

Safe Arrival depicts a pioneer family of four who came with Thomas Hooker to settle Hartford in 1636. The group walked from Cambridge for 30 days and 30 nights with the goal of establishing a colony in which religious freedom would prevail. The base bears the quotation "He who brought us here sustains us still." The dichotomy created between the narrative detail of the costume and the abstracting depiction of the surface creates the same discrepancy as seen in Wadsworth's *Thomas Hooker*.

GEORGE WASHINGTON MEDALLION MEMORIAL
Wadsworth Atheneum
Atheneum Square North
Hartford, CT

This medallion on the north wall of the Atheneum, placed in 1932, reads "George Washington was entertained by Colonel Jeremiah Wadsworth in his home on this site on June 30, 1775, when on his way to assume command of the army. On September 21, 22, 23, 1780 with Lafayette, General Knox and Governor Jonathan Trumbull, Washington here held his first conference with French Commander Count Rochambeau and Admiral Ternay to concert joint military and naval plans. During his tour through the eastern states in 1789, Washington was in Hartford on October 19, 20, 21 and November 9, 10. On October 20 he was entertained by Colonel Wadsworth. To mark this site associated with his name this tablet is erected by the Connecticut Daughters of the American Revolution, in abiding reverence for WASHINGTON, February 22, 1932, the two hundredth anniversary of his birth."

ACROSS THE LIMPOPO
Melvin E. Edwards, Jr.
before 1974
painted steel
Wadsworth Atheneum
Gengras Court

Across the Limpopo is made of orange painted steel. Representative of Edward's style since 1968, the piece consists of a triangular frame with a narrow ladder on top of curved supports that attach to the apex. Unlike his earlier works made from found objects, there are no political associations. Instead Edwards has created a lyrical flowing three-dimensional drawing in space.

Melvin E. Edwards, Jr. taught at the University of Connecticut in Storrs.

TRAHO
Lila Pell Katzen
1973
rolled steel and brush stainless
Wadsworth Atheneum
Terrace along Atheneum Square North

Lila Pell Katzen feels that her sculptures are not complete until they are installed. These "site-orientated" sculptures encourage interaction between site and viewer.

Traho consists of numerous parts of different shapes which were arranged to fit into their site, thus creating an endless form. This work is secluded from traffic and noise by its architectural and environmental surroundings. Katzen creates a contrast between the weathered, rust-colored steel and the soft, satiny finish of the brushed stainless steel, between curves and planes, and between solids and voids. In *Traho*, Katzen has created a work which interacts with its environment.

ECHO
Alexander Liberman
1969
painted steel
Wadsworth Atheneum
Main Street in front of the Morgan Memorial Building

Alexander Liberman is a painter, draughtsman, and photographer as well as a sculptor. He believes that art can only exist through quantity, therefor, much of his work is executed in series. These are groups of individual works produced in the same style that together create a symbolic generation. Liberman experimented with metal junk sculptures and gestural painting and then concentrated on Minimalist sculpture. Minimalist sculpture is characterized by the use of elementary forms on a geometric base, usually in a uniform color, in order to create a monumental effect.

Echo is a part of a series of constructions based on the cylinder which Liberman executed in 1969. His use of large boiler parts prompted this interest in curvilinear forms. The sculpture measures 10' x 18'.

Echo is painted orange. Its forms are geometrically simple. The interplay of forms creates a tension between horizontal and vertical, stability and instability. Dynamic force is created by the spatial relationships. Sculpture should, according to Liberman, embody the conception and refine it, without losing its original energy.

UNTITLED
Robert Morris
1969-70
Wadsworth Atheneum
Corner of Prospect Street and Atheneum Square North

 Robert Morris is associated with the Minimalist movement using simple geometric forms to convey order, stability, and permanence. The objective of the Minimalists was to create single images that could be readily and immediately perceived by the viewer. Minimalists related their work to the Gestalt concept that shapes are perceived as patterns, such as squareness and roundness. They wish to eliminate from their works anything that detracts from the unity of the work. If color is used it is homogeneous; surface texture remains unvaried. Often they will use industrial materials in their compositions. Morris also became involved with environmental works and earth works.

 Untitled is an example of an object referred to as an "I-beam gestalt" or unitary object. The sculpture is composed of five metal slabs, each weighing two tons, assembled into an I-beam shape. The five pieces of the sculpture are held in position by gravity, not by welding or riveting. Formally, the work has a horizontal emphasis which is created by the two horizontal planes connected by a vertical plane of metal. The placement of the vertical element produces a perfectly symmetrical composition creating a sense of three-dimensionality. The parallel lines formed by the metal slabs create a dynamic sense of space around the object. There is no application of color although it has rusted to a uniform warm brown with a surface rough to the touch.

SURVEYOR'S DRAWING BOARD
Arnaldo Pomodoro
1961
cast bronze
Wadsworth Atheneum
Gengras Court

Arnaldo Pomodoro's awareness of the sensuous quality of precious materials and ability to work in fine detail, learned as a goldsmith, directly influence his well-known large bronzes. These works are highly polished, dramatic in effect, and meticulously executed.

Surveyor's Drawing Board is an early bronze sculpture that predates Pomodoro's better known geometric bronzes. It is a bas-relief of drapery-like gold folds offset by organic striations. The surface is unpolished. This piece reflects the artist's transition from his early low reliefs in wood and lead to the fully three-dimensional forms in polished bronze of his latter work.

D.G., M.S., V.T.
Tony Smith
1969
welded bronze
Wadsworth Atheneum
Main Street Entrance

The pieces *D.G.*, *M.S.*, and *V.T.* were originally designed on a paper-weight scale and were intended for friends, hence the various initials. The original miniatures were done in marble sheets. In 1969 all three were executed at their present size. The three works, presently on indefinite loan from Fourcade, Droll, New York, have been on exhibit at the Wadsworth Atheneum since 1973.

PLAYGROUND
Tony Smith
1966
plywood, tar
Wadsworth Atheneum
Gengras Court

The idea for *Playground* first appeared in profile in a 1961 painting by Smith. The work is presently on loan to the Wadsworth Atheneum and has been on exhibit there for a number of years. Smith says that *Playground* reminds him of an ancient building with mud-brick walls. He claims the same relations in black and white exist in his mind.

In reference to Smith's few words about the subject and the work's title, *Playground* can be most accurately understood if it is viewed in the context of fun. Smith would probably not object if *Playground* were moved to an actual playground for recreational purposes.

THE BRIDE
Tal Streeter
1966-67
painted steel
Wadsworth Atheneum
Gengras Court

The Bride was a gift to the museum from the artist's wife. It is painted a uniform silver-gray.

The Bride consists of a vertical pillar encased by a rectangular, cagelike structure. The vertical rests on a pyramid which it seems to press down. The outer encasement is stable and geometrically proportioned. Its static nature contrasts with the dynamic tension of the interior. *The Bride* is minimalist in its use of elementary forms.

NATHAN HALE
Enoch Smith Woods
1889
bronze
Wadsworth Atheneum
Near Main Street Entrance

It is presumed that Enoch Smith Woods (1846-1919) became a sculptor after, while working as a bricklayer, he fell from the State Capitol, damaged his knee, and was unable to pursue that line of work. He was a sexton in Hartford's Church of the Good Shepherd in the 1880's. Woods's reputation as a sculptor rests on his works in Hartford. Prior to these works he did some carving in wood. Little is known about Woods, who left Hartford in 1901, and died in Manchester, N.H. in 1919.

Nathan Hale was designed for a competition sponsored by the State of Connecticut for a statue of this patriot-hero to be placed in the interior of the Capitol Building. The competition was held in the 1880's, shortly after the centennial of Hale's death. Woods's statue was the runner-up in this competition. James J. Goodwin, who commissioned the statue even though it was not the winner, presented it to the Wadsworth Atheneum in 1892. The statue was cast by M.H. Mosman in Chicopee Falls, Massachusetts, in 1889, and is the only known version extant. It was erected in 1894. George Ulrich, a collector and patron of the arts, posed for the statue.

This larger-than-life-size bronze, measuring approximately 10 feet high, heroically portrays Nathan Hale, Connecticut-born patriot, whose famous last words were "I only regret that I have but one life to lose for my country." Born in Coventry, Connecticut on June 6, 1755, Hale attended Yale University and taught school before fighting in the Revolutionary War. On his return from a mission behind the British lines for General Washington, Hale was caught. He was hanged the following day, September 22, 1776.

Interest in Nathan Hale spread, and statues by other artists can be found in South Coventry, New London, Yale University, New York City, Washington, D.C., Virginia, and St. Paul, Minnesota. A third version by Richard Hubbard as well as the winning statue of Hale by Karl Gerhardt are located in the State Capitol.

STEGOSAURUS
Alexander Calder (1898-1976)
1973
painted steel
Burr Mall between the Wadsworth Atheneum and City Hall

The son of two generations of sculptors, Calder was born in Launton, Pennsylvania. In 1933 Calder returned from Europe, setting up his studio permanently in Roxbury, Connecticut. He began producing his more monumental "stabiles" there.

Calder's mature works, rendered always in bold primary colors, are sculpted with paradoxical intentions. "Mobiles" show a fascination with colored forms in space as they interact driven by air currents. "Stabiles", in contrast, are monumental in character and in scale. Calder's "stabiles" can be found all over Europe and America.

Calder's *Stegosaurus* is exemplary of his "stabiles" produced after 1937. Named for a dinosaur from the Wyoming and Colorado regions, Calder's Stegosaurus is the culmination of a 66 year project which began with a grant to the city of Hartford by Ella Burr McManus. According to Mrs. McManus's wishes, "the most gifted and competent sculptor known" was to build a memorial to her father, Alfred E. Burr, founder of the *Hartford Times*. Calder was chosen in the late 1960's after a five-year search.

The original twenty-four inch model was presented on May 31, 1972. Constructed from the plans of the sculptor, the present bright orange-red steel structure rises 50 feet in height with a span of 32 feet. The sculpture was dedicated in 1973.

This is the only full-scale version constructed after his model and plans. The small-scale version is located at the University of Connecticut Health Center in Farmington. It is called *Stegosaurus, Jr.* and was installed in 1975. The particular appeal of *Stegosaurus*, and of all Calder's stabiles, is the subtle interplay of line and curves, of fluidity and elegance, as opposed to stability and weight. The open form of *Stegosaurus* contrasts with the massiveness of the adjacent building. Calder's abstracted sculpture of a dinosaur is placed beside a fountain in Burr Mall to suggest a beast coming to drink at a pool in the woods.

SYBIL OF THE WRITTEN WORD
550 Main Street

Commissioned by the Hartford Public Library Board and dedicated in 1958, this sculpture by O. Maldarelli, S. C. and M. Tomasi, C.R., symbolizes learning and gives "a final artistic touch" to the Hartford Public Library's handsome new headquarters.

ADVENTURERS' BOULDER
Municipal Building, 550 Main Street

Given by the Society of the Descendants of the Founders of Hartford to the citizens of Hartford on October 15, 1935: "In memory of the courageous Adventurers who, inspired and directed by Thomas Hooker, journeyed through the wilderness from Newtown (Cambridge) in Massachusetts Bay to Saukiog (Hartford) - October 1635." Those adventurers were: Mathew Allyn, John Barnard, William Butler, Clement Chaplin, Nicholas Clarke, Robert Day, Edward Elmer, Nathaniel Ely, Richard Goodman, William Goodwin, Stephen Hart, William Kelsey, William Lewis, Mathew Marvin, James Olmsted, William Pantry, Thomas Scott, Timothy Stanley, Thomas Stanley, Edward Stebins, John Steele, John Stone, John Talcott, Richard Webb, William Westwood.

STONE FIELD SCULPTURE
Carl Andre (1935-)
1977
boulders
corner of Main and Gold streets

To understand Andre's work, one needs to understand the Minimal Art movement that began in the 1960's,
for Andre is regarded as a major figure in Minimalist Art.
Supporters of Minimalism claim that it is the first American
Art movement that owes nothing to the art of Europe.
Minimalists seek simplicity through the use of geometry in
order to remove the artist's personality from the work. In
this respect, it is a reaction against the emotional self-expres-
sion of Abstract Expressionism and Assemblage art. As a
result, the outstanding features of Minimal Art are clarity and
restraint. Furthermore, Minimal Art is primarily sculptural,
since the advocates of this movement feel that the physical
space that surrounds sculpture is intrinsically more powerful
than the illusionistic space found in painting.

Stone Field Sculpture is a triangular arrangement of
36 boulders of varying material in eight rows placed on a
sloping site in the heart of the city. The conception for
this site sculpture is two-fold. On the one hand, its formal
arrangement was inspired by the tombstones in the adjacent Center Church Cemetery and Andre's visit in 1954 to
Stonehenge and other megalithic monuments in England,
including Carnac on the Brittany coast. Through these ref-
erences, it is thought that Andre is hinting at the ephemeral
quality of human existence versus the solidity and endurance
of nature. On the other hand, Stone Field Sculpture is
designed and executed to remind us of New England's once
glaciated landscape and the subsequent agrarian life style.
The rocks, weighing from one to nine tons, are massive,
stable, and durable, which Andre found befitting for an
insurance capital such as Hartford.

Stone Field Sculpture was constructed on August 2,
1977. The thirty-six rocks are arranged in eight parallel rows
of increasing length on a 290' x 53' lawn. The boulders of
sandstone, brownstone, granite, schist, gneiss, basalt, and
serpentine are carefully arranged so that no two adjacent
stones are of the same color and texture. The largest boul-

der is placed at the apex of the triangle, which is also the lowest point on the site, and is followed by progressively smaller stones positioned in progressively longer rows. Subsequently, the base of the triangle is comprised of the eight smallest rocks placed on the highest point on the site. Furthermore, the distance between the rows becomes increasingly large towards the base of the triangle. This gives the viewer who is sitting on the low rocks the same effect as looking through a telephoto lense because the area becomes spatially compressed *Stone Field Sculpture* is playful in this way, and Andre invites the public to explore and relax within his work. As the sun moves, the shadows shift and change the character of this sculpture.

Andre received the commission for Stone Field Sculpture from the Hartford Foundation for Public Giving and the National Endowment for the Arts. It is important to note that this work has been controversial ever since it was completed. David Bourdon, writing for *Arts Magazine* says that "*Stone Field* is an unusually commanding site sculpture and Hartford is fortunate to have it." George Athanson, mayor of Hartford, was cited in this same article saying that he believed that Andre was coming back to sculpt the rocks. When Athanson found out that the sculpture was already complete he said, "I think he chiseled the city."

LAFAYETTE
Paul Wayland Bartlett (1865-1925)
Model c. 1907, cast 1932
Bronze, granite base
Capitol Avenue at Lafayette Circle

Lafayette was commissioned to commemorate French-American amity. American school children would contribute toward the creation of an equestrian statue of the "hero of two worlds," the Marquis de Lafayette. The project was designed as a reciprocal gift to the French nation for the Statue of Liberty, erected in New York harbor in 1886.

In 1908 Bartlett's *Lafayette* was erected in Paris, in the Place du Carrousel, visible from the court as well as from the windows of the Louvre. A year later Bartlett presented the final plaster form to the State of Connecticut in hopes that a duplicate would be made. The form was stored in the State Armory until 1913 when the plaster statue was reassembled for public display in the State Capitol. The bronze statue in Hartford exists as the second casting made from Bartlett's final plaster form. It was cast and dedicated in 1932.

Lafayette, the Frenchman who helped secure the freedom of the American colonies, is commemorated in a plaque added in 1957.

KENEY MEMORIAL CLOCK TOWER
Corner of Main & Ely streets

"It commemorates a woman whose only claim to greatness was that of being a good parent" is the reason usually ascribed for the building of the Keney Tower. The l30 foot high Victorian Gothic masonry clock tower was constructed in 1898 on the site of the Keney homestead and business as a memorial gift to the city of Hartford.

COLONEL THOMAS KNOWLTON
Enoch Smith Woods (1846-1919)
1895
Bronze
State Capitol, East Entrance

Woods conceived of *Colonel Thomas Knowlton* as a companion piece to the *Nathan Hale* statue. This work was commissioned by the General Assembly of 1893 in memory of the colonel who was killed at the Battle of Harlem Heights in 1776. Woods modeled the statue after the portrait of Colonel Knowlton by John Trumbull, 1785.

RICHARD D. HUBBARD
Karl Gerhardt (1853-1915)
1890
Bronze
State Capitol grounds, southeast side

Hubbard was Connecticut's first prominent lawyer and its greatest orator. He was the governor of Connecticut from 1873-79 and was a noted advocate of women's rights. Gerhardt depicted Hubbard in a restrained yet bold pose, as if poised to address a crowd.

ANDERSONVILLE BOY
Bela Lyon Pratt (1867-1917)
1907
Bronze; granite base
State Capitol grounds, southeast side

The *Andersonville Boy* represents the Connecticut soldiers imprisoned during the Civil War. It is a second casting of a statue that stands in the National Cemetery in Andersonville, Georgia, site of the infamous prison in which so many Union soldiers were inhumanely confined.

MAJOR GENERAL CLARENCE RAMSOM EDWARDS
George Holburn Snowden (born 1902)
1942
Bronze, granite base
State Capitol grounds, west side

General Edwards was Commander of the Twenty-Sixth Division of the United States Army during the years 1917 and 1918, when he led many victories on the battlefields of France.

The north facade is dedicated to the founding fathers of the Connecticut Colony up to the Revolution. The north facade was conceived as the principal entrance to the Capitol. It is composed of six statues in gothic niches above five tympana above the portals.

The Capitol building was designed with twenty-six niches for sculpture and sixteen tympana. Each facade was to have a specific theme reflecting important events in American and Connecticut history. The north side celebrates the founding fathers of Connecticut and the early history of the colony up to the Revolutionary war. The east facade is dedicated to the Revolutionary war and the founding of the Republic. The west side is devoted to figures who distinguished themselves in the War of Independence and in government service. The south facade is dedicated to citizens who distinguished themselves in the Civil War or since. The sculpture on the east facade was started first because that part of the building was completed first. The central tympanum of the east facade, *The Charter Oak* by Salewski, was the first piece of sculpture done for the Capitol.

STATE CAPITOL: EXTERIOR

After completion of the State Capitol building in 1878, the Connecticut State Commission of Sculpture named Richard E.Brooks, Paul Wayland Bartlett, and Albert Entress as sculptors who would decorate the north front.

STATUES IN NICHES HIGH ON THE NORTH FACADE

from left to right.

JOHN HAYNES
Richard E. Brooks(1865-1919)
marble
State Capitol, North facade, first statue on left

John Haynes (1594-1654) became the first governor of the Connecticut Colony after he migrated to Hartford from Essex, England in 1637.

JOSEPH WADSWORTH
Paul Wayland Bartlett (1865-1925)
circa 1906
marble

The savior of the Royal Charter.

JOHN WINTHROP, JR.
Paul Wayland Bartlett
1906
marble

The sixth governor of Connecticut and the procurer of the Royal Charter for the colony in 1662.

REVEREND THEOPHILUS EATON
Paul Wayland Bartlett
circa 1907
marble

The co-founder and first governor of New Haven colony.

CAPTAIN JOHN MASON
Paul Wayland Bartlett
1908
marble

The chief of the Connecticut militia and the founder of Windsor.

ROGER LUDLOW
Richard E. Brooks (1865-1919)
1909
marble
Windsor lawyer Roger Ludlow drafted the Fundamental Orders, a constitution adopted by the Connecticut Colony in 1639.

The Tympana represents important events in the history of the Connecticut colony.

TYMPANA IN SPACES ABOVE THE DOORWAYS

From left to right.

ATTACK ON AN INDIAN FORT
P.W. Bartlett
1908
marble
Depicting the Pequot war of 1637.

CAPTAIN JOSEPH WADSWORTH HIDING THE ROYAL CHARTER IN THE CHARTER OAK
R.E. Brooks
1916
marble tympanum
The colonial hero is shown with the Royal Charter and the Charter Oak.

THE SEAL OF THE STATE OF CONNECTICUT
Anonymous
1908

ISRAEL PUTNAM LEAVING HIS PLOW TO GO AND FIGHT IN THE REVOLUTIONARY WAR
H.A. McNeil
circa 1916
marble tympanum
According to legend, upon hearing of the battle of Lexington, Putnam left his plow in the field and rode off to Massachusetts. The central figure of Putnam is seen turning away from his plow toward the direction urgently being pointed out to him by a man on horseback.

WILLIAM HOLMES PASSING THE DUTCH FORT
P.W. Bartlett
1908
marble

Showing the founder of Windsor, Connecticut defying the Dutch traders in the House of Good Hope, their fort.

GENERAL JOSEPH ROSWELL HAWLEY
Herbert Adams (1858-1945)
circa 1908
bronze high relief medallion

Hawley served as Governor of Connecticut from 1866-1867. Lists include dates of his military service, and of political offices held.

ORVILLE HITCHCOCK PLATT
H.A. McNeil (1866-1947)
circa 1908
bronze high relief medallion

Platt served his native Connecticut as a State representative, a State senator, and also as a United States senator.

EAST FACADE

The East entrance was the first completed with works dating from 1878 to 1895. The subjects are drawn from the early history of the Connecticut Colony or memorialize prominent citizens born in the 18th century.

STATUES IN NICHES

From Left to Right.

REVEREND THOMAS HOOKER
C. Neihaus

ROGER SHERMAN
Chauncey B. Ives (1810-1894)
1878
marble

Sherman was first Mayor of New Haven, a delegate to the first Continental Congress and a signer of the Declaration of Independence.

JONATHAN TRUMBULL

C.B. Ives

1878

marble

Trumbull was a noted soldier, statesman, and figured prominently in Connecticut commerce. He was Governor of Connecticut from 1769 to 1784.

REVEREND JOHN DAVENPORT

C. Neihaus

JOEL BARLOW

Charles Henry Niehaus (1855-1935)

circa 1895

marble

Barlow, who was a poet, Hartford wit, and leading Connecticut intellectual, is dressed in the clothing of late 18th-century America.

REVEREND GEORGE BERGE BERKELEY

C. Niehaus

circa 1895

marble

Reverend George Berkeley was a prominent theologian in Connecticut, after whom the Berkeley Divinity School was named.

REVEREND HORACE BUSHNELL

Carl H. Conrads (1839-?)

circa 1895

marble

Reverend Horace Bushnell was a local Congregtional minister and civic leader who was the primary force behind the creation of Bushnell Park.

MEDALLIONS BELOW THE STATUES AND ABOVE THE ARCHES OF THE TYMPANA.

Roundels from left to right.

NOAH WEBSTER
C. H. Conrads
circa 1895
marble
      Webster was the author of the first American Dictionary and spelling book.

REVEREND JONATHAN EDWARDS
C. Niehaus
circa 1895
marble
      Edwards was a leading Congregational theologian of the 18th century.

JONATHAN TRUMBULL
circa 1895

TYMPANA

from left to right

THOMAS HOOKER LEADING THE FIRST WHITE SET-TLERS TO HARTFORD
C. Niehaus
circa 1895
marble

THE CHARTER OAK
Charles D. Salewski
1876
marble
      In 1867 the Colony's Royal Charter was hidden in an oak tree. This action was taken in order to prevent the document's being taken by representatives of the British Crown.

THE REVEREND JOHN DAVENPORT PREACHING TO THE PURITAN SETTLERS OF NEW HAVEN
C. Niehaus
circa 1895
marble

Neither the five tympana nor the medallions on the South have ever been carved. Only three of the six niches have been filled with sculpture. Today used as the main entrance to the Capitol, the figures represented here distinguished themselves in the Civil War or since.

The first niche is vacant.

GIDEON WELLES
Hermon Atkins MacNeil (1866-1947)
circa 1934
marble
Gideon Welles was part owner and editor of the now defunct *Hartford Times* and Secretary of the Navy under President Lincoln.

JOHN SEDGEWICK

ALFRED HOWE TERRY
H.A. MacNeil
circa 1934
marble
Civil War General Terry is seen in military dress.

Fifth and sixth niches are vacant.

WEST FACADE   *OLIVER WOLCOTT OF LITCHFIELD*
          Governor of Connecticut (1796-97) and signer of the
          Declaration of Independence. His son, Oliver, Jr., champi-
          oned the new constitution which retired the old Royal
          Charter, disestablished the Congregational Church, and
          weakened the political control of the Standing Order, the
          largely Congregational Federalists who had dominated the
          colony and the state.

          DAVID HUMPHREYS
          One of the Hartford Wits, founder of Humphreysville,
          a model mill town.

          DAVID WOOSTER
          A Revolutionary War hero killed at the battle of Danbury.

          OLIVER ELLSWORTH

INTERIOR   *NATHAN HALE*
          Karl Gerhardt (1853-1915)
          1886
          bronze
          East Lobby
          One of Connecticut's earliest heroes, the young
          school teacher was hanged by the British as a spy in 1776.
          The statue's marble base is inscribed with the patriot's final
          words to his executioners, "I only regret that I have but one
          life to lose for my country."
          Hale's strong hands and straining neck emphasize the
          intense emotion of the coming event. His outstretched arms
          indicate the sacrifice he has accepted.

THE GENIUS OF CONNECTICUT
Randolph Rogers (1825-1892)
bronze
destroyed 1942
Replica in State Capitol, Rotunda

The Genius of Connecticut is a winged female figure
which crowns the Capitol dome. She is crowned with oak

leaves, the emblem of strength. With uplifted arms she extends wreaths of Laurel in her right hand and of Everlasting in her left hand.

The original *Genius* was designed in a delicate balance unequal to the fierce winds which assailed her 250 feet above Bushnell Park. On October 6, 1938, following the great hurricane, the *Genius* became unstable and swayed dangerously. She was removed, and four years later, during World War II, she was melted down for armaments.

Fortunately, the original plaster model was placed in a niche in the west hall. In 1973 the restored plaster model was placed in the Rotunda of the State Capitol. A much lighter, fiberglass replica of *The Genius of Connecticut* was cast to take the place of the original figure, and anchored to the Capitol's pinnacle.

ALLEGORICAL FIGURES
John Quincy Adams Ward (1830-1910)
1877
marble
Statues around the drum of the dome

In 1877 Ward was commissioned to make six models of free-standing, allegorical, female figures to adorn the drum of the capitol dome. The figures represent Agriculture, Commerce, Education, Music, Science, and Force. Each model was reproduced twice in marble to make twelve statues, arranged as two identical sets of six figures. The original plaster models have been preserved and are on a stairway in the capitol.

Each emblematic statue is sculpted in a classical style with symbolic iconography. The statue holding a ball represents Commerce; the figure with a flute represents Music; the figure with the scroll represents Education; the figure with the fruit and vegetables is Agriculture; the statue with one raised arm represents Force; and the one with the cloak is a symbol of Science.

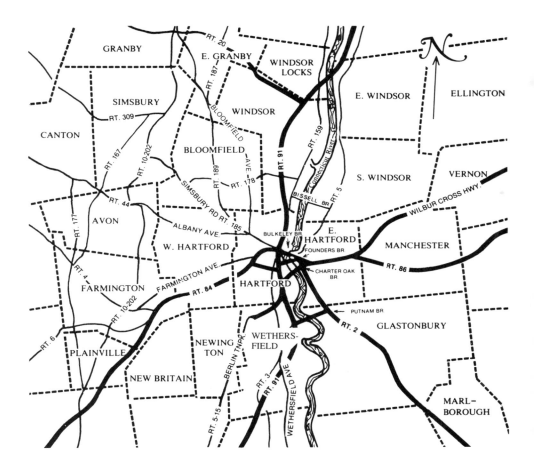

WEST HARTFORD

Taken from Hartford
in 1854
Population 61,300

Because Connecticut was founded as a Puritan theocracy, all towns in this state originated as Congregational ecclesiastical societies. In 1636 the entire Connecticut Colony was composed of Hartford, Windsor and Wethersfield. These towns covered a vast area. Hartford, for example, extended east to include the present town of Manchester and west to the border of Farmington. As Hartford residents moved out from the center of town, new ecclesiastical societies were formed and new Congregational churches built. When these settlements grew stronger, local citizens applied for town status. Thus West Hartford, created by Hartford as the Western Division in 1679, became an independent ecclesiastical society in 1711 and a separate town in 1854.

West Hartford citizens have promoted three significant "firsts." Noah Webster, born here in 1758, became the author of the first American dictionary. In 1919 the town became the first in the state to adopt a council-manager form of government. Four years later West Hartford was the first in Connecticut and one of the first in the country to form a zoning and planning study group.

St. John's Episcopal Church
679 Farmington Ave., West Hartford   Tel: 523-5201

St. John's Episcopal Church, founded in 1841, was originally located on Main Street on the present site of the Morgan Memorial. By the turn of the century this neighborhood had become quite run down, and many Hartford Episcopalians had moved west to the suburbs. The members of St. John's debated whether or not to move the church. Finally, their minds were made up for them by J. Pierpont Morgan, a prominent churchman, who wanted the Main Street site for a building he planned to erect in his father's memory: the Morgan Memorial wing of the Wadsworth Atheneum. He even encouraged the move of St. John's to the suburbs by contributing $100,000 to a building fund!

After appropriate arrangements had been made, the old church was sold and eventually demolished. The last service was held on Easter Sunday, 1907, and on July 14, 1908 the cornerstone for this handsome English Gothic sanctuary was laid. Architects were Cran, Goodhue and Ferguson. As frugal Yankees, the building committee took pride in the fact that the cost of the new church was, to the dollar, exactly as planned! In 1929, under the direction of the same architectural firm, a cloister and parish house were added.

Temple Beth Israel
701 Farmington Avenue, West Hartford
Tel: 233-8215

Under the leadership of Rabbi Abraham Feldman the Beth Israel congregation moved here from their old temple at 21 Charter Oak Avenue in 1935. The new Temple Beth Israel, designed by Charles Greco, was dedicated the following year. It is a fascinating architectural tribute to the faith and traditions of the Jewish people. The Santa Sophia dome, the Byzantine ceiling, the magnificent stained glass windows and the countless art and religious treasures combine to create an impressive edifice. The exquisite Alfred M. Silberman Chapel containing a wealth of interesting symbolism was dedicated in 1951.

Hartford Insurance Group Education & Conference Center
Hamilton Heights, West Hartford

Since November 1982 the imposing five-story brick building atop Hamilton Heights, between Fern Street and Farmington Avenue, has been the training center for the Hartford Insurance Group, containing meeting rooms and 77 bedrooms. Previously, it was the Mount Saint Joseph Academy, the oldest private school for Catholic young women in the state. The Sisters of Mercy opened the Academy on Allyn Street in Hartford in 1852, and in 1908, after several moves, settled in West Hartford. The architect was J. J. Dwyer of Brooklyn, whose firm had designed the original brownstone Cathedral of St. Joseph and St. Patrick's Church as well as Asylum Hill Congregational Church. The extensive grounds were laid out by Frederick Law Olmsted. The Patrick Garvan family gave the beautiful Romanesque chapel with its marble loggia and stained glass windows, the former library and science laboratories.

Kingswood-Oxford School
170 Kingswood Road, West Hartford
Tel: 233-9631

Hartford's first private, country-day, college preparatory school for boys was opened in 1916 with 12 boys in a small house on Farmington Avenue near Laurel Street. The boys ranged from 8 to 15 years of age. Two years later Kingswood moved to the former Mark Twain house at 351 Farmington Avenue then owned by Mr. and Mrs. Richard M. Bissell. Mr. Bissell was president of the Hartford Fire Insurance Company and his son a Kingswood student.

In 1922, with almost 100 boys, Kingswood moved to its present location which had been the Niles G. White farm. It was purchased by Dr. and Mrs. Melancthon Jacobus who deeded the land to the school as they, too, had a Kingswood son. Dr. Jacobus was the dean of the Hartford Theological Seminary. The architect of the new campus was Edwin Sherrill Dodge of Boston who subsequently designed Bennington College in Vermont. Over the years Kingswood's campus has been considerably enlarged.

Kingswood's guiding spirit and first headmaster was George R. H. Nicholson, who came from Kingswood School in Bath, England. Later William O. Williams from the same school followed Nicholson to Hartford. Together these two Britishers set high standards of behavior and scholarship, and their students referred to them affectionately as Nick and WOW. They were assisted by a loyal faculty, many of whom devoted their entire working lives to Kingswood.

Oxford School opened in 1909 in two small houses that were appropriately located on Oxford Street, with 25 boys and girls. They were enrolled in classes that ranged from kindergarten to the 12th grade. Both college preparation and general courses were given. Ten years later the school moved to the former Ensworth house at 510 Farmington Avenue; then, in 1924, to the present location at 695 Prospect Avenue. By this time the student body included almost 90 boys and girls.

The spacious house at 695 Prospect Avenue was erected by Charles E. Shepard, president of the Aetna Insurance Company, in 1900. The architects are unknown. It was subsequently owned by the family of Clark F. Sturhan who headed the old Rossia Insurance Company that was located where the new YWCA now stands.

The two guiding spirits of Oxford School were Mary Martin, the first headmistress, and Ruth Gurnsey who followed in her footsteps. The school thrived under their leadership and, in time, became an all-girl educational institution. They were assisted by a devoted female faculty who, way beyond the call of duty, took a personal interest in the girls and the success of the school.

By 1969 the educational climate of this country had considerably changed. Once more a student body consisting of both boys and girls was considered preferable. Great emphasis, too, was placed on attracting students of every race, creed and color from throughout the Capitol Region. In 1963 Kingswood and Oxford Schools merged, but did not graduate their first combined senior class until 1974.

The Middle School (grades 6-8) campus is on Prospect Avenue. The Upper School (grades 9-12) campus is located on Kingswood Road. The Roberts Theater, built in 1972, is a major cultural asset to the entire Town of West Hartford.

Science Museum of Connecticut and Gengras Planetarium
950 Trout Brook Drive, West Hartford
Tel: 236-2961

Open Mon.-Sat. 10 a.m.-5 p.m. Sun. 1-5 p.m. Adults $3.50; children (12 & under) $2.00. Planetarium: $.50.

Founded in 1927, the fifth of its kind in the nation, the Science Museum is quite literally a very lively place. Numerous exhibits of live animals, birds and reptiles are artfully arranged in attractive cages in and out of doors. The Aquarium contains equally fascinating fish, crabs and other underwater life. Perhaps even more delightful to the young is the adjoining Hands-On Room, in which some of these creatures may actually be handled.

The Gengras Planetarium contains one of New England's largest star projectors. It seats 150 people under a 40-foot dome. Star shows feature over 4,000 stars, motion of the planets and the many phenomena of deep space. It is just like having a window on a space ship!

The museum buildings were designed by Huntington and Darbee, Hartford architects.

First Church of Christ, Congregational
12 South Main Street, West Hartford   Tel: 233-9605
On October 12, 1710 the residents of the Western Division of the Town of Hartford petitioned the General Assembly of the Colony of Connecticut for permission to form a separate ecclesiastical society, the fourth in the township. Some of the reasons given for not wishing to journey into the center of town to one of the two Congregational churches on Main Street were the great distance, the bad roads, "the uncomfortableness overhead" and "a river not seldom difficult and sometimes impassable" which, of course, was the Little or Park River.

After due examination the petition of the Western Division was granted in 1711, and the Rev. Benjamin Colton was selected as pastor of the new church society. When West Hartford became a town in 1854 the church changed from being the Fourth Congregational Church of Hartford to being the First Congregational Church of West Hartford. The present handsome meeting house is the fifth in the church's history. Hobart Upjohn of New York City was architect.

Before this new meeting house was completed in 1947 the former one was destroyed by fire. Many offers of hospitality were extended to the Congregationalists by neighboring religious institutions, but the first came from Rabbi Feldman of the Temple Beth Israel. Accordingly the Congregationalists held their services in the temple for the next six months, then united with the Baptists and Universalists during the summer season.

June 15-Sept. 30: Mon., Tues., Thurs., Fri. 10-4; Sat., Sun. 1-4 Oct. 1-June 14: Mon., Tues., Thurs., Sun. 1-4. Closed Wednesdays. Adults $2.00; Sr. Citizens, children (12 & under) $1.

Noah Webster House and Museum
227 S. Main Street, West Hartford   Tel: 521-5362
Mailing Address: P.O. Box 1758, West Hartford 06107
Noah Webster was born here in the "Western Division" of Hartford in 1758. His birthplace is an excellent example of an 18th century Connecticut farmhouse. Noah Webster himself was a typical Connecticut Yankee . . . energetic, practical and idealistic. He had his finger in numerous local "pies"

including banking, law, politics, and teaching as well as writing. Literally millions of our forebears studied from the spelling and grammar books written by Webster. His greatest triumph, however, was to compile the first American dictionary for which he is deservedly renowned as the "father of his country's language." Modern dictionaries still bearing his name are based on the original *American Dictionary* that he published in 1828. It contained 12,000 words and from 30,000 to 40,000 definitions that had not appeared in any earlier dictionary.

A museum building to the rear of Noah Webster House was opened to the public in 1974. There are ever-changing displays relating to Noah the man, the 18th century and West Hartford memorabilia.

The Noah Webster House is a National Historic Site owned by the Town of West Hartford but supported privately as a non-profit institution under the auspices of the Noah Webster Foundation and the Historical Society of West Hartford.

Noah Webster South Main Street, West Hartford 06107

Although the sculptor, Korczak Ziolkowski, donated his services in order to make this statue of West Hartford's great lexicographer, insufficient funds were raised to pay for the materials and much controversy ensued about both the financing and style of the work. The statue was created in 1941.

Hours: Sunday, Tuesday and Thursday 1-4 p.m. Visitors welcome. No admission fee.

West Hartford Art League Gallery 37 Buena Vista Road, West Hartford Tel: 521-1332

Located in a charmingly refurbished 18th century farmhouse, this art gallery has more than 200 running feet of hanging space. It is staffed by Art League volunteers, including a five-member selection committee which reviews art work submitted.

The Gallery is owned by the Town of West Hartford but supported by Art League membership fees, a 20 percent commission on all art work sold, and contributions.

Boulder in Old Cemetery
North Main Street, West Hartford

This boulder was placed here by the D.A.R. to memorialize the French and American soldiers who died of
smallpox while encamped on Talcott Mountain during the
Revolutionary War. The boulder is flanked by two flags, one
American and one French.

Dr. Gallaudet and Alice Cogswell
North Main Street, West Hartford 06107

This charming statue of Dr. Thomas Hopkins Gallaudet
and his first student is an exact replica of one made by Daniel
Chester French in 1889 for Gallaudet College in Washington, D.C. Named for Hartford's great teacher, this college
was the first and only college for the deaf in the United
States. On the occasion of the one hundredth birthday of
the American School for the Deaf, the National Association
for the Deaf commissioned Mr. French to make this replica.
They presented it to the school in 1925.

The American School for the Deaf
139 No. Main St., West Hartford Tel: 236-5891

The American School for the Deaf is an important part
of our history. Founded in Hartford in 1817, it is the oldest
school for the handicapped of any kind in the entire Western
Hemisphere.

Originally named the Connecticut Asylum for the Education and Instruction of Deaf and Dumb Persons, the
school was located on the present site of the Hartford Fire
Insurance Company on the corner of Asylum Avenue and
Cogswell Street. Asylum Avenue was so-named because of
this school, and Cogswell Street recalls the school's first
pupil, Alice Cogswell.

Classes range from nursery through high school. The
high school has three tracks: academic, technical-vocational
and vocational.

Although ASD is a private educational institution, sizable portions of regular tuition expenses are covered by the
state. Additional funds are provided by endowments and
gifts from private individuals, foundations and corporations.

Renbrook School
2865 Albany Avenue, West Hartford
Tel: 236-1661

 Renbrook was founded in 1935 as Tunxis School with
17 students. First located on Albany Avenue in a house just
east of Bishop's Corner, the school soon moved to another
large house on the corner of Farmington and Outlook avenues and was renamed Junior School. In 1938 Junior School
settled into a new building on Trout Brook Drive and, less
than a decade later, added two more buildings to its campus,
which is now the site of the Science Museum.

 In 1957 the Junior School changed both its location
and name when it made a final move to "Renbrook," the 48-
acre former estate of the Rentschler family. Frederick B.
Rentschler had been the founding genius of United Aircraft
Corporation. His magnificent home, designed by Chester A.
Patterson, was built on Avon Mountain in 1931. "Renbrook"
was presented to the school by the Fay Belden Rentschler
Foundation on a long-term 99-year lease for $1 a year.
Additional school buildings at Renbrook were designed by
Hartford architect Louis Drakos.

 The guiding spirit behind Renbrook's phenomenal
success and growth was headmistress Florence Greene.
Although preceded by two other headmistresses, both of
very short duration, it was Mrs. Greene's gentle but firm
leadership that enabled Renbrook to become one of the
outstanding country-day schools in Greater Hartford. Her
philosophy of "individualized teaching to meet individual
student needs" laid the basis for the school. Co-educational
classes run from junior kindergarten through ninth grade.
During the summer months the school campus is used by
Summer Adventure Day Camp and by Summer Challenge,
an academic program.

UConn--Hartford Branch
Asylum Avenue & Trout Brook Drive.
West Hartford Tel: 241-4700

 In 1940 the University of Connecticut established the
Hartford Extension Center to help meet the educational
needs of the students in the Hartford area. The demand
for educational offerings became so great that the University

organized the Hartford Branch in 1946 and extended its program.

Open twelve months of the year, the Branch has full-time and part-time freshmen and sophomore undergraduate students. Students transfer to the main campus at Storrs for the junior and senior years. Two six-week summer sessions are offered. The fully accredited freshman-sophomore program includes offerings in ten areas of study: Agriculture and Natural Resources, Allied Health Professions, Business Administration, Education, Engineering, Fine Arts, Home Economics and Family Studies, Liberal Arts and Sciences, Nursing and Pharmacy. No distinction is made between the credits earned for courses taken in Hartford and those earned at Storrs, either within the university or in transferring credits to another institution.

Graduate courses in Education and Social Work are offered in the late afternoon and evenings toward the Masters and Doctorate. However, graduate students must meet a residency requirement.

The non-credit and certificate programs offer such diversified programs as Real Estate, Genealogy, Solar Heating, Sexuality, Business Management Law and others meeting the demands of the times.

The architects for the buildings on this campus were Harry Danos and Associates of West Hartford.

Tours by appointment.

Saint Joseph College
1678 Asylum Avenue, West Hartford
Tel: 232-4571

Shortly after the turn of the 20th century, the Congregation of the Sisters of Mercy, pioneers in Connecticut education since 1853, became increasingly aware of women's need for higher education and of society's need for educated women. Desiring to direct their efforts and their own resources to meet these needs, the Congregation in 1925 obtained from the Connecticut state legislature a college charter granting power to confer degrees. The college was incorporated under the laws of Connecticut, and Mount Saint Joseph Junior College welcomed its first class in 1932. Three years later, as a senior college, it occupied its beautiful new buildings on Asylum Avenue.

The spacious campus of Saint Joseph College was laid out by Frederick Law Olmsted, Jr., son of Hartford's famous landscaping pioneer, who is now buried in the Old North cemetery. The college's first two colonial-type buildings, Mercy Hall and McDonough Hall, were both designed by Maginnis & Walsh of Boston. All the other buildings, with the exception of the chapel, were designed by Russell Hills and completed between 1955 and 1962. The Gengras Center for Exceptional Children, however, was completed in 1965. The Conner Chapel of Our Lady, an exquisite example of modified Georgian Colonial style, was designed by Eggers & Higgins and completed in 1966.

Although Saint Joseph College is still a college for women, men were admitted to graduate courses in the late 1950s. Because Saint Joseph is a member of the Greater Hartford Consortium, male students from area colleges also attend classes here.

Unitarian Meeting House
50 Bloomfield Avenue
Tel: 233-9897

The first Unitarian Society of Hartford was organized July 27, 1844. The following year on May 25th the cornerstone of their first meeting house was laid. An impressive brownstone structure, the Church of the Savior stood on the northeast corner of Trumbull and Asylum streets. It was dedicated on April 22, 1846, and the Rev. Joseph Harrington was installed as the first settled minister.

Unfortunately the congregation proved to be too small to support the church adequately, so it was sold to a local bank in 1862 to defray expenses. The bank later sold it to the Episcopalians who moved the building, piece by piece, to Sigourney Street, reassembled it, and renamed it Trinity Church!

The Unitarian congregation was reactivated in 1877 and attempted, but failed, to purchase the Temple Beth Israel Synagogue on Charter Oak Avenue. The Rev. John C. Kimball, a strong and dynamic man, was chosen the Society's minister the following year. After diligent preparations the congregation erected Unity Church at 68 Pratt Street which they dedicated in 1881. The meeting house was uniquely practical in that it was designed like a theater and could be rented throughout the week to other organizations. Unity Hall thus became Hartford's chief lecture and concert hall. Because the pastor was an outspoken liberal, champions of unpopular causes such as Woman's Suffrage, negro rights and labor reform were always welcome here.

In 1924 the Society built a third and larger meeting house at 215 Pearl Street. Milton E. Hayman was the architect.

Lack of adequate space for a growing membership again forced the Unitarians to move, this time to 50 Bloomfield Avenue. Their fourth meeting house, dedicated on December 4, 1964, is a fascinating architectural expression of the Unitarian concept that "there are many paths towards Truth." The free-standing reinforced concrete radial walls, each different with respect to height, sharpness and distance from its neighbor, symbolize the respect for individual differences and the freedom of belief on which the Unitarian faith is founded. Designed by Victor Lundy of Guilford, Connecticut, the meeting house has received national recognition. Its picture has appeared on the cover of *Fortune Magazine*, special articles have described it in the *New York Times Magazine*, and it was judged the best architectural design of the year by the Connecticut Chapter of the American Institute of Architects.

In 1961 the independent Unitarian and Universalist associations in this country and Canada joined together to form the Unitarian Universalist Association headquartered in Boston. The Universalist's first sanctuary, the Church of the Redeemer, was located on Central Row. Today this church may be found at 433 Fern Street in West Hartford. Over the years both Unitarians and the Universalists have developed into the broad liberal religious faith they represent today.

Watkinson School
180 Bloomfield Avenue
Tel: 236-5618

Watkinson School was originally chartered by the Connecticut General Assembly in 1862 as the Juvenile Asylum and Farm School for Orphan Boys. It was created by David Watkinson, a Hartford merchant born in England in 1778, the seventh child in a family of twelve. He was an uncle of the Collins brothers who manufactured axes and machetes in Collinsville. When Mr. Watkinson settled in Hartford he became a merchant and amassed a considerable fortune in the West Indies trade. He and his wife had no children of their own but took a deep interest in the welfare of others.

Upon his death David Watkinson left an estate that was the largest ever probated in Hartford up to that time. Among his bequests were $100,000 to the Watkinson Library, now at Trinity College, $40,000 to Hartford Hospital, and $60,000 to establish the Juvenile Asylum and Farm School. Henry Barnard, the great educator, was entrusted with the task of establishing the new institution, which was not actually opened until 1880. The first home of the Watkinson Juvenile Asylum and Farm School was located on the former Penfield Farm, bounded by Park Street to the south, Putnam Street to the east, the Park River to the west and the old Weed Sewing Machine factory to the north. Next door was the Hartford Orphan Asylum which had recently moved from Washington Street.

By this time the Rev. Francis Goodwin had become president of Watkinson's Board of Trustees, and no one could have been better suited to the task. He served as president from 1880 to 1901 and as a member of the board until his death in 1923.

On May 2, 1884 Watkinson's trustees voted to build a dormitory for 16 boys and to construct or refurbish suitable farm buildings on their new campus. They also arranged for 12 students to be housed temporarily at the nearby orphan asylum. Less than a decade later Mr. Goodwin, keenly aware of the fact that this part of town was fast becoming a busy factory district, reported that he had purchased the extensive Prosser Farm that fronted on Bloomfield and Albany Avenues. He wanted to use some of the acreage later as a site for handicraft instruction but also wanted Watkinson to be located there.

A large new building, now the main school building, was constructed and the school opened its new quarters in 1895. Fifty students were enrolled but most of the boys, while making their home at Watkinson, attended the local public school. In 1924 assets of the handicraft school were transferred to the Watkinson Juvenile Asylum and Farm School and the whole renamed Watkinson School. Life at Watkinson School continued to be plain, with emphasis on Christian principles and outdoor work. There was some time for play, however, because a gymnasium was added to the school building in 1924 and named Francis Goodwin Hall. Most of the headmasters continued to be Episcopal clergymen.

During World War II the school ran into financial reverses and was closed until 1945 when a college preparatory curriculum was instituted. After fire destroyed the school's chapel in 1952, it was quickly replaced by the present chapel, St. David's, designed by Hartford architect John W. Huntington, who contributed his professional services.

Watkinson today is a co-educational day school for grades 7 through 12. The school seeks to provide average and gifted students "who might be lost in the public school system or in a very highly competitive private school" with flexible, individualized programs. Accredited by the New England Association of Schools and Colleges, Watkinson offers both college preparatory and specialized arts curricula and its graduates are now represented in the best colleges.

Watkinson's unique Creative Arts Program is conducted with the following cooperative institutions that are part of the University of Hartford which adjoins the Watkinson campus: Department of Theatre and Communications, Hartford Art School, Hartt College of Music, and the Julius Hartt School of Music. A dance curriculum is coordinated with the Hartford Ballet. Through this Creative Arts Program students have the opportunity to receive highly professional instruction in the fine arts, music, dance and drama. During their stay at Watkinson capable students can complete the requirements for a high school diploma and at the same time earn college credits.

The old Prosser Brick Barn (circa 1870) on the campus has been remodeled by students and parents for use as an arts center and social gathering place.

In 1919 the Hartford Orphan Asylum which had been Watkinson's neighbor on Putnam Street moved out to a portion of the old Prosser Farm that fronted on 1680 Albany Avenue. There in 1925-27 a unique Children's Village was created to care for orphans in small groups rather than in a typical institutional orphan asylum. Architects were Stowe, Phelps and Tompkins of New York City.

BLOOMFIELD

Separated from
Windsor in 1835

The present town of Bloomfield was originally part of this historic township of Windsor, and later included small pieces of Farmington and Simsbury. An Indian deed, dated 1660, records the purchase of this area ... then called "the wilderness" ... by white pioneers. The first settlement was named Messenger's Farms.

In 1736 Connecticut's theocratic General Court passed on Act which transformed the area into the Parish of Winton-bury so that all who lived here could build and attend their own Congregational Church. The new name was a combina-tion of *Win*dsor, *Farming*ton, and Sims*bury*. When this became a separate town in 1835, Senator Francis Gillette, the squire of "Wildwood," suggested the name Bloomfield.

St. Thomas Seminary
467 Bloomfield Avenue, Bloomfield
Tel: 242-5573

St. Thomas Seminary opened in the old Chinese College on Collins Street in Hartford in 1898 with 37 students. The lovely Gothic buildings on this Bloomfield campus were completed in 1930. The architect was Louis A. Walsh of Waterbury and the general contractor was William F. O'Neil.

Training is provided here for the Roman Catholic priest-hood. The seminary offers educational programs at the high school level and the first two years of college. It is also a res-idence for junior and senior class students attending area colleges that are members of the Greater Hartford Consor-tium for Higher Education. St. Thomas graduates go on to post-graduate work at major seminaries in this country and abroad.

Francis Gillette House "Wildwood"
511 Bloomfield Avenue, Bloomfield

Francis Gillette built this stone house in 1834. A strong abolitionist, U.S. Senator, chairman of the State Board of Education from 1840-1865, leader in the temperance movement, and a founder of the Republican party, Senator Gillette was a man of eloquence and action. He used his home as a station for the "underground railroad" until he moved to Nook Farm in 1853. There he continued to aid escaping slaves. (See Nook Farm Complex.)

Francis Gillette's son, William, became a famous actor. Since the Gillettes were not pleased by their son's choice of profession, Mark Twain helped the young man get started by lending him money. (See Gillette's Castle.)

CIGNA Companies

When CIGNA Companies (formerly Connecticut General Life Insurance Company) was founded in 1865, the company's original purpose was to insure persons whose health was below normal standards. However, it soon observed "that the infirmities buried in the human system [are] too deceptive and variable to respond to any ... law of averages." Today CIGNA is one of the largest stockholder-owned insurance companies in the United States. During the past quarter century, the company has grown at twice the rate of the insurance industry.

The company's spectacular office building designed by Skidmore, Owings and Merrill is a major aesthetic accomplishment. Completed in 1957, it was selected by the American Institute of Architects as "one of the ten buildings in America's future." Incorporated into the total architectural plan are four unique garden courts created by the noted landscape architect and sculptor, Isanu Noguchi. These courts artfully relate the vast edifice to its beautiful natural setting-- 300 acres of rolling pasture and woodland.

The overall concept of a total, self-contained, inspiring corporate headquarters out in the country rather than in the center city was developed by CIGNA's former president, Frazar B. Wilde. Mr. Wilde joined the company in 1914, became president in 1936, chairman of the board in 1960, and chairman emeritus in 1966. His astonishing versatility, vigor and vision as a corporate executive have received national recognition.

In 1973 CIGNA purchased the former headquarters of the Emhart Corporation at 950 Cottage Grove Road when that company moved to Farmington. Completed in 1962, the slim, glass rectangular building hovering lightly on precast supports is a fascinating structure. The architects were also Skidmore, Owings and Merrill of New York City.

Outdoor Sculpture
Family Group by Isanu Noguchi.

Old St. Andrew's Church
59 Tariffville Road, Bloomfield
Tel: 242-4660

In 1740 one of the oldest Episcopal parishes in Connecticut was assembled in the "Scotland" District of Ancient Simsbury. It consisted of six members. This was the mother church of Christ Church Cathedral in Hartford and several others. A year later it had grown to about 30 families, augmented by those who were involved in copper mining operations in the area. Many were newcomers from England and thus staunch members of the Church of England.

The Episcopalians' first church, a plain white frame building, was constructed in 1743. Its original organ, second oldest in the United States, now belongs to the Simsbury Historical Society. During the Revolution the Episcopalians in Connecticut were often badly treated by local Congregational patriots who suspected them of being Tory sympathizers, ... which many of them actually were! The Rev. William Gibbs, first rector of this little church, accused of being a traitor by some of his strong-armed neighbors, was led upside-down onto a horse and driven into Hartford to be judged. The poor man was so frightened he subsequently became insane. The church's second pastor fled to Canada.

In 1806 the little church was moved about two miles south to "Duncaster" and, in 1828, moved again to its present location.

Farm Implement Museum
434 Tunxis Avenue, Bloomfield
Tel: 242-7961

*April-November, Tues.-Sun.,
10- 5 by donation*

Exhibits of farm implements and techniques dating back to 1790. Petting animal zoo and picnic area are available.

EAST HARTFORD

Taken from
Hartford in 1783

Before the arrival of the white man, East Hartford was the home of Podunk Indians whose chief, in 1631, traveled to Boston and Plymouth to invite the Puritans to settle here. Chief Wanginnacut's purpose was to enlist the support of the English against fierce Pequot invaders who had subjugated the peaceful river tribes living on the Connecticut.

Seven years later John Crow and William Goodwin, both of whom had come to Hartford with Thomas Hooker in 1636, constructed the first sawmill east of the great river. The following year Crow became East Hartford's first white resident.

In 1775, stimulated by the threat of war against the mother country, the first gunpowder mill in America was built here. Fourteen years later Hudson and Goodwin, Hartford publishers of the *Connecticut Courant* (now the *Hartford Courant*) built a paper mill in this town to supply their flourishing business.

In 1843 an East Hartford man manufactured the first machine-made watch in the nation.

Two years later a Connecticut historian, John W. Barber, applauded the resourcefulness and enterprise of East Hartford's Yankee residents. "East Hartford was for many years distinguished beyond any other town in the state for the variety and amount of its manufactures." Although raising tobacco, succulent East Hartford melons and other produce has also occupied many area inhabitants, East Hartford's primary emphasis on manufacturing was greatly enhanced by the arrival of Pratt & Whitney Aircraft in 1929. As the largest employer in New England, P & W is the dominant influence in the community today.

Edward E. King Museum
840 Main St., Raymond Public Library
Tel: 289-6429

The story of tobacco and aviation, local industries with world-wide impact, is told through pictures, models, actual tools, implements and products.

Huguenot House (1761)
Martin Park, 307 Burnside Avenue
Tel: 528-0716

The restored home of a Connecticut saddlemaker features a Connecticut gambrel roof, and vaulted dormer windows. Located on the grounds is the 1820 Goodwin Schoolhouse.

Mon.-Fri. 9-9 p.m.; Sat. 9-5. Free.

First Congregational Church
837 Main Street, East Hartford
Tel: 528-3133

For many decades citizens of Hartford who lived east of the Connecticut River were required to attend the First Congregational Church or the South Congregational Church on Main Street in the center of town. Finally, in 1699, a Third Ecclesiastical Society of Hartford was formed here to accommodate the local residents. However, East Hartford people continued to be buried in Hartford until 1712. Because there was no separation between church and state in Connecticut until 1818, this church was the most powerful single force in the community.

Memorial Day-Labor Day: Thurs., Sun. 1-4 p.m.

In 1783 when East Hartford became a separate town from Hartford, this became the First Church. Despite their unique position of authority in the community, Congregational pastors sometimes were forced to cope with rebellious parishioners. In 1823 Colonel Giles Olmsted, a gruff and outspoken member of the congregation, interrupted the Sunday sermon to loudly voice his disagreement with the pastor's interpretation of a particular passage of scripture. On another occasion the Colonel lost his temper over the music being played in the church and stomped out saying that he "didn't come to meeting to hear any damn fiddling!" The pastor eventually resigned in disgust, and Olmsted was excommunicated.

The original sanctuary of the First Church, when it was still the Third Ecclesiastical Society of Hartford, was located on the corner of Pitkin and Main Streets. This lovely meeting house was constructed in 1835. A chapel was added in 1952.

St. John's Church
12 Rector Street, East Hartford 06108
Tel: 528-1474

This small church is of particular interest to admirers of architect Edward Tuckerman Potter who also designed the Mark Twain House and the Church of the Good Shepherd in Hartford and Trinity Parish in Wethersfield.

A charming brownstone sanctuary with an ornate slate roof and an equally delightful interior, St. John's was constructed in 1867. Some of its most prominent early parishioners were members of the McCook family in Hartford.

Corning Hall, constructed behind the church in 1909, is used for office and recreational purposes.

GLASTONBURY

Taken from
Wethersfield in 1690

As early as 1639 a few residents of Wethersfield crossed the Connecticut River to settle here on land purchased from Sowheag, Sachem of the Wangunks. When the town separated from Wethersfield in 1690, it was known as Nabuck, an Indian name meaning "flooded land." Two years later it was renamed Glastonbury, traditionally pronounced "Glassenbury," by the English Puritans.

Over 175 homes here were built prior to 1800 and many more before 1900. The Glastonbury Historical Society's headquarters are located in the Museum on the Green. The Society also operates the Welles-Chapman Tavern on Main Street in Glastonbury Center. The birthplace of Gideon Welles, President Lincoln's Secretary of the Navy, is located on Hebron Avenue and is being used as a Senior Center by the town.

No doubt modern feminists would be most interested in a house (now a private residence) at 1625 Main Street which used to be the home of the famous Smith sisters. Abby and Julia Smith were two of the five daughters of Zephaniah Hollister Smith and his wife, Hannah Hadassah Hickok. The father was a minister, lawyer, scholar, mechanical genius, and rugged nonconformist. The mother was equally talented and independent. For example, Mrs. Smith and 40 other ladies drew up one of the earliest anti-slavery petitions to be presented before Congress by John Quincy Adams.

Abby and Julia and their sisters shared their parents' anti-slavery sentiments and fighting spirits. However, it was not until 1873 when they had reached the venerable age of 77 and 82 respectively that Abby and Julie achieved real fame.

Because of an unfair new tax assessment upon their property, the two old spinsters refused to pay their taxes. In retaliation, the tax collector seized their herd of seven cows and some of their farm land, then sold them at auction, the land going very cheaply to a covetous next-door neighbor.

Outraged, the elderly sisters protested the tax collector's action as illegal because they, as disenfranchised females, had been denied their rights as citizens, and took their cause to court. Until a sympathetic gentleman came to their rescue, Abby served as their lawyer.

For over two years the case was argued from court to court, and the fame of the determined old ladies became world-wide. Newspaper editors in France and England praised them, and they achieved a strong national following, especially among advocates of women's suffrage. In great demand as public speakers, they even appeared at a hearing before Congress where they received a standing ovation. Finally victorious, Abby wrote a pamphlet about their experiences entitled, "Abby Smith and Her Cows." It was published by Julia in 1877.

One of Glastonbury's most unique contributions to the male sector of our population was the first American shaving soap introduced by the J. B. Williams Company in 1840.

Museum on the Green
1944 Main Street, Glastonbury
Tel: 633-6890

Mon. 10-2; Thurs. 1-5; Sun. 2-4.

    The former Town Hall (c. 1840) houses displays on local history, early industry, Indian artifacts, and changing exhibits. The museum is adjacent to the old town cemetery, dated from 1690.

Connecticut Audobon Society, Holland Brook Center
1361 Main Street Tel: 633-8402

Tues.-Fri., 1-5; Sat., 10-5; Sun. 1-5

    Exhibits focus on native flora, fauna and Connecticut River ecosystem. There is a hands-on discovery room. The Society is adjacent to 38-acre Earle park and trail system.

Welles-Shipman-Ward House
972 Main Street, South Glastonbury Tel: 633-6890

For access to the house and for special tour arrangements, call the Glastonbury Historical Society.

    This house has received national recognition for "possessing exceptional architectural interest" and "as being worthy of the most careful preservation." It was constructed in 1755 by the Welles family, local shipbuilders. Unfortunately John Welles Jr., a staunch American patriot, went bankrupt during the Revolution, so his house was taken by one of his creditors, Stephen Shipman, another shipbuilder. Members of the Shipman family owned it until 1925 when it was purchased by Mr. and Mrs. James Ward. In 1963 Mrs. Berdena Hart Ward willed the house to the Glastonbury Historical Society.

Situated at the head of the navigable waters of the Connecticut until a spring freshet changed the river's course in 1698, Wethersfield is a magnificent example of a colonial river port. Founded in 1634, the town is fortunate to still possess over 140 homes built prior to 1800. Some were constructed by ship's carpenters and cabinetmakers, and details of ornamentation are often very fine. In 1962 the area known as Old Wethersfield was set aside as an historic district, the first in the state to be so designated under the new Historic District Act. No doubt one reason why so many lovely old homes still stand in this town is that the Wethersfield Volunteer Fire Department is the oldest of its kind in continuous operation in the United States!

Since the river was shallow, the bar at its mouth a hazard, the river captains' ships were necessarily of shallow draft. They could not carry home large, rich cargoes like the big vessels that plied to and from the great seaports of Boston and New York. But the river captains were numerous and diligent and as a group did very well indeed. Their modest but charming homes reflect both their affluence and good taste.

In 1649 the *Tryall* was built by Thomas Deming of Wethersfield, the first American-made ship to trade in the West Indies. Deming's shipyard kept busy until the middle of the 19th century. For many years red onions were Wethersfield's chief cash crop for trade. They grew well in the fertile meadows, and kept well during the long haul down to the Caribbean. For this reason Wethersfield was popularly known as Oniontown. The West Indian trade was the backbone of the economy of all the Connecticut River towns until the War if 1812. Besides onions, Connecticut River captains and merchants also exported the colony's surplus of lumber, horses, beef, skins, barrel staves, bricks, fish, furs, and grain. They generally imported molasses, sugar, spices and rum-popularly, and correctly known as "Kill Devil"!

Combination tickets to all nine of the major historic properties in Wethersfield may be purchased at the Visitors' Center. For information call 529-8611, ext. 266 or ext. 280. The Center is open May 15th to October 15th daily from 9:30 a.m. to 4:30 p.m.

Visitors' Center 105 Marsh Street, Wethersfield

The Visitors' Center is an excellent place to begin your tour of Wethersfield. Here hosts and hostesses will distribute information, assist you in arranging your tour and answer questions about the past and present of the community. This facility is maintained by the Town of Wethersfield.

Wethersfield Historical Society
150 Main Street, Wethersfield
Tel: 529-7656

Located in Old Academy Museum, built in 1804, a federal style brick building, the Academy served Wethersfield in many ways. The building has housed public and private schools, a pioneer female seminary, religious groups, a public library, the Town Hall, an armory, and a draft induction center for two World Wars. It is now a local history museum, with archives and a library. Fascinating exhibits and authentic artifacts orient visitors and students to the three-century span of Old Wethersfield's lively past.

In 1633 when a restless adventurer named John Oldham first came here from Dorchester, Massachusetts, to explore and to trade with the Indians, this area was known as Pyquag in honor of the local tribe. The settlers from Watertown, Massachusetts, who arrived in 1635 named the place Watertown. Two years later it was officially renamed Wethersfield.

First Church of Christ, Congregational
corner Main & Marsh streets, Wethersfield   Tel: 529-1575

Founded in 1635, this is the third meeting house of Wethersfield's First Church. Completed in 1764, it is the oldest extant brick meeting house in Connecticut and a superb example of early masonry. In the 18th century Connecticut citizens were taxed to support the local Congregational church. This brick meeting house, therefore, was paid for by the town of Wethersfield. Because the town's tax receipts were insufficient to cover the total cost, the citizens of Wethersfield raised additional funds by contributing ropes of red onions which were then sold for sixpence a bunch! For this reason the meeting house became known as "the church that onions built"!

When John Adams visited Wethersfield in 1774, he recorded in his diary, "Went up to the steeple of the meeting house, from whence is the most grand and beautiful prospect in the world." Seven years later George Washington attended services here while visiting the Webb family.

In 1971-73, at a cost of almost $1 million, the interior of the old meeting house was beautifully and authentically restored, and an attractive passageway now connects the church to the parish house facilities. The architects were Jeter, Cook and Jepson and the builder Robert Swain.

The ancient burying ground behind the meeting house is particularly fascinating. Many graves date back to the 17th century, the oldest being 1648. One small headstone marks the grave of Dr. Primus, the black slave of an early Wethersfield physician. Primus, by serving as an apprentice to his master, became a doctor himself and ultimately earned his own freedom. He had a number of talented descendants including Nelson Primus, a successful portrait painter. The buying ground is beautifully maintained.

Webb-Deane-Stevens Museum
211 Main Street, Wethersfield
(one-half mile west of Exit 26 off Interstate 91)
Tel: 203-529-0612

	One House	Two Houses	Three Houses
Adults	$2.00	$4.00	$5.00
Children 14 & Under	.75	1.50	2.25

Open year round, Tues.-Sat., 10 a.m.-4 p.m.; additional hours, May 15-Oct. 15: Sundays, 1-4 p.m.

The Museum is a complex of three 18th century houses restored on their original sites in the heart of Old Wethersfield, Connecticut's largest authentic historic district. The Joseph Webb House (1752), an impressive Georgian mansion, was home to a prominent family of merchants and patriots. In May 1781, General George Washington stayed with the Webbs during a conference with the French Comte de Rochambeau to plot strategy for the final campaign of the

Revolution. In the 20th century, the house was owned and renovated by photographer and furniture historian Wallace Nutting. Today, Webb House is furnished with fine Connecticut furniture and other decorative arts of the 18th and early 19th centuries. The original bright paint colors have been restored, and English red flocked wallpaper hung in 1781 remains on the walls.

The Silas Deane House (1766) was built for a young lawyer and merchant who went on to represent Connecticut at the First Continental Congress and to serve as America's first diplomat at the court of France. Furnished to the Revolutionary era, the house is graced by an elaborate cherry bannister and a carved brownstone fireplace. Portraits of Silas and Elizabeth Deane hang in the parlor, over a tea table owned by Silas (the latter loaned by The Connecticut Historical Society).

The furnishings of the Isaac Stevens House (1788-89), built for a leatherworker and his bride, traverse the years form the aftermath of the Revolution through the Jacksonian era. Many of the furnishings belonged to the Stevens and Francis families, who dwelled there for over a hundred years.

Gardens behind the Webb and Stevens houses illustrate the decorative, medicinal and culinary uses of herbs and flowers before 1800.

Hurlbut-Dunham House
212 Main Street Tel: 529-7636

Apply to Wethersfield Historical Society for admission.

One of the most interesting chapters in Wethersfield's maritime history is the tale of the ship *Neptune* which began a voyage to circumnavigate the world in November of 1796. The ship's captain, Daniel Green, died en route, so First Mate John Hurlbut of Wethersfield took command of the vessel. In 1804, after he returned home with his share of the proceeds of the three-year trading mission in the Orient and Pacific Islands. Hurlbut built this home, one of the finest and largest Federal structures in town. The following year Captain Hurlbut became master of the ship *Leader* and, in 1807, of the brig *Bordeaux*. The young man unfortunately died of smallpox in New York City the following year at the age of 38. His wife and one daughter also died of smallpox. A surviving daughter was raised here by an aunt and uncle.

In 1852 Levi Goodwin, a tavern keeper, purchased the house from the Hurlbuts and added a kitchen ell and piazza. Goodwin became the husband of John Hurlbut's grand-daughter.

Silas W. Robbins, a prosperous businessman, pur-chased the house in 1879 for his son and daughter-in-law, Elisha and Ida Robbins. Their daughter, Jane, ultimately inherited the place and lived here all her life. Her husband was Colonel Howard Dunham who served the State of Connecticut for many years as Insurance Commissioner. The Dunhams had no children, so Mrs. Dunham willed the house and property, with an endowment for its maintenance, to the Wethersfield Historical Society. The house is beauti-fully furnished chiefly with 19th century antiques that belonged to the former occupants, and the first floor and grounds are used for social and cultural events.

Trinity Parish
300 Main Street Tel: 529-6825
Starting January 12, 1867 the first members of Trinity Parish began holding services every other Sunday in the old Academy. Three years later they purchased this land on which to build their church. The corner stone was laid June 1, 1871. The architect was Edward Tuckerman Potter,who also designed the Mark Twain House, the Caldwell Colt Memorial and the Church of the Good Shepherd in Hartford. The latter was the mother church of Trinity Parish and Mrs. Samuel Colt was a great benefactress. Two stained glass win-dows in the back of the sanctuary were gifts from the Sunday School of the Church of the Good Shepherd. Another nota-ble window is "The Tiffany Cross" on the north side of the church. The brownstone came from Portland, Connecticut. This was a favorite building material in the 19th century. The first permanent rector of Trinity Parish was the Rev. Howard S. Clapp.

Trinity Parish Rectory, also known as the Lockwood House, is located at 290 Main Street. Originally the rectory of the Congregational Church, the house was built in 1766-77 for the Rev. James Lockwood by public subscription. Mr. Lockwood was the last minister to serve in the Congregational Church's old wooden meeting house (located where the flag pole now stands) and the first to serve in the present brick meeting house. Widely respected, he was invited, but declined, to become president of both Yale and Princeton.

Comstock, Ferre & Co.
263 Main Street, Wethersfield
Tel: 529-3319

Comstock, Ferre & Co., founded in 1820, is the oldest independent seed company in continuous operation in the United States, and is located in the Wethersfield Historic District. One of the warehouses in use was owned by the patriot Silas Deane in the mid-1700's. Antique seed bins are in use in the Seed Store--an authentic historical note for this old wholesale-retail company. The Seed Store, Garden Shop, Nursery Center, and Holiday Decorating Shop are open all year.

The Cove Warehouse
Cove Park, Wethersfield

Open Sundays, 2-5 p.m., Memorial Day through October 1st. No admission charge.

The Cove Warehouse is the only remaining one of six warehouses built on Wethersfield Cove before 1700 to handle the valley, coastal and West Indian trade. Trade continued to thrive until well into the 19th century. The designation in 1799 by the U.S. Congress of Wethersfield as an official port of entry indicates the amount and scope of the town's trading activity. This warehouse, constructed in 1690, now holds a fine collection of marine charts, ship models, fishing and net-making gear and nautical instruments. This warehouse is maintained by the Wethersfield Historical Society.

Buttolph-Williams House
249 Broad Street, Wethersfield
Tel: 247-8996

May 15 to October 15, Tues.-Sun., 12-4 p.m. The house is maintained by the Antiquarian & Landmarks Society. This house is a Registered National Historic Landmark.

The Buttolph-Williams House, built in 1692, is the oldest restored dwelling in Wethersfield. It is correctly furnished with authentic antiques. "Ye Great Kitchin" is considered the most completely equipped 17th century kitchen in New England. It contains many simple but practical gadgets made of wood, wrought iron and horn, an extensive collection of wooden plates and trenchers, and other intriguing accessories for open hearth cooking.

Captain James Francis House
120 Hartford Avenue, Wethersfield

Captain James Francis was a master builder, skilled in woodworking and house construction. He was a local expert on the framing of brick houses and over 20 examples of his work still stand in Wethersfield. Captain Francis built this home for himself in 1793, and it remained in the Francis family for seven generations. It is now a crafts-oriented restoration and contains only Francis family furnishings and artifacts, tracing a single family through 170 years. Since 1963 the house has been maintained by the Wethersfield Historical Society.

Open Thursday 1-4 p.m., May 15th through October 15th.

Solomon Welles House
220 Hartford Avenue, Wethersfield

One of the most unusual homes of the Revolutionary period is that built by Solomon Welles, a descendant of Thomas Welles, the only governor from Wethersfield. The house was begun in 1774, but as soon as the shell was finished the carpenters left their tools and marched off to war. According to tradition, the men retrieved their tools after the war and completed their work. The fine interior is a tribute to the excellence of their craftsmanship.

Apply to the Wethersfield Historical Society for admission.

FARMINGTON

Founded in 1640 as "an ideal Christian commonwealth," Farmington is one of the most charming old towns in the country. At first a simple agricultural community, the town became very prosperous and important after the Revolutionary War. Then, for almost half a century, Farmington was a major center of mercantile and commercial activities and developed a number of thriving local industries. The Yankee peddlers who distributed the products of these industries and brought others back to trade became prosperous merchants. Some formed the Farmington East India Company, and went overseas as well as overland. The grand list of the town became the third largest in the state, larger than that of Hartford, and the affluent citizens built themselves the many handsome houses that may still be admired. The Farmington Canal, completed in 1828, created even more business wealth. But by 1848 the canal was outmoded by the railroad, and the mercantile importance of the town began to yield to cities like Hartford.

During the years preceding the Civil War, Farmington was a major station of the underground railroad used by slaves escaping from the south. In 1839 the town was also the temporary refuge of a number of Africans who, destined for slavery in Cuba, revolted on the Spanish slave ship, *Amistad*, seized control of the vessel, killed two of their captors, but allowed two of the Spanish crew to survive to help them navigate their way back to Africa. Duped by the Spaniards, the Africans sailed into Long Island Sound where the ship was taken by federal authorities. Disposition of the ship and the Africans proved to be so highly complicated that the affair became an international incident.

Although President Martin Van Buren agreed with the claims of the Spanish government that our courts had no jurisdiction, and that the slaves should be returned to their Spanish owners, sufficient public opinion was aroused in favor of the Africans so that a prominent New Haven attorney, Roger Sherman Baldwin, accepted their case which finally reached the U.S. Supreme Court. In the trial former

President John Quincy Adams supplemented Baldwin's efforts with a bitter and eloquent attack upon the legalistic position of the Federal government. The Supreme Court finally decided the case in favor of the Africans, who, it declared, had been illegally kidnapped from Africa and forced into slavery. The Africans spent the next eight months living in Farmington, until in late 1841 the survivors returned to their homeland. A portrait of Cinque, the Africans' leader, may be seen in the Sarah Porter Memorial.

The *Amistad* affair is of national historic significance as an important case in American history involving foreign slave. It was also a *cause celebre* for the abolitionists and gave impetus to their movement. As a legal matter, it established the fact that Africans, under specific circumstances, were free men as opposed to slaves and therefore entitled to the rights of free men.

During the past century historic Farmington has gradually evolved into a quiet, elegant, residential village. Containing over 100 houses dating prior to 1835, most of the original village was declared an Historic District on July 1, 1965, under a special act passed by the Legislature to preserve for posterity the best of Connecticut's old towns.

Farmington's Historic Main Street

Along this street may be found some of the most beautifully restored 17th, 18th and 19th century houses in the nation. Many styles of architecture are represented, including Colonial, Federal, Georgian, Greek Revival, Republican and Victorian. Most are private homes. Some are owned by Miss Porter's School, including the old Union Hotel that once accommodated patrons of the ill-fated Farmington Canal.

Farmington Congregational Church
Main Street, Farmington
Tel: 677-2601

Built in 1771, this church is the third meeting house of the Farmington congregation and one of the most beautiful in New England. Until 1818 when church and state were officially separated in Connecticut, this building quite literally served both as the place of worship and as the town hall for Farmington.

The church was designed by Captain Judah Woodruff, a self-taught architect and carpenter who went to Boston to personally select the timber for the building. While there he was probably inspired by the design of the Old South Church, which the Farmington meeting house resembles. This is only one of the several buildings designed and constructed by the captain, a number of which still stand in the town. For example, the house at 66 Main Street was a gathering place for the abolitionists during the Civil War, and the house at 4 High Street, a tavern for many years after the Revolution. The captain himself lived at 37 Mountain Road. Some of his carpenter's tools are on exhibit at the Farmington Museum.

In his later years Captain Woodruff for some unrecorded reason stopped attending church, a very radical decision in those days when Connecticut was a rock-bound theocracy. The church fathers demanded an explanation for his absence but, for three years, he ignored them and even refused to appear at his own excommunication!

Miss Porter's School
Main Street, Farmington 06032
Tel: 677-1321

One of the country's most prestigious educational establishments, Miss Porter's School was founded in 1843 by Miss Sarah Porter, sister of the president of Yale University and daughter of Noah Porter, who served for 60 years as pastor of the Farmington Congregational Church. As learned as the male members of her family, Sarah Porter took particular delight in reading Greek before breakfast! She began her career as an educator by teaching local girls. As her reputation spread and students from far and wide traveled to Farmington to attend her school, she purchased the hotel built during the heyday of the Farmington Canal bubble. This is still used as the school's main building.

Today the campus of Miss Porter's School includes about 50 buildings located in the center of the town. Dormitories were formerly private homes and reflect many architectural periods from Colonial to Victorian to contemporary. There is no single classroom building. Classes are held in special rooms in many of the dormitories and in the former arts and science building. A gymnasium/auditorium complex designed by Moore and Salsbury of Avon was completed in 1961 and an arts and science center, designed by Edward Larabee Barnes of New York, opened in 1976.

The boarding students come from 27 states, the District of Columbia and 11 foreign countries. Ninety-five percent of the graduates enter colleges and universities and the rest enroll in programs for specialized training.

Lewis-Walpole Library
Main Street, Farmington

Wilmarth Lewis devoted his life to collecting, cataloging and editing Horace Walpole. In his Farmington home are the largest collection of Walpoliana in the world and the world's largest collection of political and satirical prints and drawings of the second half of the 18th century.

Not open to the general public. Scholars wishing to use these resources must request permission in writing.

Mr. Lewis willed his collection to Yale University. The library is a major international resource for students of this particular period of history.

Since Horace Walpole was sympathetic to the cause of American colonists, it is appropriate that his writings should repose in Farmington, a fountain head of Federalism during the American Revolution.

Stanley-Whitman House
37 High Street, Farmington
Tel: 677-9222

The Stanley-Whitman House, built around 1720 and now a Registered Historic Landmark, recently underwent the most painstakingly accurate restoration ever done on a Colonial New England Home. The house is furnished with authentic period pieces.

Hill-Stead Museum
35 Mountain Road, Farmington
Tel: 677-9064

Open for tours throughout the year except mid-Jan.
to mid-Feb., Wed. through Fri., 2-5 and weekends 1-5 p.m.
Closed Mon., Tues. and on major holidays. Guided tours for
groups can be arranged, but reservations must be made in
advance. Admission $5 adults, $4 senior citizens and students,
$2 children under 12. Friends of Hill-Stead may tour free of
charge.

On May 7, 1915 the *H.M.S. Lusitania*, suspected of
carrying munitions, was torpedoed en route from New York
to Liverpool by a German U-boat just off Kinsale, Ireland.
She sank, and of her 1,524 passengers only 726 were saved.
(Among the survivors was Theodate Pope of Farmington,
Connecticut.) The following year she became the wife of
John Wallace Riddle, a former U.S. Ambassador to Russia
and, from 1921 to 1925, Ambassador to Argentina.

In 1901, long before these dramatic events had changed
her life, Theodate Pope, in cooperation with the distinguished
architect Stanford White, had designed Hill-Stead as a home
for her parents, Mr. and Mrs. Alfred A. Pope. Mr. Pope was
one of the founders and first president of the Cleveland
Malleable Iron Company. He was also an art enthusiast and
Hill-Stead was created not only as a home but as a place to
house his fine collection of French Impressionist paintings
and other art objects which he had collected over the years.
He died in 1913. After her marriage to Mr. Riddle, Hill-Stead
became the permanent home of Theodate Pope Riddle and
her new husband.

Mrs. Riddle, who had become a pioneer female licensed architect in 1912, designed Westover School for Girls and Avon Old Farms School for boys, both tributes to her fine taste and originality. After her death in 1946, she bequeathed Hill-Stead and its contents to be maintained as a museum in which the furnishings were to remain just as she had left them. The house, in its unspoiled vast country setting, is an important social document. Few house museums in the world can match its outstanding works of art.

The grounds are kept in a natural state, and the museum is part of the Farmington Historic District of the National Trust for Historic Preservation. The garden has been restored as designed by Beatrix Ferrand.

Grist Mill
Mill Lane, Farmington 06032
Tel: 677-0848

Originally constructed by Deacon Stephen Hart in 1650, Farmington's grist mill has been owned by Roger Hooker, a descendant of Hartford's founder; by Winchell Smith, a prominent theatrical producer; by Emmet and Mary Rourke, who sold the mill's stone-ground flour; and by Helen Winter. The old mill has been transformed into an unusual and delightful center that includes an antique gallery, two art galleries, needlework shop and book store. The natural beauty of the area, the Farmington River flowing over the old dam, the mill pond and mill wheel all combine to make this a most unique spot.

Heublein Incorporated
Farmington Tel: 677-4061

Heublein, Inc. is a diversified food and beverage company headquartered in Farmington. Heublein's beverages are headed by Smirnoff Vodka, once the official vodka of the czars of Russia, now the largest selling liquor brand in America and a leader overseas.

Heublein's specialty food items include such familiar names as A-1 Steak Sauce, Kentucky Fried Chicken, Gray Poupon Dijon Mustard, Snap-E-Tom Tomato Cocktail, Regina Wine Vinegar, and the Ortega brand of Mexican-style foods.

The company markets other highly popular beverage brands including Lancers Wines from Portugal, Harvey's Bristol Cream, Black Velvet Canadian Whiskey, Black and White Scotch, Arrow Cordials and Flavored Brandies, Malcolm Hereford Cows, Heublein and Club Cocktails, Italian Swiss Colony Wines, Inglenook Wines, Beaulieu Vineyard Wines, Popov Vodka, Jose Cuervo Tequila, Don Q. Puerto Rico Rum, Relska Vodka, and Annie Green Springs and T.J. Swann refreshment wines.

The company has liquor plants in Hartford, Connecticut; Allen Park, Michigan; and Menlo Park, California; wineries in the Napa Valley and other principal grape growing areas of California; and food plants in Oxnard, California and Douglas, Arizona.

The company traces its roots back over 100 years when Andrew Heublein migrated from Bavaria, Germany to Hartford and opened a small restaurant and hotel. Old Hartfordites fondly remember the Heublein Hotel which stood for many years on Jewell Street between Mulberry and Gold, and was finally torn down to make way for Bushnell Plaza. Andrew Heublein's two sons, Gilbert and Louis, moved the family firm into the distilled spirits business in 1875 when they founded G. F. Heublein & Bro. Company. The brothers' first great success came about quite by accident in 1892. The Connecticut Governor's Foot Guard, planning an outing, gave them an order for one gallon of Martinis and one gallon of Manhattans. The brothers filled the order reluctantly because of concern over mixing such a large batch of cocktails in advance. What would happen to the flavor?

It rained the scheduled day of the picnic, and the two gallons of cocktails were set aside for the following Saturday. Again it rained and again the party was called off. The cocktails were forgotten until some time later when they were discovered in storage. The brothers ordered them to be thrown out, but a curious helper took a taste and dutifully reported that they were even better than before. Thus was created the first of Heublein's bottled Club Cocktails which eventually achieved wide popularity. In 1907 the company moved into a new and larger building and began the manufacture of Milshire Gin. By 1914 it had become an international company with branch offices in New York, Frankfurt and London. Its chief import, starting in 1908, was Brand's A-1 Steak Sauce, a fortuitous acquisition that later enabled Heublein to survive more than a decade of Prohibition.

Following the repeal of the Volstead Act, John G. Martin, grandson of Gilbert Heublein and president of Heublein, Inc., made a decision which had a far-reaching effect not only on Heublein but on the entire liquor industry. In 1939 he acquired the U.S. rights to Smirnoff Vodka. At first the new drink was not popular. One batch, however, happened to be incorrectly labeled "Smirnoff White Whiskey. No Taste. No Smell." The mistake triggered a very positive customer response and vodka soon became an American favorite! It is not surprising that Heublein products today are marketed in more than 100 countries throughout the world.

The company's headquarters in Farmington were officially opened in 1973. Architects Russell, Gibson and von Dohlen Inc. of Avon designed the building which they describe as "Mirador" in style ... meaning "overview" or "lookout" ... a most appropriate style considering the fact that the company was founded by the man who built Heublein Tower on Talcott Mountain back in 1914!

University of Connecticut Health Center
263 Farmington Avenue, Farmington Tel: 679-1000
The Health Center of the University of Connecticut was occupied in 1972. Its first students, who had started classes in temporary quarters in 1968, graduated here that same year. In 1977 the Center was formally dedicated with a total enrollment of about 1,000 medical and dental students. The architects for the 1.1 million square-foot complex were Vincent G. Kling and Associates of Philadelphia (now the Kling Partnership). Construction was directed by the State Department of Public Works.

This enormous Health Center consists of five major components:

> An Academic Wing which contains teaching facilities for medical and dental students in first two years, and administrative offices for the School of Medicine and the School of Dental Medicine.

> The Main Building which contains faculty offices, research laboratories, a 100,000 volume health science library, a computer center, and personnel, purchasing and other administrative services.

> The John Dempsey Hospital which contains a 212-bed general hospital.

> An Ambulatory Services Wing which contains medical and dental outpatient services.

> A Center for Laboratory Animal Care which contains quarters for animals used in research and education.

Also located on the 150-acre campus are the Greater Hartford headquarters of the American Red Cross and its state-wide blood bank; Connecticut's Office of the Medical Examiner; a family practice office building; a firehouse; warehouses and maintenance buildings; and a few small research laboratories.

The major programs of the Health Center are: education of future physicians and dentists; graduate education of interns and residents; education of Ph.D. candidates and post-doctoral fellows; continuing education for practitioners; patient care; research.

The Health Center is affiliated with Hartford, St. Francis and Mount Sinai Hospitals and the Institute of Living in Hartford as well as other hospitals throughout the state.

AVON

Taken from Farmington in 1830

Probably settled around 1645, the present Town of Avon was known originally as Nod. Some say this unique name developed from the fact that this part of the Farmington was known as the *North District*. Others say it came from the Indian word *Noadt*, which means "a great way off" or "far, far away." To the early settlers of Nod, often spelled Node, this district really was far away from the center of town!

In 1750 Nod was allowed to become a separate ecclesiastical society and to have its own Congregational Church. Thus Nod's inhabitants no longer were required to attend the First Church on Farmington's Main Street. At this time the name of the district was officially changed to Northington (North Farmington). After Northington separated from its mother town in 1830, its name was changed once again to Avon.

Avon Congregational Church
6 West Main Street, Avon

Constructed in 1819, this beautifully proportioned meeting house is the work of Connecticut's first self-taught architect, David Hoadley. He built a number of other churches including the one in Norfolk.

When the end of the Civil War was proclaimed the citizens of Avon rang their church bell so joyously that it cracked and had to be recast! It has recently been reconditioned and is now in regular use. The church's steeple, badly damaged in the 1938 hurricane, was subsequently repaired.

By 1944 the membership had grown so large that new community rooms and a new parish house were constructed.

Avon Park North
Avon 06001

In 1976 Stanley D. Fisher, the creator of Avon Park North as well as seven other unusually beautiful industrial parks in the Greater Hartford area, was presented with a Distinguished Service Award in Environmental Planning by the Industrial Development Research Council and Conway Publications Inc. The park includes Avon's Town Hall and other town services.

The charming brownstone buildings of Avon Park North were originally constructed in 1852 by the Climax Fuse Company. Later they were purchased by the Ensign-Bickford Company of Simsbury, manufacturers of safety fuse, detonating cord and blasting accessories. In 1967 the company began to move its operations either to other parts of the country or to consolidate them into its facilities in Simsbury, so the Avon buildings stood empty by the end of 1968.

Thanks to the energy and imagination of Stanley Fisher and the management of Ensign-Bickford, the old factories were not torn down but renovated for their present use. The Avon Town Hall complex now occupies five acres of the new park and ten of the old brownstone buildings. The remaining brownstones, all tastefully restored, are spread over 80,000 square feet of land. Some are occupied by architects, engineers, realtors, banks, attorneys, an insurance claims office, and a computer center.

One unique complex contains 22 lofts which have been converted into the Farmington Valley Center for Creative Arts. The facilities were established to assist artists with limited means. The art center has achieved a wide reputation because of the excellent craftsmanship of the artists who work here. The Fisher Gallery Shop is open for the sale of those arts and crafts. Studios are open to the public at varying times at each artist's discretion.

Another complex within the park is the Farmington Valley Association for Retarded and Handicapped, Inc. which prepares retarded people for work within their capabilities, either in a workshop or an actual job in the community.

Avon Old Farms School
Avon Tel: 673-3201

As a school community, an architectural design and an educational ideal, Avon Old Farms is the inspiration of a remarkable founder, Theodate Pope Riddle, (see *Hill-Stead*). A pioneer female architect and fantastically creative human being, her multi-faceted genius still casts a spell over the enchanting campus that she designed, built and financed in 1927 at a cost of almost $10 million. It is located on 1,000 acres of fields and woodlands to which the buildings are related as natural and integral parts of the total landscape. Mrs. Riddle's dream was to erect an "indestructible school for boys" which would inspire successive generations with its unusual beauty and imaginative detail. The massive walls of the buildings are created from roughly split local red sandstone, and the oak woodwork and trim came from forests on the school property and axed on the building site. Seventeenth century tools were used for almost all the construction, while modern plumb lines, rules, and machines were rigorously banned from the premises. The roofs of the buildings are capped with uneven, hand-split red slates, and all the interior and exterior iron and wood work was fabricated by hand in the school's forge and carpentry shop.

In conventional terms Avon is a residential school for boys in grades 9-12. True to the ideals of its founder the school fosters the concept of students and faculty families living together in a community of shared concern for excellence, individuality and integrity.

The school opened in September, 1927. It was closed in 1944 when the U.S. Army took over the buildings and 200 acres of the surrounding land for the duration of World War II. For six months afterwards it was used as a rehabilitation center for blind veterans. The school reopened in 1947 under Headmaster Donald Pierpont. Since then it has grown steadily and is now running at full capacity.

SIMSBURY

Simsbury was first settled in 1642 as Massacoh Plantation by pioneer entrepreneurs who were attracted to the area by large stands of pine trees needed to make tar, pitch and turpentine. These products were in great demand in the shipyards along the Connecticut River. (Massacoh is an Indian word meaning "the great brook's mouth.") The English settlers came chiefly from Windsor. In 1647 Massacoh Plantation and the manufactures were destroyed by fire, supposedly of Indian origin, for which large amounts of tribal land were deeded to the English in reparation.

In 1670 Massacoh Plantation became the independent township of Simsbury. It was approximately 10 miles square and included East Granby, North Bloomfield, Canton, and West Simsbury as well as villages like Scotland, Spoonville and Tariffville. Six years later the scattered settlers were forced to flee back to Windsor because of the King Philip's War. On March 26th of that year everything they could not carry with them was burned by the hostile Indians. King Philip himself is supposed to have watched the flames from a cave on Talcott Mountain that still bears his name. A year later the settlers, assisted by generous Windsor neighbors who took up a collection on their behalf, returned to Simsbury, repossessed their farms and manufactures, rebuilt their homes and, in 1683, constructed their first Congregational meeting house within a few feet of the present reproduction on Massacoh Plantation.

In 1705 a rich vein of copper was discovered in the East Granby sector (Old Newgate Prison) of Ancient Simsbury. Mining commenced almost immediately, the first mining company being composed of Simsbury land proprietors. In lieu of taxes on their new enterprise, the association agreed to pay the town 10 shillings on each ton of copper produced, of which two-thirds was used to support "an able schoolmaster in Simsbury" and one-third was donated to Yale College!

Although entirely illegal under English law, which required the copper ore to be sent back to England for refinement, a certain amount of smelting into pure copper was carried on by a few persons within the town of Simsbury. To further instruct them in this process, the proprietors imported expert smelters from Hanover, Germany. Dr. Samuel Higley of Simsbury, who had been well-educated at Yale, was one of the ten outstanding surgeons in the colonies and a man of infinite curiosity. He took a particular interest in the smelting of local ore ... both copper and iron ... and, in 1728 achieved an American "first" by developing a process for making steel out of iron. Better known are the copper coins he struck nine years later. These Higley Coppers were the first coins made in North America and are now treasured collector's items. They were very popular because adequate coinage was in short supply in those days and barter was, of necessity, the usual medium of trade.

Copper mines in Simsbury continued to be worked into the middle of the 19th century when an influx of copper from richer mines near Lake Superior destroyed the market. Even so, a new business was born from the old. In 1831 an Englishman named Bickford invented a safety fuse to be used for blasting in mining operations. Impressed by its superiority, Richard Bacon of Simsbury, in charge of the local copper mine, acquired from Bickford the rights to manufacture this fuse in the U.S.A. In 1836 the firm of Bacon, Bickford and Eales was formed and brought forth the first safety fuse to be manufactured in this country. As changes in ownership occurred, the name of the company evolved to Ensign-Bickford. In 1851 the present factory, constructed from local red sandstone, was built on Hop Brook to take advantage of the water power.

Manufacturing in Simsbury actually began in the Tariffville and Spoonville sections of town at the Falls on the Farmington River. There, in 1845, the first silver-plated spoons were made by Asa Rogers and William Cowles. However, the setting of the Ensign-Bickford Company, surrounded like an old mother hen by its charming company houses, is a fascinating relic of what used to be a typical Connecticut manufacturing village. Today, of course, the town has evolved into a prosperous suburb of post-industrial Greater Hartford.

Massacoh Plantation
800 Hopmeadow Street, Simsbury
Tel: 658-2500

Open daily, 1-4 p.m., May-October

Massacoh Plantation, an artful reconstruction and preservation of an earlier Simsbury, is a delightful encounter with an historical era that spans more than three centuries. Phelps Tavern, built as a residence by Captain Elisha Phelps in 1771, is the headquarters of the Simsbury Historical Society as well as a museum. The Historical Society acquired the house in 1964.

Just north of this building is an authentic replica of Ancient Simsbury's first Congregational meeting house which served as a place of worship, town hall and school in the 17th century. Outside are an old well sweep, a stocks and pillory and a genuine old ice house.

The Yankee peddler used to be a familiar sight in New England as he distributed "Yankee Notions" manufactured in Connecticut. In 1869 Lucius W. Bigelow, deciding to "take up an outdoor occupation," became a peddler of wooden and tin kitchen items. In 1925 he and his old horse both retired. After his death his widow gave his cart to the Simsbury Historical Society. This, with related relics, is displayed in a barn behind the old meeting house. Other barns and sheds on Massacoh Plantation contain fine exhibits of horse-drawn sleighs and carriages as well as a horse-drawn hearse and explosive wagon.

Reconstructed equipment used in the old days by Ensign-Bickford Company to make safety fuse is well presented in another small building. This company, started as Bacon, Bickford and Eales back in 1836, the oldest manufacturers of safety fuse for mining operations in the nation, is still going strong. E-B's nearby factory, constructed of local red sandstone, is handsome as well as historic. The company also has branch plants in Colorado and Kentucky. Today its chief product is Primacord detonating cord, with safety fuse running second. It has also been an active participant in our country's Space Program. A wholly-owned subsidiary, Darworth, Inc., makes specialty chemicals and wood preservatives.

The Ellsworth Gallery, in another portion of the building with the old fuse-making machinery, presents revolving art exhibits.

In the Hathaway cottage old looms, spinning wheels, home-made textiles, and rag rugs-in-progress are well displayed as are various Victorian artifacts. Simsbury's two leading garden clubs share the care of well-kept herb and parlor gardens in season. Children will take particular delight in the authentic Little Red Schoolhouse of 1740 with its pot-bellied iron stove that was used during Connecticut's long winter months. In those days the three R's were vigorously drummed into well-disciplined scholars, as was the fourth "R"--religion. A "New American Map" hangs on the wall of the school room. It was printed in 1865 and shows most of the land west of the Mississippi River as Indian Territories! Indians used to inhabit Ancient Simsbury, too, and the Indian Village on Massacoh is reconstructed in their memory.

First Church of Christ, Congregational
689 Hopmeadow Street, Simsbury Tel: 658-4422
The original meeting house of Simsbury's first Congregational Church was constructed in 1683 near the present site of the reproduction on Massacoh Plantation. A second meeting house was built here on Drake's Hill in 1743 and a third in the same place 87 years later. The architect was Isaac Damon. Unfortunately this church was destroyed by fire in May, 1965, but reconstructed the following year. Jeter, Cook and Jepson were the architects in charge of restoration.

There is a mistaken notion that Puritan pastors were, of necessity, humorless and stiff-necked human beings. The following story, taken from Dr. Barber's history of Simsbury, illustrates the contrary. It is about the Rev. Samuel Stebbins, minister of this church after the Revolutionary War.

"Mr. Stebbins was an extensive farmer. He owned more than 260 acres of land of which a large proportion was adapted to the raising of grain. Rye was his specialty, of which he raised annually several hundred bushels, which he sold profitably at the distillery of his brother clergyman and friend Dr. Nathan Strong of Hartford. He necessarily employed a large number of men, especially in harvest-time. His knowledge of human nature enabled him to obtain from these men a much more than ordinary amount of labor.

"Having marshalled his men in the harvest field, he would appoint one whom he knew to be ambitious as foreman to lead the field. The sickle was the only harvesting implement. Grain cradles and reapers were not known. One after another, the men fell into their work. 'Now men,' quoth Mr. Stebbins, leaning on the fence, 'I want to see how quick you can go through.' Fresh and vigorous they went across the field with a rush, each striving to 'cut out' the man immediately before him. Having reaped through, they walked back to the starting point, as was the wont of reapers. 'Surprising,' said Mr. Stebbins, 'I don't think you can go through again so quick ...' Again they set in, and rush across the field and return in less time than before. 'Amazing! I didn't think it possible to reap across the field in so short a time. I'm sure you can't do it again--but if you think you can, take a drink of rum and you may try once more--an I'll hold the watch.' They go through with greater speed than before. 'Ah, I had a minute less time than before.' And thus, under the influence of the Dominie's rum and flattery, a vast amount of work was accomplished ..."

A strong Federalist, when Thomas Jefferson won the presidency of the United States over John Adams, Mr. Stebbins "forgot" to pray the following Sunday for the new Chief Executive. Reminded of his omission he complied. "We pray, O Lord, for our new rulers. May they be good men, ruling in the fear of God. Especially we pray for the President of the United States, give him Wisdom--give him understanding--for God knows, he needs them."

Simsbury United Methodist Church
799 Hopmeadow Street, Simsbury Tel: 651-3356
The Methodists, like the Episcopalians, did not begin to grow in numbers in Connecticut until after the Revolution as most of their preachers were Tories and left the country at the start of the war.

The first Methodist church building in Simsbury, a wooden frame structure, was replaced by this handsome English Gothic Church in 1908. The architect was George Keller of Hartford. Native brownstone with terra cotta trimming was used for the edifice, which is cruciform in plan with a low, square belfry tower in which swings the same bell that for nearly 70 years tolled its welcome from the old church. Five magnificent windows in the sanctuary are the work of Louis Comfort Tiffany. The two windows on the left side of the nave were executed in Germany and are very fine examples of stained glass artistry.

Heublein Tower
Talcott Mountain Trail, Simsbury

The Tower is located within Talcott Mountain State Park.

Enter Talcott Mountain Trail off Rte. 185 en route between West Hartford and Simsbury. Be prepared for a one-mile hike. Memorial Day-Labor Day. Open daily 10-5 p.m. Tel: 677-0662

Most human beings seeking power and romance are attracted by mountain tops. Gilbert Heublein of the food and liquor family--G. F. Heublein & Bro. Co.--was no exception to this rule. In 1914 he purchased this lofty site on Talcott Mountain and commissioned West Hartford architect Roy Bassette to build a solid concrete seven-story tower strong enough to withstand violent storms, if necessary, or the ravages of fire. This tower is thought to have been the first structural steel building in the nation, its frame extending ten feet into the rock cliff and anchored there by five feet of concrete. It took nearly two years to build because all the materials--stone, steel and concrete--had to be hauled up the side of the mountain by horse and wagon. The cement walls would require a wrecking ball to bring down. The observation deck windows are framed in heavy copper and some of the doors are two-inch thick oak. Even so, during severe wind storms, such as the hurricane of '38, the tower is reported to have swayed and shuddered dramatically ... but it has never fallen. The cost of the tower alone, excluding later additions and a servants' quarters built nearby, was more than $95,000.

The Heublein family used the tower for 25 years as a summer residence. Mr. Heublein's study was on the main floor; the second floor was the master bedroom and sleeping porch; the third floor the Pink Room; the fourth floor the Green Room; the fifth floor the Peacock Room; and the sixth floor the Ballroom, where the observatory is now located.

One can see New Hampshire to the north on a clear day, and as far in every other direction.

Shortly after its completion, the tower played a part in causing Gilbert Heublein to be suspected of being a German spy. One evening during World War I Mr. Heublein was entertaining guests in his new home. To show his friends the area and the other summer homes which dotted the hillside, he took them up to the seventh floor and turned on a large 2,000-watt floodlight he had installed in the cupola. The light was turned on several times to highlight different features of the landscape. At 2 a.m. that morning Mr. Heublein was confronted at his door by a naval officer and a group of men who accused him of signaling to German submarines lying off Newport, Rhode Island! The poor gentleman was so upset by this accusation that he offered his estate as a training ground for Connecticut troops and his English bowling green as a parade ground, but the offer was refused and the spy rumor persisted.

Gilbert Heublein was not the first romantic to build a tower on Talcott Mountain. Daniel Wadsworth, Hartford's first citizen who was wealthy enough to indulge a fancy for lofty lookouts, built a 55-foot tower atop this same mountain in 1810. It was part of his country estate, Montevideo. When his tower blew down in a windstorm, he erected another in 1840. The Wadsworth Tower was subsequently purchased by David Collins, a pioneer Connecticut industrialist who, with his brother, had founded the Collins Company in Collinsville to manufacture axes and machetes. The tower was destroyed by fire in July of 1864.

More than 40 years later two speculators, M. H. Bartlett and Charles Kellogg, built a third tower just north of this site as a commercial venture. For 50 cents they offered the general public a tempting array of attractions: "Telescope, Tower, Summer House, Tables, Croquet, Swings, Flying Alley, Piano and Dancing Platform." Children were admitted for half price, and horses were provided with four quarts of oats in the shade for 35 cents! The venture prospered until 1888 when Robert Roe, a wealthy manufacturer of printing presses, purchased the property for his private estate. This tower was removed when Gilbert Heublein built the present one in 1914.

In 1944 the *Hartford Times* acquired the tower and the surrounding land for $70,000. The newspaper planned to use the site for a radio transmitter and executive retreat. The *Times* held many glamorous parties here. One of its most honored guests was General Dwight D. Eisenhower just before he ran for the presidency of the United States. Because the cost of maintaining the tower and the mile-long entrance road finally became too burdensome, the *Times* sold the tower and 340 acres to a developer in 1962. The latter proposed to use the mountain top as sites for expensive homes and to convert the tower into a restaurant or nightclub.

Public opposition to this proposal was immediate. In the forefront of several non-profit citizen groups interested in preserving the area as open space were John E. Ellsworth of the Farmington River Watershed Association and Roger W. Eddy of the Connecticut Park and Forest Commission. In 1963 the Capitol Region Planning Agency recommended that the state purchase the tower and land as a state park. A "Save Talcott Mountain Committee" then was formed, headed up by Buist Anderson, general counsel for Connecticut General Life Insurance Company. The committee soon raised $75,000, and the Hartford Foundation for Public Giving matched this sum.

Negotiations, however, were slow and laborious. The developers held out for $595,000 which the state refused to pay. Even worse, the State Department of Agriculture and Natural Resources wanted to tear the tower down. Finally, in September of 1966, after much public anguish, the state purchased the land and the tower from the developers for $377,000 plus $150,000 raised by the private sector, and the tower was refurbished for public enjoyment.

Visitors entering the grand foyer of the tower are greeted by portraits of Gilbert and Louis Heublein, founders of G. F. Heublein & Bro. How astonished these gentlemen would be now to learn that the little food and liquor processing company they established back in 1875 has become a top corporation.

The name Heublein, over the years, has been pronounced three distinctly different ways. The brothers Gilbert and Louis called themselves "Hoy-bline." Later the company changed to "High-bline." Now the correct pronunciation is

"Hugh-bline" for the obvious reason that this is what the spelling of the word most clearly indicates. Old Hartfordites, however, stubbornly stick to "Hoy-bline" ... probably just to show off the fact that they knew the family before the company achieved world renown!

Westminster School
995 Hopmeadow, Simsbury   Tel: 658-4444

Founded in 1888 as a school for boys, Westminster today is a coeducational school for grades 9-12. Students come to Westminster from all over the country and represent many ethnic, social, religious, economic and regional differences. One importance of this much diversity is that a student's background seldom hurts or helps him once he is on the hill. At Westminster the big question is not "Who is your father?" but "What are you ready to do?"

The school is situated on 200 acres of plateau overlooking the Farmington River Valley. Its plant includes excellent academic, athletic and recreational facilities, a chapel, administrative offices, student dormitories, and faculty homes. The majority of these facilities have been erected or significantly remodeled since 1950.

Westminster's graduates attend a broad spectrum of the best colleges and universities in the country.

Ethel Walker School
Bushy Hill Rd., Simsbury Tel: 658-4467

Walker's is a small school. More of an educational family than an educational institution, the school offers a four-year boarding and day program for grades 9 through 12. Students come here from more than 30 states and 10 different foreign countries.

The school was founded in 1911 by Ethel Walker as a college preparatory school for girls. Situated on a lovely 800-acre wooded campus, the school provides its students with a wealth of academic, artistic and athletic activities. The graduates attend major colleges and universities in the United States and abroad.

Walker's campus is particularly attractive with handsome buildings designed by prominent architects: Moore and Salsbury and Milton Hayman of Hartford; Douglas Orr of New Haven; Farrar and Majers of St. Louis, and others.

Old Newgate Prison and Copper Mine
Newgate Rd., East Granby

This museum is a National Historical Landmark owned and operated by the Connecticut Historical Commission. Mid-May - Mid-Oct. Wed.-Sun. 10-4:30.

GRANBY

In 1707 the copper mines of colonial Simsbury were the first to be chartered in North America. By 1773 work at the mines had ceased to be profitable to the owners, so the Colony of Connecticut took possession. After constructing essential buildings adjacent to the main mine shaft and surrounding the entire area with a formidable stone wall, the colonists created a prison named Newgate after notorious Newgate Prison in England. Prisoners, mostly thieves and counterfeiters, were quartered in the bowels of the old copper mines where they were kept busy digging ore. (In those days felons convicted of more serious crimes were executed, not imprisoned!) Later the inmates of Newgate were allowed to emerge from their subterranean cells every day and placed in shops within the prison yard where they were taught to make nails and shoes.

Many fabulous escapes from this dungeon at Newgate were attempted, and some succeeded. One ingenious man contrived to remove the body of a fellow prisoner from a newly made coffin and to climb in himself. The coffin was carried outside the prison walls and was about to be buried when the prisoner suddenly "rose from the dead." The guards were so stupified with fear and astonishment that he was able to flee, never to be recaptured!

During the Revolution, prisoners of war and Tories were confined here since Connecticut, the most solidly pro-revolution of all the colonies, was considered a logical spot for impounding persons unsympathetic to the patriots' cause.

Later it became a state prison. This Connecticut landmark thus has the rather lugubrious distinction of being the first state prison in America! Newgate continued to be used until 1827 when the convicts were marched to new quarters in Wethersfield. The Wethersfield Penitentiary ... a place where prisoners were supposed to become penitent and repent their crimes ... was considered a model penal institution designed after the avant-garde Auburn plan. In 1964 the penitentiary was closed and a new State Prison at Enfield took its place.

WINDSOR

Guided by friendly Indians, the first white settlers came to Windsor from Plymouth Colony in 1633 to establish a trading post. Later more settlers came from Massachusetts Bay.

For about 150 years the little colony developed in much the same manner as Hartford and Wethersfield, concentrating on agriculture, trade and shipping. However, Windsor's soil was especially fertile. Tobacco was grown, but an inferior grade unsuitable for export. The white farmers learned about tobacco from the Indians. It was the only crop Indian males deigned to cultivate, and they grew it only for their own smoking pleasure. To those warriors and hunters, all other agriculture was "woman's work."

At first the English copied the Indians and grew the local tobacco just to smoke themselves. But, being men of business, they finally tried to improve the quality of the leaf and to export it. In 1801 a Mrs. Prout of East Windsor made

the first American "long nine" cigar. Windsor farmers began
to concentrate on broadleaf tobacco for cigar wrappers. By
1825 Connecticut Valley Broadleaf was a quality product
that could compete on a world-wide market with all other
tobaccos. In 1875 Havana Seed was introduced because it
yielded a higher percentage of wrappers than Broadleaf.

By this time Connecticut's only real competitor in the
cigar wrapper market was Sumatra in the East Indies. There
a particularly fine-textured, mild-tasting and smooth-burning
leaf was grown, thanks to the hot, humid climate of the region.
Sumatra leaf began to be preferred for cigar wrappers,
although Connecticut leaf continued in heavy demand for
cigar fillers and binders.

Challenged, Windsor Yankees devised a unique
method for simulating Sumatra's climate. In 1900 they began
to spread tents of white netting over their fields. The atmosphere under their netting was indeed like that of the East
Indies--hot, moist and ideal for developing a strong, light
leaf!

During the growing season it is interesting to drive
around the Windsor area to see the tobacco being cultivated.
The acres and acres of white and yellow tents and the many
busy farm workers are an amazing sight in this highly indus-
trialized "land of the Puritans." However, increasing amounts
of former tobacco land have been turned into industrial parks.
Today, only 1800 acres are planted in broadleaf or under shade.

The Palisado Green
Windsor

This small green, or common, is surrounded by the
most historic portions of Windsor. Easterly, along the sandy
banks overlooking the Great Meadows and the Connecticut
River, the settlers from Dorchester, Massachusetts, lived in
dugouts during the bitter winter of 1635. Two years later a
great palisado or fort 1,100 feet square was built to protect
the newly built homes and the first meeting house from the
Pequot Indians. It was again a place of refuge during the
King Philip's War of 1675.

During the last half of the 1700s this area was the scene
of vigorous commercial activity. The internationally known
trading firm of Hooker & Chaffee unloaded ships from Boston,

the West Indies and Liverpool at the foot of North Meadows Road and shipped livestock and produce to distant ports.

Prominent on the green is a monument commemorating the "gathering" of Windsor's First Church in England, the oldest Congregational Church in America. A tablet portrays a replica of the *Mary and John*, the ship which carried this pioneer congregation to New England. The monument marks the site of their first meeting house and lists the names of the original settlers from Dorchester, Massachusetts.

The Palisado Cemetery ... Ye Burying Place of Windsor ... dates back to 1637. One gravestone marks the resting place of Ephraim Huit, 1644, the oldest original gravestone in Connecticut. Huit shares this ancient cemetery with many of the original settlers and others who have shaped American history. Nearly 115 veterans of the Revolution and earlier colonial wars against the Indians and the French lie here behind the First Congregational Church on Palisado Avenue.

Interested persons should also visit the Old Poquonock Burying Ground on Marshall Phelps Road near Poquonock Avenue. This cemetery also contains ancient graves and is reported to have been used initially as an Indian burying place.

The Palisado Green was designated an Historic District by the Connecticut Historical Commission in February. Many other fine old homes still stand in other parts of the town.

First Church in Windsor
107 Palisado Avenue, Windsor
United Church of Christ Tel: 688-7229

In March of 1630 the Rev. John White of Dorchester, Devon, in southwestern England, assisted by the Rev. John Maverick and the Rev. John Warham, gathered together approximately 140 persons to form what would become the oldest Congregational Church in America. The congregation included a number of talented lay leaders like Roger Ludlow, Captain John Mason and Matthew Grant. The company assembled at Plymouth where they held a day of solemn fasting and praying. In the morning White preached a farewell sermon, and in the afternoon the people formally elected Maverick and Warham as their ministers. Soon after they boarded the ship *Mary and John*. It is recorded that they "came by the good hand of the Lord, through the Deeps comfortably; having Preaching or Expounding on the Word of God every day for Ten Weeks together, by our Ministers." On May 30, 1630, they landed at Nantasket, the first of the Massachusetts Bay Company of 17 ships to arrive in New England. Shortly afterwards they settled in Dorchester, Massachusetts. They were not, however, completely satisfied with their new settlement.

In 1633 the colonists in Plymouth, Massachusetts, sent out a bark under the aggressive leadership of William Holmes to explore the land above the Dutch Fort at Hartford for trade with the Indians. Defying the guns of the Dutch, Holmes reached the present site of Windsor on October 26th and quickly erected a prefabricated house frame which he had carried with him from Plymouth. Around this he then built a stockade against possible attack by both Dutch and Indians. The Dutch protested, but to no avail, so it was in this manner that a fur trading post was established by the English and the future Town of Windsor officially founded.

In 1635 a number of settlers at Dorchester, hearing about the fertile land along the Connecticut in this area, decided to migrate here too. Unfortunately they arrived late in the year, and an early winter soon descended upon them. A few fled back to Dorchester. However, in the spring of 1636 the Rev. Mr. Warham led more than half of the Dorchester population to Windsor, including a majority of the most influential landowners and leaders. The simple fact that they controlled greater resources of wealth and manpower meant the eventual overwhelming of the few traders from Plymouth. In 1637 Plymouth officials sold their interests to the Dorchester pioneers more or less under duress!

This meeting house was the fourth church constructed by the Windsor congregation. It was designed and built by Ebenezer Clark in 1794, and Oliver Ellsworth was on the building committee. In 1844 the church was extensively repaired and altered and the Greek-Doric portico added.

Wood Memorial Library
783 Main Street, South Windsor, CT Tel: 289-1783
Wood Memorial Library, erected in 1926 by William Wood in memory of his parents, is a privately funded institution established to maintain a library for the benefit of the

general public, to promote an understanding of the Northeast Woodland Indian, and to preserve the history of South Windsor. Exhibits depicting early American Indian life and an extensive collection of ancient Indian artifacts are highlights of a visit to the Library. Also on display are fine examples of the work of early Connecticut River craftsmen, such as clockmaker Eli Terry, cabinetmaker Eliphalet Chapin, and metalsmith/clockmaker Daniel Burnap, and local artists Albertus Jones, and Edith and Amelia Watson. In addition to its circulating and reference collection of over 12,000 volumes the library also houses archives for the paper history of South Windsor. Events held at Wood include a Sunday Concert Series, ongoing quilting demonstrations, story hours, and special programs and classes for children.

Part of the charm of visiting Wood Library is the chance to explore its quiet, rural setting on one of Connecticut's oldest Main Streets. The avenue is lined with beautiful historic houses, representing a wide variety of architectural styles and the diversity of South Windsor's history.

The Fyler House and Wilson Museum
96 Palisado Avenue, Windsor Tel: 688-3813

The Museum Research Library is available by appointment.

The Fyler House has been the headquarters of the Windsor Historical Society since 1925.

The land upon which the Fyler House stands was given to Lieutenant Walter Fyler for his services in the Pequot War of 1637. Captain John Mason of Windsor commanded the little army of approximately 100 men from Hartford, Windsor, Wethersfield and Saybrook who took part in this decisive war which saved the Connecticut Colony from destruction by hostile Pequot Indians. At that time the people of Windsor, fearing an attack upon their tiny settlement, constructed a fort for protection. According to early maps, Lieutenant Fyler's land lay within the palisado.

Lieutenant Fyler built his home around 1640. He died in 1685 and his will contained a most unusual clause: his wife had the use of his estate during her lifetime and also 100 pounds to bestow upon another husband or to use as she pleased! Members of the Fyler family continued to live here for the next 123 years. The place was purchased in 1763 by Alexander Allyn and later by Nathaniel Howard, a sea captain. Legend has it that the latter added a room after each successful voyage! The location of the house made it a natural place to receive mail, so during the Howards' residence it became the first post office in Windsor. Later it became the home of the Stiles sisters, relatives of Henry Stiles, the Windsor historian.

The Windsor Historical Society has restored the distinctive features of the Fyler House with painstaking care, and furnished it with period furniture and artifacts. It is one of the oldest surviving frame houses in Connecticut.

The Wilson Museum

The Wilson Museum, built in 1962, joins the Fyler House by a connecting vestibule and breezeway. It is built in an architectural style typical of Windsor houses in the mid-eighteenth century. The museum houses a fine historical and genealogical library. There are also on display many Indian relics and varied collections of early Americana.

It is interesting to note that when the fur traders from Plymouth, Massachusetts, first came here in 1633 the area was called Poquonock in honor of the local Indians. However, when the settlers from Dorchester arrived in 1635 they called their plantation Dorchester. Two years later the town was officially renamed Windsor.

The Oliver Ellsworth Homestead
778 Palisado Avenue, Windsor Tel: 688-8717

When the United States sent Oliver Ellsworth to France as minister plenipotentiary in 1799, Napoleon Bonaparte noted his dignified face and majestic form in the crowd of new envoys and commented to a companion, "We must make a treaty with that man!" Upon Ellsworth's return to America in 1803, Napoleon presented him with a Gobelin Tapestry, "The Shepherd Boy," in appreciation for his services in resolving differences between the two countries. It still hangs in Ellsworth's old homestead.

May 1 - Nov. 1; Tues. - Sat. 1-5 p.m.

In 1665 Josiah Ellsworth acquired the land on which his son Jonathan built this gentleman's estate in 1740. The house has always been well kept and is filled with fine antiques. Oliver Ellsworth was born here on April 29, 1745.

Both President George Washington and President John Adams subsequently visited here.

A brilliant lawyer, Oliver Ellsworth was a strong leader during the Revolution. He was elected a delegate to the Connecticut Congress in 1777 and became a Judge on the Superior Court of Connecticut in 1784. He was one of the five framers of the Constitution in 1787 and personally hand-wrote the entire Judiciary Act which forms the basis of our whole Federal Judiciary System. It was adopted without amendment. He was elected to the first Senate in 1789, serving until 1796 when he was appointed Chief Justice of the Supreme Court by his friend John Adams. Oliver Ellsworth and George Washington were also close associates, and a letter from Washington is one of the exhibits in the Ellsworth's homestead.

Despite his distinguished career and wide travels, this home-loving Connecticut puritan once wrote to a friend: "I have visited several countries, and I like my own the best. I have been in all States of the Union, and Connecticut is the best State. Windsor is the pleasantest place in Connecticut. I am content, perfectly content, to die on the banks of the Connecticut." And on November 26, 1807, he did.

Bissell's Ferry

In 1618 the Connecticut General Court made a contract with John Bissell "to keep and carefully attend the Ferry over the Great River in Windsor ..." The Bissell Ferry Landing was located about 1,000 feet north of the Ellsworth homestead. In 1665 the landing was moved about one mile south where it remained until it was discontinued in 1917. Today this ferry, the first in Connecticut, has been replaced by Bissell Bridge.

Loomis-Chaffee School
Batchelder Rd., Windsor Tel: 688-4934

In 1874 four Loomis brothers and a sister, bereft of heirs, decided to pool their considerable estates and found an institution for secondary education in the hopes "that some good may come to posterity through the harvest, poor though it may be, of our lives." The site for their new school was approximately 300 acres of land at the confluence of the Farmington and Connecticut rivers on which stood their ancestral homestead, built by Joseph Loomis in 1639.

Loomis Institute for boys and girls was opened in 1914 but soon evolved into a school for boys alone. Chaffee School for girls opened in 1926. The two schools existed separately for many years. However, a program in coordinate education between the two schools which began in 1970 led to their reunification two years later. Loomis-Chaffee enrolls boarding boys and girls, and day students.

Over the years, Loomis and Chaffee, separately and together, have earned a reputation for the highest standards of academic excellence. Both schools, with the advantage of a large endowment and substantial scholarship monies, have admitted and graduated the most able students without regard to social status or financial background, thus remaining true to the democratic principles in the founding character.

How delighted the one Loomis sister would have been to know that the school she and her four brothers founded graduated the first woman elected governor in her own right; Governor Ella Grasso of Connecticut!

Loomis-Chaffee's campus and buildings are particularly attractive and well-equipped. In 1944 the historic Loomis Homestead became a faculty residence.

WINDSOR LOCKS

Separated from
Windsor in 1854

This part of old Windsor was originally known as Pine
Meadow and, for many years, was considered to be the best
place to ford the Connecticut. In 1829, after the locks which
formed the Enfield Canal were constructed here, the name
of the area changed to Windsor Locks.

Enfield Canal
Windsor Locks

For a brief period in the Connecticut River's history,
canals and steamboats played a significant economic and
romantic role. In 1795, at South Hadley, Massachusetts, a
canal was built to circumvent a falls, so the Connecticut
River was the first in the country to be improved by the addition of a man-made waterway. The Enfield Canal, dug by
the Irish workmen and financed by Hartford merchants, was
open for business November 11, 1829. Five and a half miles
long and 70 feet wide, the canal was equipped with four locks
capable of carrying boats up to 70 tons in size.

Up to this time, the shallow rapids and falls at Enfield
had been serious deterrents to up-river traffic. The cargoes
of boats going to Massachusetts and Vermont had to be
unloaded and sorted at Warehouse Point. Then the goods
were loaded on flatboats that were poled over the rapids by
strong men. It was a very cumbersome method. So, when
steamboats began to be used, Hartford businessmen determined to bypass the rapids with a canal.

For fifteen years a steady procession of freight and passenger steamers passed through this canal, and both down-
river merchants and up-river farmers prospered from the
increase in trade. But the canal was gradually outmoded by
the railroad as steamboats were supplanted by freight trains.

Today this old canal, still in good condition, was included in the National Register of Historic Places.

Dexter Corporation
One Elm Street, Windsor Locks
Tel: 623-9801

C. H. Dexter, a division of Dexter Corporation, was founded in 1767. It is one of the oldest companies in the United States and the oldest company listed on the New York Stock Exchange. It began as a sawmill on the banks of the Connecticut River at the same location where both C. H. Dexter and Dexter Corporation are headquartered today in Windsor Locks.

In the 1840s under C. H. Dexter, the third generation in the family line that still manages Dexter today (7th generation), the company entered the papermaking business and developed into a producer of graphic arts papers, wrapping tissues and condenser tissue. (Along the way the company invented nontarnish paper for wrapping silverware and introduced the first packaged toilet paper which was sold complete with hook for hanging it on the outhouse wall.)

In the 1930s Dexter became a producer of specialty nonwoven papers with the invention of its wet forming nonwovens process. This new process yielded the first filter paper which, in turn, made it possible for teapackers to produce teabags on a high volume basis. The Dexter system also produced the first processed meat casing base paper and the first machine-made mimeograph stencil base.

The company developed Dextex, a family of non-woven fabrics which has since gained broad use in surgical disposables and has now been expanded with new varieties for durable nonwoven applications.

Bradley International Airport
Windsor Locks Tel: 623-3940
Manager of Airport and 566-4598 Dept. of Aeronautics.

Under the management of the Connecticut Department of Transportation, Aeronautics Division, and strategically located between New York and Boston, Bradley International is one of the four most important international airports in the northeastern part of the United States. Bradley is equipped with the latest in navigational aids, making it accessible for regular flights and diversions when larger coastal airports are closed because of poor weather conditions. Its inland location makes it a true all-weather airport as the field very rarely shuts down because of unfavorable climactic conditions.

Most recently the State of Connecticut has equipped the airport with a new international concourse that is rapidly becoming a major port of entry for the world's biggest carriers.

Like all modern airports, Bradley International is much more than a facility for aircraft, passengers and freight. It is as well a very active center of commercial economic activity for many merchants and related aerospace industries and a place of work for thousand of employees. Bradley has a full range of ground support services including health, immigration and customs offices, restaurants, hotels and transportation facilities. It is a great place to take children to view incoming and outgoing aircraft.

New England Air Museum
Route 75, Bradley International Airport, Windsor Locks, Connecticut Tel: 623-3305

Open daily, 10-5 p.m.
Because the Hartford area is an important center of the aircraft industry, this museum is of particular interest. Founded in 1959, it has achieved international recognition for its unique collection of fighters, bombers, helicopters, and gliders dating from 1909 through World War II to the present. The display includes the Constellation once owned by billionaire flight pioneer, Howard Hughes, in which he visited practically every major airport in the world. Also on display is a Boeing B-47E stratojet, the forerunner of today's wide-bodied, swept-wing jetliners and the first airplane designed to approach supersonic flight. The oldest surviving aircraft in America may be seen here, too. It is the balloon *Jupiter* built by Connecticut Yankee Silas Brooks in 1886.

The aeronautical history of this Capitol Region began in 1800 when a young man named John Graham came to Hartford with some "captive" balloons described by the *Hartford Courant* as "Archimideal Phaetons," "Vertical Aerial Coaches" and "Patent Federal Balloons." He ensconced himself and his aerial devices near the South Green, now Barnard Park, and delighted the men, women and children of Hartford by giving them sky rides.

In 1878 the first dirigible flight in the United States took place in Hartford. Thirty-eight years later the U.S.

Navy's first blimp, DN-1, was assembled in the Connecticut State Armory located on Broad Street. Although the blimp had actually been built in New Haven, the State Armory was the only enclosed area in Connecticut at that time large enough to contain the inflated airship while it was being rigged.

Hartford's entry into the air-age, however, did not really "take off" until local industrialists had managed to develop a work force of skilled mechanics and the mechanical and managerial know-how essential to coping with complex design and manufacturing operations. This was accomplished over a period of about 80 years in the process of inventing and fabricating guns, sewing machines, screw machines, bicycles, automobiles, and precision machine tools.

Connecticut led the nation in establishing laws regulating aviation. On January 4, 1911, Governor Simeon E. Baldwin noted in his message to the General Assembly: "The rapid progress of the art of aviation during the past few years calls for legislation. Flying machines and ... dirigible balloons put in danger all over whom they sail ... It is not improbable that they will be used before long as a regular mode of transportation between distant places ... I recommend the passage of a statute providing for their registry in the office of the Town Clerk in each town in which one is owned; forbidding their use for flights within this state unless in charge of someone approved by competent authority as capable of directing their course with due skill and care ..." The following June appropriate laws were passed. They were the first of the kind in the nation, and perhaps in the world, to regulate aviation. Not until 15 years later did the Federal Government enact national aeronautical regulations.

The manufacture of aircraft engines in this area began in the early 1920s when financing by the Pratt and Whitney Machine Tool Company attracted young Frederick Rentschler and George Mead to Hartford. Here they designed and built their first Wasp engine in 1925. Since then the aircraft industry and related enterprises have gradually dominated Greater Hartford's manufacturing scene. United Aircraft, Hamilton Standard, Kaman Aircraft and their hosts of local subcontractors and suppliers now employ one out of every two persons engaged in manufacturing in the Capitol Region.

In 1921 the only airfield in Hartford was a so-called

"barn-storming field" in Goodwin Park. When two young Army fliers were killed there trying to make a landing, Hartford's Mayor Newton Brainard championed the creation of a suitable airport in the city's South Meadows. It was named Brainard Field in his honor.

The following year Connecticut invoked its pioneer aviation law for one of its first cases. This involved a dare devil pilot who flew too low over Yale Bowl during the Army-Yale football game, terrifying and outraging the spectators! It is not surprising that Travelers Insurance Company in 1919 issued the world's first airplane liability policy.

In May of 1927 Connecticut became the first state to establish a Department of Aeronautics. This same month and year Charles Lindbergh thrilled the world by his solo, non-stop flight across the Atlantic Ocean. Connecticut Governor John H. Trumbull achieved fame by becoming a qualified pilot, thus earning the honor of being the first "flying governor" in American history.

Eleven months before the Japanese attack on Pearl Harbor, the Army indicated that it wished to create a fighter plane base in Connecticut as part of the air defense of this section of the nation. The state purchased almost 2,000 acres of flat tobacco land in Windsor Locks for this purpose, then leased it to the federal government for $1 a year. By summertime the new airfield was put into active operation. Then, on August 21, 1941, at 9:15 a.m. a young pilot, Eugene M. Bradley of Antlers, Oklahoma, taking off from the field in a Curtiss-P40, developed engine trouble over the landing strip and crashed to his death. He was the first pilot to be killed here, and the following January 20th the airfield was officially named in his memory by the War Department. (There is a picture of Lt. Bradley in the Airport Officer's office in the Air Force Museum.)

Bradley Field continued to be used throughout the war as a transitional training field for men before they actually flew in combat. Scores of flying fortresses and other bombers were parked here awaiting overseas flight. From October 8, 1944 until the latter part of 1946, Bradley was also used as a prisoner-of-war camp for German soldiers. These men were assigned to many tasks at the base. In the last months of the war, the number of women at Bradley Field increased greatly. The WAC contingent required special barracks. At one time 40 percent of the mechanics working on airplanes at the base were women!

The most extensive use of Bradley came in 1945 when bomber planes stopped here en route from the European to the Pacific theater of war. Homecoming airmen spoke of the Bradley Field Tower as their "Statue of Liberty." Fortunately the war soon ended with the capitulation of Japan and most of the planes did not leave this country.

Bradley Field, like so many similar installations throughout the country, became relatively dormant after World War II. Then on June 12, 1946, an unusually dynamic and far-sighted man, Francis S. Murphy, became chairman of the Connecticut Aeronautic Commission. The fact that he was also general manager, later publisher, of the *Hartford Times* was of crucial importance. Mr. Murphy was a man of ideas ... new ideas. The newspaper became his tool for educating the public-at-large about Connecticut's potential future in the dawning Space Age. His was at first a one-man battle to convert the defunct bomber base of Bradley Field into a top-notch commercial airport. He acted with the speed of lightning. On August 28th the State of Connecticut, led by the new Commissioner of Aeronautics, sent a telegram to the U.S. Government announcing that the State was seizing Bradley Field and all its buildings and would take immediate possession.

After the takeover of Bradley Field by the Aeronautical Commission, most newspapers and other opinion makers backed up Francis Murphy's boldness. Endorsements poured in from ministers, priests and rabbis, service clubs and veterans' organizations, as well as from the political and economic leaders of Connecticut. Support was so enthusiastic that plans for the modernization of Bradley Field developed rapidly and climaxed on May 23, 1950, when popular General Dwight D. Eisenhower flew in and personally broke ground for a superb new Bradley Field Terminal Building. Two years later on September 15th the building was dedicated amid gala ceremonies attended by prestigious air pioneers, war heroes and political-industrial moguls. Francis Murphy was the "star" of the occasion, as he should have been, and the terminal building was officially named in his honor.

Connecticut Fire Museum

58 North Road (Rt. 140), Warehouse Point Tel: 623-4732

July-Aug. Open daily 10-4; April-Oct. Sat. & Sun. 10-4.

Many old-time fire trucks on display dating from 1850 through 1950. The exhibits include models and outline the history of firefighting.

Connecticut Trolley Museum

58 North Rd. (Rt. 140), Warehouse Point
Tel: 623-7417

Memorial Day - Labor Day: M-F, 10-4; Sat., 10-5; Sun.12-6 p.m. Labor Day - Memorial Day: Sat. & Sun., 12-5.

To recreate an important phase of New England's business and social life from 1890 to 1945, a three-mile round trip streetcar ride with an educational narrative is provided to the visitors. The museum's collection consists of passenger and freight trolley cars, interurban cars, electric and steam locomotives, freight and passenger cars, cranes and service cars.

Over the years the volunteers have been able to not only build miles of track and the associated overhead for power distribution, but all of the yard and storage track, the power substation, the storage barns, and a restoration shop.

NEW BRITAIN

New Britain Museum of American Art

56 Lexington Street, New Britain
Tel: 229-0257 Tues.-Sunday 1-5 p.m.

No admission charge. All are invited to contribute voluntarily to the museum by becoming a Friend.

Opened in 1937 in the former home of Grace Judd Landers, this privately endowed museum contains outstanding collections of American paintings, prints and sculptures. It is the first museum collection of exclusively American art in the world, from 1740 in the present.

You may find here the works of Trumbull, Stuart, Copley, Whistler, Sargent, Borglum, Cassatt; a very fine landscape of Connecticut by Frederick Church; sculpture by Samuel Morse, also known for his telegraphic genius; many paintings by Andrew Wyeth; and a whole room of Thomas Hart Benton murals entitled, "The Arts and Life in America." The quality of the collections and the informal charm with which they are displayed make this a truly delightful place to visit.

Art lovers also should visit Yale University Art Gallery and Yale Center for British Art and British Studies in New Haven and Wesleyan University's Davison Art Center in Middletown.

New Britain Youth Museum
30 High Street, New Britain 06051 Tel: 225-3020
Tue.-Fri., 10-5; Sat., 10-4.

Tue. - Fri. 10-5; Sat., 10-4

Hungerford Outdoor Education Center
191 Farmington Ave., Kensington 06037 Tel: 827-9064
    Today the resources and collection of the Youth Museum are contained at two sites. The New Britain Youth Museum is in downtown New Britain. Exhibits at this site are cultural or historical in nature, usually focusing on the culture of the child.
    The second site is in Kensington. This is the Hungerford Outdoor Nature Center. This site has indoor and outdoor exhibits, gardens and nature trails. Exhibits include plants, geology, pets, farming tools, live exotic and native and farm animals. Gardens include a working herb, vegetable and rose and flower gardens.
    Each site has special events, programs and Saturday afternoon programs.

Copernican Space Science Center
(Planetarium & Observatory) Central Connecticut State University, 1615 Stanley St., New Britain   Tel: 827-7419
    The second largest public telescope in the U.S. Special programs for children and adults throughout the year. Call for schedule.

Tue.-Fri. 105; Sat. 10-5; Sun. open seasonally 1-5.

Canton Historical Museum
11 Front Street, Collinsville
Tel: 693-2793

*April 1-Thanksgiving;
Tues.-Thurs., 12-4; Sun. 2-5.*

This museum is a treasure trove of 18th and 19th century artifacts. The tools used in the home and on the farm to ease the burdens of daily living are intriguing examples of Yankee ingenuity and practicality. The General Store with its period post office, pot-bellied stove, cracker barrel stools, chess board, penny candy, and many other typical items is delightful. So are the blacksmith shop, the toy and doll collections, the Nickelodeon, the craft center with women carding, spinning and weaving, and the boutique at which their products may be purchased.

The museum itself, part of the old Collins Company, is a refreshingly authentic and uncontrived setting for various collections most of which have come directly from ancestral attics and barns in the immediate community.

Collinsville, founded in 1826 by the Collins brothers who manufactured the famed Collins machetes and axes (on display in the museum), is now an historic district. By a scant margin of two votes local citizens avoided the ravages of modern urban renewal and are now preserving and recycling the unique buildings of this typical Connecticut manufacturing village of yesteryear. Water power from the Farmington River made manufacturing practical in Collinsville, as it did for the more than 200 such villages that once dotted the length and breadth of Connecticut.

Roaring Brook Nature Center
196 Gracey Road, Canton 06019
Tel: 693-0263

No admission charge.

The Nature Center features natural history displays and dioramas. It is situated in Werner Woods, 115 acres of trees, a bog, a swamp, and a pond all accessible by trail on foot. It is a place to fully understand ecology during each of the four seasons, as well as to observe the interrelationship of Man and Nature.

Hitchcock Museum
Rt. 20, Riverton   Tel: 379-1003

The Hitchcock Museum, formerly the old Union Church of Riverton, was established in 1972 by John Tarrant Kenney as a tribute to Lambert Hitchcock, America's greatest maker of decorated chairs. From 1826 until his death in 1852 Hitchcock mass produced chairs in Riverton, then called Hitchcocksville. Since this handsome granite church was constructed by Hitchcock and his fellow parishioners in 1829, and because he was married here the following year, a museum honoring his memory is particularly appropriate.

The museum houses an assemblage of selected antique painted furniture, including not only Hitchcock's work but that of other 18th and 19th century craftsmen, all pieces carefully collected by Mr. Kenney throughout the years.

To carry on the tradition of the cherished Hitchcock chairs, Mr. Kenney in 1946 restored the old Hitchcock factory on its original site along the Farmington River. A tour of the museum may be pleasantly combined with a stop at the Hitchcock factory showroom--a short walk down the road from the museum--where craftsmen skilled in the arts of weaving, rushing, woodworking, and stencilling demonstrate their crafts.

The little town of Riverton itself offers attractive possibilities for walking, shopping, antiquing, dining, or just plain picnicking by the edge of the river.

American Clock & Watch Museum
100 Maple Street, Bristol Tel: 583-6070

Founded in 1952, this clock museum is the only one of its kind in the country. The extensive collection of clocks and other timepieces is beautifully displayed in two connecting buildings. The main part is a lovely old mansion house constructed in 1801. In 1955 the Ebenezer Barnes Wing was added, greatly increasing the museum's facilities. The library vault contains rare horological historical materials.

Clockmaking was a very important business in early Connecticut. Eli Terry of East Windsor pioneered mass production of clocks in 1793 when he opened his factory in Plymouth, near Bristol. During the 19th century, this area of the state was a center of the American clock industry.

Lake Compounce

822 Lake Ave., Bristol   Tel: 582-6333

This is the oldest amusement park in America. The park has been carefully restored and includes a 1911 carousel, rides, an all-wood Wildcat rollercoaster, games, the antique Gillette Railroad, paddleboats, swimming and live entertainment daily. Call for schedule and rates.

ROCKY HILL

The ferry runs from April 1st to November 30th, weather permitting. Call 566-7635 when in doubt.

Rocky Hill-Glastonbury Ferry

Rocky Hill 06067

This is the oldest continuously operated ferry in the United States. Since 1655 public transportation across the Connecticut River has been provided at this site connecting the towns of Rocky Hill and Glastonbury, both formerly part of Wethersfield.

Rocky Hill's first ferry is believed to have been a barge, poled back and forth across the river. Motive power has also been supplied by oars and a horse treadmill. At another time a steam-powered vessel was in service. The present ferry is a tug and barge.

Privately owned for 200 years, this ferry became a state facility in 1915. It is now operated by the Department of Transportation.

Dinosaur State Park

West Street, Rocky Hill 06067

Tel: 529-8423

This remarkable find of dinosaur tracks was uncovered by a bulldozer operator in 1966 when excavations were in process for building a new testing laboratory for the Connecticut State Highway Department. Steps were immediately taken to preserve and display the tracks, and Dinosaur State Park was created. The Jurassic Period dinosaur tracks (185 million years old) are housed under a giant geodesic dome. The Park offers 40 acres of nature trails.

Dinosaur buffs should also visit the Peabody Museum in New Haven.

Chester-Hadlyme Ferry
Chester 06412

For over 200 years the Chester-Hadlyme ferry has provided public transportation across the Connecticut River at this site. The first ferry crossing was made in a sailboat by Jonathan Warner of Chester in 1769. Warner subsequently presented this ferry boat to his son as a wedding gift. However, he stipulated that should the income from tolls exceed $75 a year, the excess must be returned to his father! Warner's Ferry continued to be privately operated until 1877 when it became a town facility.

This is the second oldest ferry in continuous use in Connecticut and has been owned and operated by the Department of Transportation since 1917.

The Chester-Hadlyme ferry makes its crossing in one of the most scenically attractive sections of the Connecticut River, in the shadows of Gillette Castle, the mountain-top retreat of the late actor and author, William Gillette of Hartford.

Gillette Castle
67 River Rd., Hadlyme Tel: 526-2336

The 184-acre estate includes hiking trails, outdoor picnicking areas, a picnic shelter and a food concession.

This remarkable structure, reminiscent of German castles on the Rhine, was built in 1915 on a high bluff overlooking the Connecticut River by the famous American actor and playwright, William Hooker Gillette. Nothing about the external architecture or interior decor of the place is traditional, and many of the embellishments and strange contraptions that adorn Gillette's home are his own design. All the hardware, for example, is made of wood; much of the furniture is built-in, and the arrangement of the rooms is unique. He named his castle Seventh Sister, and the structure expresses his highly unorthodox character. Unfortunately, the wonderful small-gauge railroad that he constructed and the little train in which he enjoyed driving all around his estate and along the river's edge have been sold to an amusement park. Gone too are the mysterious Japanese butler and the dozens of cats that kept the actor company when he lived here.

Born in Hartford in 1853, Gillette came from a distinguished lineage. His father, Senator Francis Gillette, was a founder of the new Republican Party and a strong abolitionist whose home was a station for the "underground railway," a network of anti-slavery activists who assisted runaway slaves en route to Canada. His mother, Elizabeth Hooker, was a sixth generation descendant of the great Puritan theologian, Thomas Hooker, spiritual leader of Hartford's first settlers in 1636. Young Will was born and grew up in the city's literary neighborhood known as Nook Farm whose residents included Mark Twain, Harriet Beecher Stowe and Isabella Beecher Hooker, Will's aunt, who founded the Connecticut Woman Suffrage Association. The families of Nook Farm were aristocratic, intellectual and inter-related which provided the maturing youth with considerable stimulation and support.

When Will Gillette decided to become an actor, he realized his choice of career would not be altogether pleasing to his parents, so his neighbor Mark Twain gave him the necessary funds to make a start. By 1879 he had written and played the leading role in a delightful comedy entitled *The Professor*. This initial success was followed by many more before he wrote *Sherlock Holmes*, one of his best-known roles. This play and a number of other melodramas which he wrote and in which he always played the leading character were full of intrigue and espionage and extremely popular with American audiences. He played in *Sherlock Holmes* as late as 1933 and gave his last performance as the lead in Austin Strong's *Three Wise Fools* in 1936 at the age of 83.

Of William Gillette it has been written that he "combined breathtaking artistry on the stage with uncanny inventive ability, a precocious and daring initiative and a total disregard for accepted standards and ways."

His last concern before his death in 1937 was that his unique home should not "fall into the hands of some blithering saphead . . . " He is buried in Farmington, Connecticut.

Goodspeed Opera House
East Haddam Tel: 873-8664

Guided tours available. Call for appointment.

The Goodspeed Opera House was built on the banks of the Connecticut River at East Haddam by William H. Goodspeed, who had shipping, banking and other mercantile interests in that community, but who also had a great love for opera and the theater. Completing the six story edifice in 1876, Goodspeed included a perfect gem of a theater atop his building, which also housed his shipping office, a bar, a steamboat passenger terminal, and general store.

Guided tours available. Call for appointment.

For a quarter-century Goodspeed's flourished as a theater. Sometimes complete Broadway shows were brought here by steamboat. After the 1920's the building declined and was finally marked for demolition by the State of Connecticut in 1958. Local preservationists, alarmed by these proposals for destroying such an obviously attractive and historical building, formed the Goodspeed Opera House Foundation the following year and persuaded Governor Abraham Ribicoff to intercede.

Through the efforts of the Foundation and its many supporters, the building has been delightfully restored and refurbished and is now listed on the National Register of Historic Places. During the summer season the very best of musicals, revivals and tryouts are produced here. Six have gone on to Broadway -- *Man of La Mancha (1965), Shenandoah (1974), Very Good Eddie (1975), Something's Afoot and Going Up (1976) and Annie (1977).*

The theater has a very active apprentice program to train and develop talented young people in the performing arts and related crafts. Another major project of Goodspeeds' is its program for handicapped children. Lectures and motion pictures are major attractions during the winter months.

HADDAM NECK

CT Yankee Energy Information Center
Injun Hollow Rd.
Tel: 267-9279
    Situated on the east bank of the Connecticut River, on the grounds of the state's first nuclear power plant, the center features hands-on exhibits, multiprojector shows, computer games and self-guided nature trails.

ESSEX

Call for schedule.

The Valley Railroad
Railroad Ave. Tel: 767-0103
    Nothing could be more thrilling than this trip into America's past aboard the century-old Valley Railroad's authentic, full-sized steam train as it chuffs and whistles its way up the picturesque Connecticut River Valley from Old Essex Station to Chester. There you may board an equally romantic riverboat, *Silver Star*, which will take you for a one or two-hour cruise farther up the valley, then down the majestic Connecticut to Deep River and back to the steam train, which will return you to Essex.
    This is a "must" adventure for railroad and riverboat buffs of all ages!
    While in the vicinity, an extra delight is a side-trip to the village of Essex with its lovely 18th century homes and tempting shops and restaurants. This beautiful old riverport has been a haven for sailors since Colonial times.

Connecticut River Museum
Main St., Essex Tel: 767-8269

April-Dec., Tues.-Sun.
10-5 p.m.

    Steamboating began on the River in 1823 when the *Experiment*, built at Middletown, began regular trips between Hartford and Saybrook twice a week. Landings were made at the many ports along the River and at Starkey's wharf in Essex. Goods were sheltered in the West Indies warehouse until William H. Parmelee built a new dockhouse in 1878.
    The three-story, white clapboard building with the graceful cupola soon became a landmark on the river. All of the goods shipped to and from the port of New York passed through this and similar warehouses at the river ports.

The cargo hoist, hanging on the third floor, raised the goods to the second and third floors, keeping the ground floor clear for unloading wagons. Passengers awaited the steamers on the broad dock or on the second floor porch, and approaching steamers, signalled by their whistles, were greeted by crowds of curious residents anxious for the latest news.

The Connecticut River Foundation, formed in 1974, has restored the exterior of the dockhouse and a portion of the interior to its warehouse days. Today it houses a River Museum dedicated to preserving the history of the river and the people of the Valley.

The benches in Wolcott Park, the waterside green, invite visitors to enjoy the quiet majesty of the river or the colorful activity of this yachting port.

The Connecticut River Foundation owns a growing collection of artifacts that reflect the diverse history of the river. A portion of the collection is on permanent exhibit, but temporary exhibitions on changing themes permit the visitor to view new artifacts on loan or from the study collection.

Ship and boatbuilding along the river are represented by a strong collection of tools, half models, and cased full-rigged models such as the *Oliver Cromwell*. The role of Connecticut mariners in the rise of the port of New York is interpreted through a fine collection of navigation instruments and paintings.

"Yankee ingenuity" is perhaps best represented through the life-size reproduction of David Bushnell's *American Turtle*, the first submarine.

The War of 1812 can be seen in dramatic paintings and the Golden Age of Steamboating through models, prints, and paintings and broadsides.

The warehouse itself, with its cargo doors, hoist, barrels and sacks of valley produce, provides a trip back into time. Those who love the river or are seeings its gentle waters for the first time will more fully appreciate the importance of the river in the history of New England and the nation after their visit to The Connecticut River Foundation at Steamboat Dock.

MYSTIC

Spring/Summer open daily: 9-5
Fall/Winter open daily: 9-4

Mystic Seaport Museum
Mystic Tel: 572-0711

Mystic Seaport is an absolutely fascinating reproduction of a 19th century maritime village. It is one of the largest repositories of American maritime memorabilia in the nation and includes authentic ships, buildings, and shops. The *Charles W. Morgan* is the last of the wooden whaling ships. Many thousands of people from all over the world visit this unique museum all year-round. Members often go by boat and tie up at the excellent docking facilities. This is a wonderful place for family excursions.

Mystic Marinelife Aquarium
Coogan Blvd., Mystic
Tel: 536-3323

The Aquarium is open daily at 9 A.M. except Christmas, Thanksgiving and New Year's Day.

In this excellent aquarium more than 37 living exhibits, ranging in size from 200 to 30,000 gallon tanks, emphasize sea life in the tropical and temperate waters of North America, featuring 6,000 specimens.

Starting at 10 A.M. hourly, dolphin, sea lion, and whale demonstrations may be viewed by the public.

A two and one-half acre outdoor complex called Seal Island simulates the natural habitat of seals and sea lions.

Olde Mistick Village
Coogan Blvd., Mystic   Tel: 536-4941

Mon.-Sat. 10-5:30;
Sun. 12-5:30.

This is a replica of a colonial settlement in a carefully landscaped setting. The village offers shops, restaurants, the Memory Lane Doll & Toy Museum, and the Mystic Shoreline Information Center.

Tantaquidgeon Indian Museum
Rte. 32, Norwich-New London Road, Uncasville
Tel: 848-9145

May-Oct.: Tues.-Sun., 10-4.

This museum was built by the late John Tantaquidgeon and his son Harold, in 1931. The Tantaquidgeons are direct descendants of the Mohegan Chieftain Uncas, Captain Tantaquidgeon and the Rev. Samson Occum, a Christian Indian missionary and educator. These Indians all played prominent roles in Connecticut history.

This unique museum houses a collection of objects of stone, bone, and wood made by Mohegan and other New England Indian artists and craftsmen, past and present. Featured in this Northeastern Woodland section are baskets, bowls, and ladles made by John Tantaquidgeon a skilled woodworker and lst Mohegan basketmaker. Many of the stone artifacts on display were found in the Mohegan area.

Other points of interest in the area include the Mohegan Congregational Church, the homesite of Samson Occum, and Fort Shantok State Park.

Governor Jonathan Trumbull Homestead
West Town Street, Lebanon   Tel: 642-7558

Built in 1735, this is the home of "Brother Jonathan," George Washington's able and stalwart friend, the only governor of the 13 original colonies to side with the revolutionists.

The house is a proper Yankee dwelling, solid but unpretentious, good proportions, plain furnishings. Even the useful but slightly battered broad-brimmed hat of the beloved old governor may be seen, placed casually on his little day-bed as though he might still be needing it.

Recent restoration has disclosed the narrow staircase down which the governor's artist son fell as a child, blinding one eye. John Trumbull, many of whose patriotic canvasses now hang at the Yale Art Museum, also designed the unique brick church of Lebanon.

Governor Trumbull's War Office, built in 1727 as the Trumbull family store, is located near his home, also the old stable of Jeremiah Wadsworth of Hartford, where George Washington once slept.

William A. Buckingham, Connecticut's Civil War governor, was also a native of Lebanon. His home still stands but is not open to the public.

Eleazer Wheelock's famous Indian school, forerunner of Dartmouth College, was located in Lebanon. It was here that the Rev. Samson Occum was educated.

Jonathan Trumbull, Jr. House
Rt. 87, Lebanon Tel: 642-6040

May-Oct.: Tues.-Sat. 1-5 p.m.

Home of Governor Trumbull's son, this center chimney farmhouse, with eight corner fireplaces, is furnished with antiques of the period.

COVENTRY

Nathan Hale Homestead
South Street, Coventry Tel: 742-6917

May-Oct. Open daily 1-5 p.m.

Nathan Hale, Connecticut's best-beloved hero, never actually lived here, but he was born and raised in a house on this site. Deacon Richard Hale and his family moved into this homestead just one month after their brave son was hanged for spying on the British lines. Now the Hale home is kept as a shrine to the memory of the patriotic young school teacher. Many of his possessions are in this lovely mansion which is beautifully and appropriately furnished.

Caprilands Herb Farm
Silver St., Coventry Tel: 742-7244

This rustic, 18th century farmhouse is surrounded by 30 herb gardens, featuring over 300 varieties. There is a greenhouse, bookshop, gift shop, and dining room. Herbal lectures and garden tours are available.

Riverboat Cruises
Deep River Navigation Company, River Street, Deep River Tel: 526-4954.
2 ½ Hour Cruise to Rocky Hill Ferry Landing
Beginning at the Charter Oak Landing in Hartford.

Call for schedule and rates.

The journey takes you south from Hartford, along remarkably unspoiled tree-lined shores ... the river narrows and follows a series of winding turns. As the *Lady Fenwick* cruises along, you will begin to feel a sense of the quiet magic that Mark Twain found in life along the river. Your Captain will comment on sights along the way including the Hartford skyline and bridges, the East Hartford waterfront, Trinity Boat House, a tour of Wethersfield Cove, the Rocky Hill Ferry and the wide array of Nature's offerings.

2 ½ Hour Haddam Island Cruise

Beginning at Harbor Park in Middletown. Cruises are also available from Saybrook Point.

Board the *Aunt Polly* and set sail for a relaxing 2 ½ hour cruise to Haddam Island. This is a particularly interesting and scenic stretch of the Connecticut River dotted with boatyards, stately homes, pine shrouded bluffs, waterfowl and an occasional bald eagle. Your Captain will comment on sights along the way including the history of shipbuilding in Middle Haddam, Bodkin Rock, Dart Island, Hurd State Park, Higganum Creek, Rock Landing and the colonial settlement at Haddam Island. A delightful way to enjoy a summer or fall afternoon.

The American Indian Archaeological Institute
Off. Rte. 199, P. O. Box 260, Washington Tel: 868-0518

WASHINGTON

Mon.-Sat. 10-4:40 p.m.; Sun. 1-4:30 p.m. Closed on major holidays.

Admission by membership or donation. The Museum Shop offers the visitor a variety of gifts for all ages. Books, Indian crafts, jewelry, pottery, weaving and basketry as well as special collector's pieces.

The purpose of the American Indian Archaeological Institute is to discover and preserve information about Native American peoples of the Northeastern Woodlands and to make such information known through educational programs, exhibits, lectures, the Institute's libraries and publications. As a center for research and education, the Institute conducts surveys for prehistoric and historic evidence of human occupation and, under the direction of the Research Department, sponsors controlled archaeological excavations. Equally important is the interpretation of this information through exhibits and educational programs for children, serious students and the general public. The AIAI staff works to heighten awareness of the thousands of years of Indian peoples' cultures and to develop appreciation and understanding of their cultures, achievements and integrity.

Permanent exhibits at the Institute include both artifact displays and interpretive panels. The exhibits include: 12,000 years of prehistory and history; Connecticut's most complete mastodon; simulated archaeological site; reconstructed longhouse; Quinnetukut Habitats Trail and an array of changing exhibits.

The Ethnobotanical Herbarium is a special reference library of pressed and mounted plant specimens that reflects Native American usages. This collection is available, by appointment, for study by botanists, naturalists, artists and students. Included are the native harvests of shrubs, trees, herbs, seaweeds, mosses, lichens and ferns.

Outdoor plant labels identify AIAI's living herbarium which flourished as a Native American Garden Walk as the Quinnetukut Habitats Trail--a quarter-mile woodland loop walk reflecting the changing environments encountered by the Native Americans during the past 10,000 years and in "Yo Appituck" (Narragansett for "Let us sit here"), the gathering ground.

PLAINVILLE

Plainville Historic Center
29 Pierce Street, Plainville
Tel: 747-0705/747-6577

April-Dec.Wed. & Sat. 12-3:30   The former Town Hall (1890) now houses a museum of Plainville's early days, including the era of the Farmington Canal (1827-1847). The collection includes toys, period costumes, tools, clocks and a bakery wagon.

SOUTHINGTON

Barnes Museum
85 N. Main Street, Southington
Tel: 628-5426

Mon-Fri. 9-11, 1-2:30   Home of the prominent local family for more than a century, the museum displays original furnishings and operates an historical and genealogical library.

TOLLAND

Tolland Green
The Green became the center of the town of Tolland with the building of its first meeting house in 1722. This was the beginning of the village, and since at this time state and church were inseparable, all activity, both civic and religious, centered around the meeting house. As early as 1723 the east-west Old Post Road was an important thoroughfare carrying mail and supplies from Hartford to Boston. The town bustled with activity when Tolland was designated the county seat in 1785. Taverns, hotels and little shops opened around

the Green. A complex network of toll roads developed and Tolland Street became a toll road center, the intersection of many turnpikes. Stage coaches became the accepted way to travel.

Today, of the structures on the Green, most are over 100 years old, and some are from the eighteenth century. In architecture one is a saltbox, many are Colonial, some Federal and others Victorian, and even a Swiss chalet. In front of many of them are sidewalks of large flat stones, some garnet studded, all quarried locally.

After decades of change the Green still retains the appearance and tone of an early New England Village.

The Daniel Benton Homestead
(c. 1720) Metcalf Rd.

Throughout the house one can find indications of the distant past: huge timbers held together with wooden pegs, beams hand hewn and brown with age, five fireplaces of stone, one with an oak lintel, oil lamps, hand-made rugs, old chests and much more.

May-Oct. Sun. & Wed. 1-4 p.m.
Tel: 875-7552

Hicks-Stearns Museum
42 Tolland Green

Begun in the 1700s as a colonial inn with iron pots hung in a deep stone fireplace and a typical bake oven, the house has been added to and embellished through the ages.

Three generations of the Hicks family have lived here. In 1842, the house was purchased by Judge Elisha Stearns and given to his daughter Maria and son-in-law Charles R. Hicks as a wedding present. Captain Ratcliffe Hicks, father of Charles, was a renowned sea captain in the early 1800s. His grandson Ratcliffe also made many ocean voyages in connection with his business and served in the Connecticut legislature. The last member of the family, Miss Elizabeth Hicks, died in 1974 and the Museum was established under her will.

Feeling more like a home than a museum, the house is filled with family heirlooms and simple treasures from cloth tea balls and the old Victrola to faux bamboo furniture. The house was always changing, with a new kitchen every century

May-Oct. Sundays 1-4 p.m.
Tel: 872-8673

and new trim for every style in fashion. The three-story tower and carriage house were added during the Victorian period when the simple Colonial white exterior became the three-color ornate style still found today.

The Old Jail Museum
(c. 1856) Tolland Green

May-Oct. Sundays 1-4 p.m.
Tel: 872-8673

For two hundred years a jail has stood on this site. The first two proved insecure. The third built in 1824 was built of large blocks of stone quarried from solid rock well doweled together. Rebuilt in 1856 this fourth jail was enlarged, extended and connected to the County House where the jailor and his family lived. The County House also offered food and lodging to judges, lawyers and others who had to travel a distance to carry out the business of the court just a few steps across the Green.

MANCHESTER

The area now known as Manchester began its recorded history as the camping grounds of a small band of peaceful Indians--the Podunk tribe. English settlement began about 1673, some 40 years after Thomas Hooker led a group of Puritans from Massachusetts Bay Colony to found Hartford. "Manchester" was part of Hartford in what was called "Five-Mile Tract." Later the area came to be called Orford Parish, and was part of East Hartford. Residents of Orford Parish began agitating for incorporation as a separate town as early as 1812. Their petitions were not successful until 1823, when it was incorporated as the town of Manchester.

Cheney Brothers, founded in South Manchester in 1838, gradually became world famous for premium quality silk thread and fabrics as well as for the invention of innovative silk processing techniques. It was as an employee of Cheney Brothers that young Christopher Spencer (inventor of the Spencer repeating rifle) won early fame as a mechanical genius by inventing a silk spooling machine. Cheney Brothers were renowned as well for their generosity and public spiritedness, building over the course of 50 years a "model community" of workers' housing and contributing assets such as schools, Cheney Hall, a public library, the Hall of Records, public utilities, and land for churches.

The Civil War disrupted many lives, taking 268 young men from Manchester; 48 never returned. After the war, a time Mark Twain called "The Gilded Age," people in town launched many new commercial enterprises. Manchester had been called "Silktown" because of the immense influence that the Cheney Bros. Silk Manufacturing Co. had on South Manchester. In the 19th century the town could just as well have had the nickname "Papertown," since there were five successful paper mills in operation.

Manchester was a "boomtown" by 1900. Cheney Bros. employed about 25 percent of the residents, recruited new European immigrants to work in the mills, and continued its corporate generosity.

Manchester celebrated its Centennial in 1923 with a huge parade and weeks of special activities. The town could pride itself on a century of progress in education and public benefit, and could applaud such commercial advances as the innovative Hale's Store--one of the first self-serve groceries in the United States. "Made in Manchester" was one of the mottos of the Centennial; products in that category ranged from precision industrial gauges through fine silk fabrics to Bon Ami cleansing soap.

The Great Depression of the 1930s hit Manchester hard, especially with the decline and eventual failure of Cheney Bros. There was a modest upswing in housebuilding as workers in Hartford moved to Manchester to live. An offshoot of Cheney Bros., Pioneer Parachute, helped in the defense efforts in World War II. The post WWII era was a time of house building again, as many people commuted to work at places like Pratt & Whitney Aircraft. The period from 1950 through the 1970s saw commercial growth in town, improvements to the highways for the commuting public, the construction of the first Jewish synagogue, and new industrial parks. The Manchester Historical Society was founded in 1965 by a group of townspeople to preserve the town's rich historical legacy for future generations.

The Cheney Homestead
106 Hartford Road

Timothy Cheney, farmer, miller and one of America's famous clock makers, built the Cheney Homestead about

Thurs. & Sun. 1-5 p.m.
Tel: 643-5588

1780. A brook to the south of the home afforded water for the grist mill which he operated with his son George.

On October 25, 1798, George Cheney brought his bride, Electa Woodbridge Cheney to the Homestead. To the couple were born eight sons and one daughter. With the exception of Seth and John, who became well known artists, all the brothers joined in establishing the Mt. Nebo Silk Company. The firm later incorporated as Cheney Brothers and became world famous as a leader in the silk industry.

The homestead includes many 18th and 19th century furnishings, paintings, and Cheney family memorabilia.

The Keeney Schoolhouse
106 Hartford Road

April-Oct.
Thurs. & Sun., 1-5 p.m.
Tel: 643-5588

Public schools in colonial Connecticut were operated by the Colony's official, established Congregational church. The legal institution which managed them was the ecclesiastical society. Qualified voters who belonged to the official church were members of this society. In 1694, the General Court of the Connecticut Colony chartered an ecclesiastical society in the part of Hartford lying east of the "Great River." This consisted of East Hartford, and the area called the Five Miles, which later became Orford Parish and still later the Town of Manchester. In 1745, that Society gave the people in the Hop Brook section, Manchester's first settlement, the right to conduct a school. In 1751, the Society authorized the erection of five schools in the Five Miles, all to be built without cost to the Society, which would, however, provide money for operating them.

The very small size of the classroom will surprise many visitors. It is accounted for by the fact that travel was very difficult in early Connecticut. Roads were incredibly bad. Bridges were rarities. It was impossible for small children to walk any great distances, particularly in the snow of winter and mud of spring. With the large families of the old days, a village of only a few houses or a small area of scattered farms required its own school.

The Fire Museum
230 Pine Street

The history of the Connecticut fire service has been long, illustrious and exciting. To help preserve this heritage, the Connecticut Firemen's Historical Society established its museum in 1979. The museum is housed in a fire station that was built by Cheney Brothers primarily to protect their silk mills, and the south end of Manchester. The station was dedicated in 1901.

April - Nov.,
Fri. & Sat., 10 - 5 p.m.;
Sun. 12 - 5 p.m.

On display you'll find a wide variety of fire fighting equipment and memorabilia ranging from leather fire buckets used by the first settlers, to early motorized fire apparatus.

Fascinating exhibits include several hand-pulled engines which required as many as thirty men to pump water on a fire, hose reels and chemical engines pulled by willing volunteers, and colorful displays of tools, badges and lanterns.

You'll see a magnificently decorated four-wheel, hand-pulled hose reel, primarily used for parades and other occasions.

There's a horse-drawn hose wagon--similar to one actually housed in the Museum when it was a firehouse--and a steam-operated pumper that not only show the romance of yesteryear, but also demonstrate the development of fire prevention technology.

The Lutz Children's Museum
247 S. Main Street

A hands-on museum where the curious of all ages can explore nature and join in special activities. The exhibits are devoted to topics in art, history, science, nature, and ethnology. There is also a live animal exhibit of small native, domestic, and exotic animals. One of Connecticut's largest Playscape areas is located on the grounds.

Tues., Wed., Fri., 2-5 p.m.;
Thurs., 2-8 p.m.;
Sat., Sun., 12-5 p.m.
Tel: 643-0949

The *Oak Grove Nature Center* is the museum's unique outdoor educational facility of trails through 53 acres of varied habitat.

CANTERBURY

Jan. 15-Dec. 15:
Wed.-Sun., 10-4:30 p.m.
Tel: 546-9916/566-3005

Prudence Crandall House
Canterbury Green, Junction of Rts. 14 & 169.
    This is the site of New England's first school for black girls (1833). Period furnishings decorate the house, changing exhibits are featured, and a research library is available.

HAMDEN

Wed.-Sat. 10-3 p.m;
Sun. 12-5 p.m.
Tel: 777-1833/789-8681

Eli Whitney Museum
Whitney Avenue, Hamden
    Exhibits trace 200 years of industrial growth on the site. The special exhibit, "Windows of the Works," outlines achievements of the inventor of the cotton gin and firearms manufacturer who devised methods of mass production.

STORRS

Sat.-Sun. 1-4 p.m.;
Mon.
12-4 p.m.

Connecticut State Museum of Natural History
University of Connecticut Campus, Rt. 195, Storrs
Tel: 486-4460
    Established in 1985, the state's latest museum is dedicated to preserving Connecticut's natural heritage. The museum's archaeologist has identified 200 new sites within the state. Housed in the Wilbur Cross Building, at the University of Connecticut, the museum features exhibits, lectures, field trips, and workshops. Especially interesting are the collection of Rex Brasher's watercolors of the birds of North America and a 15-foot white shark, the largest mounted fish on display in the Northeast.

William Benton Museum of Art
University of Connecticut, Rt. 195, Storrs   Tel: 486-4520

Mon.-Fri., 10-4:30 p.m.,
Sun., 1-5 p.m.

    The Benton Museum's collection, strong in American art, has swiftly grown to include European and American paintings, drawings, prints and sculpture from the 16th century to the present. Benton exhibitions change frequently, and are applauded for their excellence and imagination.

Connecticut Wineries
Connecticut Department of Agriculture
Tel: 566-3671/566-4845

The Connecticut Department of Agriculture invites you to discover one of our state's best kept secrets: Connecticut's fine wines. Scattered throughout the state, on hilltop farmlands, flourishing vineyards produce quality wines of distinctly individual character.

Glimpse into the fine art of winemaking and enjoy a taste of Connecticut grown fine wines. The state's warm, hospitable wine-making families are happy to show you the unique beauty and state-of-the-art technology of their vineyards.

Call for your list of Connecticut wineries.

FOR FURTHER READING

The Colonial Period of American History
Charles M. Andrews

Structures & Styles--Guided Tours of Hartford Architecture
Gregory E. Andrews and David F. Ransom

From Colonial Parish to Modern Suburb (West Hartford)
Nelson R. Burr

Silas Deane Marcia Carleton

History of Hartford Streets F. Perry Close

King Philip's War Ellis and Norris

History of Simsbury John F. Ellsworth

The City of Hartford 1784-1984 Marion & Ellsworth Grant

The Colt Legacy Ellsworth S. Grant

Yankee Dreamers and Doers Ellsworth S. Grant

The Story of Connecticut
Robert N. Holcomb and C. C. Hemenway

Captain James Francis, Master Builder
Anne Crofoot Kuckro

The Colonial History of Hartford, gathered from original
records William DeLoss Love

Older Than the Nation John Bard McNulty

Only More So (East Hartford) Lee Pacquette

How the Other Half Lived Robert Pawlowski

Wethersfield Enters the Revolution Ronna Reynolds

Wethersfield in the Revolution Ronna Reynolds

Inner City Bicentennial Booklet John F. Rogers

The Story of Tobacco Valley
Shade Growers AgriculturalAssociation

Connecticut Past and Present Odell Shepard

The Memorial History of Hartford County
J. HammondTrumbull

Hartford in History Willis Twitchell

Connecticut Albert E. Van Dusen

New England Frontier Alden T. Vaughan

An Illustrated History of Connecticut's Capital
Glenn Weaver

INDEX

Meyer, Rabbi Isaac, 143, 115
Michalczyk, Casimir (sculptor), 36, 37
Middle East, 146
Middle Haddam, Conn., 357
Middlebury College, Middlebury, Vt., 224
Middletown, Conn., 50, 219, 352
Mill (Park) River, 240
Mills, Bishop Cedric, 132
Milton, Mrs. Rachel Taylor, 132
Minimalist (artistic) Movement, 259, 261, 265
Miss Porter's School, Farmington, Conn., 309, 310-311
Mitchell, Charles, 128
Mitchelson, Joseph C., Coin collection, 40
Mohawk Data Sciences Corporation, 171
Mohawk Indians, 18, 20
Mohegan Congregational Church, Mystic, Conn., 355
Mohegan Indians, 20, 354-355
Monarch of the Glen (painting), 66
Monk, General George, 254
"Montevideo" (country estate), 326
Mooklar, James, 93
Moore, [Mr.] H. B., 164
Moore and Salsbury (architects), 188, 201, 311, 329
Morgan, John Pierpont, 25, 48, 50, 61, 67, 138, 164, 207, 215, 247, 280
Morgan, Junius Spencer, 207
Morgan family, 123, 208; Homestead, 135
Morgan's Coffee House, 24-25, 50, 245
Morison, Allan, 102
Morison, Dr. Norman, 102
Morris, Benjamin Wistar (architect), 44, 68, 207
Morris, Robert (sculptor), 259
Morris and O' Connor (architects), 208
Morse, Samuel Finley Breese (artist), 344
Mosman, [Mr.] M. H. (bronze caster), 262
Mother Bethel Methodist Church, 129
Mount Holyoke College, South Hadley, Mass., 199
Mount Nebo Silk Company, 362
Mount Saint Joseph Academy, West Hartford, Conn., 136, 281
Mount Saint Joseph Junior College, West Hartford, Conn., 288
Mount Sinai Hospital, 185-186, 317; Auerbach Wing, 185; Samuel S. Suisman Building, 186
Municipal Art Society of Hartford, 44

Murphy, Francis S., 343
Murphy, John (architect), 115
Museum of Modern Art, New York, N.Y., 200
Museum on the Green, Glastonbury, Conn., 298, 300
Music (sculpture), 36, 278
Musiel, Rev. Stanislaus, 107
Mustad (Swedish manufacturer), 88
Mystic, Conn., 18, 354-355; Coogan Boulevard, 354
Mystic Marine Life Aquarium, 7, 354
Mystic Seaport Museum, 354
Mystic Shoreline Information Center, 354

Nannen, Howard, 217
Nannpier, Connie (architect), 80
Narragansett Bay, 14
Narragansett Indians, 21
Napa Valley, Calif., 314
Nathan Hale (sculpture), 37, 256, 262, 268, 276
National Fire Insurance Company, 70, 187
National Register of Historic Places, 114, 118, 146, 150, 162, 166, 174, 338
National Soldiers Monument, Gettysburg, Pa., 56
Native American Garden Walk, Washington, Conn., 358
Neihaus, Charles Henry (sculptor), 272, 273, 274
Nepauquash (Indian name), 176
Neptune (ship), 304
Neuhaus and Taylor (architects), 80
New Britain, Conn., 72, 104, 107, 135, 214, 344-346; High St., 345; Lexington St., 344; Stanley St., 345
New Britain Avenue Triangle (Mini Park), acreage, 239
New Britain Museum of American Art, 344-345
New Britain National Bank, 54
New Britain Youth Museum, 345
New England, 14, 18, 26, 34, 53, 72, 75, 79, 141, 143, 174, 182, 203, 218, 229, 236, 255, 265, 296, 306-307, 322, 332, 333, 358, 364
New England Air Museum, Windsor Locks, Conn., 340-343
New England Association of Colleges and Secondary Schools, 184